LEVITICUS

JIM HASTINGS

THE *WORD* connection

Houston, Texas

LEVITICUS

Dr. Jim Hastings

First Edition © 2023

ISBN – 9798863919966

All Scripture in this book entitled "Leviticus" are taken from the NEW AMERICAN STANDARD BIBLE, Copyright © 1960, 1962, 1963, 1968, 1971, 1972, 1973, 1975, 1977, 1988, 1995, 2020, by the Lockman Foundation. Used by Permission.

Cover Photo © 2023 by Jim Hastings

THE WORD *connection*

15419 Greens Cove Way, Houston, Texas 77059

Table of Contents

PREFACE 13

CHAPTER 1 17

I.   **THE TIMING OF THE LAW (1:1)** 17

II.   **THE REQUIREMENTS OF THE OFFERINGS (1:2-6:7)** 18

    A.   THE SOURCE OF THE OFFERING (1:2) 18
    B.   THE BURNT OFFERING (1:1-2:16) 26
      1.   From the Herd (1:1-9) 26
      2.   From the Flock (1:10-17) 29

CHAPTER 2 34

      3.   The Raw-Ingredient Grain Offering (2:1-2:16) 34
      4.   The Oven-Baked Grain Product (2:4) 37
      5.   The Griddle-Cooked Grain Offering (2:5-6) 38
      6.   The Pan-Cooked Grain Offering (2:7-10) 38
      7.   The Forbidden Ingredients (2:11) 39
      8.   Seasoned with Salt (2:13) 41
      9.   The Roasted Grain Offering (2:14-16) 41

CHAPTER 3 50

    C.   THE PEACE OFFERING (3:1-17) 50
      1.   From the Herd (3:1-2) 50
      2.   From the Flock (3:6-7) 53

CHAPTER 4 57

    D.   THE SIN OFFERINGS (4:1-35) 58
      1.   For the Unintentional Sin of the Person of a Priest – a Bull (4:1-12) 58
      2.   For the Unintentional Sin of the Nation – A Bull (4:13-21) ... 61
      3.   For the Unintentional Sin of a Leader – A Male Goat (4:22-26) 62
      4.   For the Unintentional Sin of the Common People (4:27-35). 65

CHAPTER 5 68

    E.   THE GUILT OFFERINGS (5:1-19) 68
      1.   Examples of Intentional Sins (5:1-4) 68
      2.   Remedies for Intentional Sins (5:5-13) 70
      3.   Offering for Unfaithful Acts Against Holy Things (5:14-16).. 73
      4.   Offering for any Intentional Acts of Sin Unaware (5:17-19). 74

CHAPTER 6 76

    5.   *Offering for Sins Against the LORD Through Sins Against Others (6:1-7)* 76

III.   **THE LAW OF THE OFFERINGS** 77

    A.   THE LAW OF THE BURNT OFFERING (6:8-14) 77
        1.   *Cooking Time (6:8-9)* 77
        2.   *Collecting Ash (6:10 – 11)* 78
        3.   *Continuous Fire (6:12-13)* 79
    B.   THE LAW OF THE GRAIN OFFERING (6:14-18) 79
        1.   *Presentation of Offering (6:14)* 79
        2.   *Amount of the Offering (6:15)* 80
        3.   *Remainder of the Offering (6:16)* 80
        4.   *Restriction of the Offering (6:17)* 81
        5.   *Ingestion of the Offering (6:18)* 82
    C.   THE LAW OF THE GRAIN ORDINATION OFFERING (6:19-23) 83
        1.   *Amount of the Offering (6:19-20)* 83
        2.   *Preparation of the Offering (6:21)* 84
        3.   *Giver of the Offering (6:22)* 84
        4.   *Restriction of the Offering (6:23)* 84
    D.   THE LAW OF THE SIN OFFERING (6:24-30) 85
        1.   *Place of the Offering (6:24-25)* 85
        2.   *Ingestion of the Offering (6:26)* 85
        3.   *Restrictions of the Offering (6:27a-28b)* 85
        4.   *Ingestion of Offering (6:29)* 87
        5.   *Blood of the Offering (6:30)* 87

CHAPTER 7 89

    E.   THE LAW OF THE GUILT OFFERING (7:1-2A-10) 89
        1.   *Place of the Offering (7:1-2a)* 89
        2.   *Blood of the Offering (7:2b)* 89
        3.   *Fat of the Offering (7:3-5)* 89
        4.   *Ingestion of the Offering (7:6-7)* 90
        5.   *Hide of the Offering (7:8)* 90
        6.   *Grain of the Offering (7:9)* 90
        7.   *Owner of the Offering (7:10)* 91
    F.   THE LAW OF THE SACRIFICE OF PEACE OFFERING (7:11-21) 91
        1.   *When it is for a Thanksgiving (7:11-12)* 91
        2.   *When it is for a Votive or Freewill (7:16-17)* 93
    G.   THE LAW OF THE FAT (7:22-27) 96
        1.   *Restriction on the Fat Offering (7:22-23)* 96
        2.   *Uses for Non-Offering Fat (7:24)* 97
        3.   *Penalty for Eating the Fat Offering (7:25)* 97
        4.   *Penalty for Eating the Blood Offering (7:26-27)* 97
    H.   THE LAW OF THE SACRIFICE OF PEACE OFFERING FOR THE COMMON PERSON (7:28-34)   98

  1. *The Giver of the Sacrifice of Peace (7:28-29)*.........................*98*
  2. *The Slayer of the Sacrifice of Peace (7:30a-34)*..................*98*
 I. THE PORTIONS FOR THE PRIESTS (7:35-38) 99
  1. *Consecrated to Aaron and His Sons (7:35)* *99*
  2. *Given to Aaron and His Sons (7:36)*................................*100*
  3. *Law of the Offerings (7:37-38)* *100*

CHAPTER 8...103

 IV. **THE ORDINATION AND OFFERINGS FOR AARON AND HIS SONS BY MOSES (8:1-9:24)** 103

  A. DAY ONE OF THE ORDINATION (8:1-36)................................... 103
   1. *The Priest and the Offerings (8:1-4a)* *103*
   2. *The Announcement to the Nation (8:4b – 5)*..................*103*
   3. *The Washing of Aaron and His Sons (8:6)* *104*
   4. *The Dressing of Aaron (8:7-9)*...*105*
   5. *The Anointing of the Tabernacle (8:10-11)*....................*110*
   6. *The Anointing of Aaron (8:12)*..*110*
   7. *The Dressing of Aaron's Sons (8:13)*...............................*110*
   8. *The Bull of the Sin Offering (8:14-17)* *111*
   9. *The First Ram of the Burnt Offering (8:18-21)*................*112*
   10. *The Second Ram of the Ordination Offering (8:22-36)*.......*113*

CHAPTER 9...116

  B. DAY EIGHT OF THE ORDINATION (9:1-24)................................ 116
   1. *The Calling of Aaron, His Sons, and the Elders (9:1-6)*.......*116*
   2. *Aaron's Offerings (9:7-8)*..*117*
   3. *Aaron's Ram Burnt Offering (9:12-14)* *118*
   4. *Elder's Offering (9:15-24)* *119*
   5. *The Grain Offering (9:17)* *121*
   6. *Ox and Ram Sacrifice of Peace Offering (9:18-21)* *121*
  C. THE APPEARANCE OF THE LORD TO ALL THE PEOPLE (9:22-24) 123
   1. *The Blessing by Aaron (9:22-23a)*..................................*123*
   2. *The Glory of the LORD from the Tent of Meeting (9:23b-24)*
    123

CHAPTER 10...138

 V. **THE REBELLION OF TWO OF AARON'S SONS (10:1-20)** 138

  A. NADAB AND ABIHU USED STRANGE FIRE AND THE LORD KILLED THEM (10:1-2) 138
  B. AARON KEPT SILENT (10:3)..141
  C. NADAB AND ABIHU CARRIED AWAY (10:4-5) 141
  D. INSTRUCTIONS TO AARON AND HIS REMAINING SONS (10:6-20)..........142
   1. *Do Not Mourn (10:6-7)*..*142*
   2. *Do Not Drink (10:8-11)*..*143*

    3.   Eat the Grain Offering (10:12-13) 146
    4.   Eat the Wave Offering (10:14-15) 147
    5.   Uneaten Goat Offering (10:16-18) 148
    6.   Aaron's Question (10:19) 150
    7.   Moses' Thought (10:20) 151

CHAPTER 11 152

VI.   THE LAW OF THE CLEAN AND UNCLEAN FOODS (11:1-46) 152

    A.   CLEAN AND UNCLEAN FOODS FROM THE LAND (11:1-2).................... 152
        1.   Clean with Divided/Split Hoof and Chews the Cud (11:3) .. 153
        2.   Unclean with any Deviation (11:4-8)..................................... 154
    B.   CLEAN AND UNCLEAN FROM THE SEA (11:9-12) 155
        1.   Clean Fins and Scales (11:9) 155
        2.   Unclean without Fins and Scales (11:10-12) 156
    C.   UNCLEAN FOWL (11:13-19) 157
    D.   CLEAN AND UNCLEAN INSECTS (11:20-25) 157
        1.   Unclean walk on all fours (11:20)... 157
        2.   Clean with Jointed Legs and Jump – Locust, Crickets,
Grasshoppers (11:21-22).. 158
        3.   Unclean if Touched until Evening (11:23-25) 158
    E.   UNCLEAN SUMMARY CONCERNING DIVIDED BUT NOT SPLIT HOOF (11:26)
159
    F.   UNCLEAN ANIMALS THAT WALK ON PAWS (11:27-28) 159
    G.   UNCLEAN ANIMALS THAT SWARM (11:29-31) 160
        1.   What They Are (11:29-31).. 160
        2.   What they Touch that is Unclean (11:32-35) 161
        3.   What they Touch that is Clean (11:36-38) 162
    H.   UNCLEAN DEAD ANIMALS (11:39-40)... 163
        1.   The One Who Touches it is Unclean Until Evening (11:39). 163
        2.   The One Who Eats or Picks It Up is Unclean Until Evening
(11:40)   163
    I.   SUMMARY OF DETESTABLE SWARMING THINGS (11:41-44) 164
    J.   CLEAN AND UNCLEAN DECLARATION (11:45-46).............................. 164

CHAPTER 12 165

VII.   THE LAW CONCERNING CHILDBIRTH (12:1-8) 165

    A.   THE LAW FOR THE MOTHER OF A MALE CHILD (12:1-4)..................... 165
        1.   Her Uncleanness (12:1-2) 165
        2.   Her Child's Circumcision (12:3).. 166
        3.   Her Days of Purification (12:4) 166
    B.   THE LAW FOR THE MOTHER OF A FEMALE CHILD (12:5AB) 167
        1.   Her Uncleanness (12:5a).. 167
        2.   Her Days of Purification (12:5b) 167
    C.   THE LAW FOR THE OFFERING OF THE MOTHER (12:6-8) 168

  1. *The Required Burnt and Sin Offerings (12:6-7)*.................*168*
  2. *The Permitted Burnt and Sin Offerings (12:8)*...............*169*
CHAPTER 13...**170**
 VIII. **THE LAW CONCERNING LEPROSY (13:1-59)**..........................**171**
  A. THE SUSPICION OF LEPROSY ON A MAN (13:1-8) 171
   1. *Three Conditions – Swelling, Scab, Bright Spot (13:1-2)*.....*171*
  B. THE CHRONIC LEPROSY ON A MAN (13:9-23) 173
   1. *White Swelling, Hair Turned White, Quick Raw Flesh – Declare Unclean (13:9-11)*...*173*
   2. *White Leprosy Covers All of Body – Declare Clean (13:12-13)* 174
   3. *Presence of Raw Flesh – Declare Unclean (13:14-15)* *175*
   4. *Raw Flesh Turned White Leper – Declare Clean (13:16-17)* *175*
   5. *Boil Turns to Deep White Swelling or Reddish White Spot – Declare Unclean (13:18-20)*...*175*
   6. *Boil, No White Hairs, and Skin Deep – Isolate Seven Days (13:21)* 176
   7. *Boil, White Swelling or Reddish Spot Spreads – Declare Unclean (13:22)*...*176*
   8. *Scar from Boil – Declare Clean (13:23)*...............................*176*
  C. THE BURN TURNED TO LEPROSY ON A MAN (13:24-) 177
   1. *Burn Turns to Deep Bright Spot, Reddish-white, or White – Declare Unclean (13:24-25)*...*177*
   2. *No White Hair No Deep Spot – Isolate Seven Days (13:26)* 177
   3. *Bright Spot Spreads Deeper – Declare Unclean (13:27)*.....*177*
   4. *Bright Spot Stays the Same – Declare Clean (13:28)*..........*178*
  D. THE INFECTION OF LEPROSY IN THE HAIR OF MAN AND WOMEN (13:29-37) 178
   1. *Deep in Skin with Thin Yellowish Hair – Declare Unclean (13:30)* 178
   2. *Skin Deep with No Black Hair – Isolate Seven Days (13:31)**179*
   3. *Not Spread, Shave – Isolate Seven Days (13:32-33)*...........*179*
   4. *No Change – Declare Clean (13:34)*....................................*179*
   5. *Change – Declare Unclean (13:35-36)*................................*180*
   6. *Spot Remains with Black Hair Growing – Declare Clean (13:37)* 180
  E. THE INFECTION OF LEPROSY IN THE SKIN OF MAN AND WOMEN (13:38-39) 180
   1. *Bright Spots Faint White Eczema – Declare Clean (13:38-39)* 180
  F. THE INFECTION OF LEPROSY ON A BALD MAN (13:40-46) 181
   1. *Just the Loss of the Hair – Declared Clean (13:40)* *181*
   2. *Bald on Front and Sides – Declared Clean (13:41)*.............*181*

3. Bald Head or Forehead with Reddish-white Infection – Declared Unclean (13:42-46) 181
G. THE INFECTION OF LEPROSY ON GARMENTS (13:47-59) 182

CHAPTER 14 188

IX. THE LAW CONCERNING THE CLEANSING OF LEPROSY (14:1-57) 188

A. INSPECTION BY THE PRIEST OUTSIDE THE CAMP (14:1-3A) 188
   1. Ceremony for the Healed Leper (14:3b) 188
   2. Leper Waits Seven Days Outside Camp (14:8-9) 190
   3. Offering on the Eighth Day (14:10-11) 191
   4. Second Male Lamb for Sin Offering (14:19a) 194
   5. One Ewe Lamb for Burnt Offering and the Grain Offering (14:19b-20) 194
   6. Offering Substitute for the Poor (14:21-32) 195
   7. The Leprosy in the Promised Land (14:33-53) 197
   8. House with Mark Not Spread after the Renovation – Declare Clean (14:48) 200
B. THE LAW OF LEPROSY CONCLUSION (14:54-57) 202

CHAPTER 15 204

X. THE LAW CONCERNING A MAN OR WOMAN WITH A DISCHARGE (15:1-33) 204

A. FOR THE MAN IN GENERAL (15:1-15) 204
   1. The Person of the Man with a Discharge (15:1-4) 204
   2. The Nurse of the Man with a Discharge (15:5-7) 206
   3. The Atonement of the Man with a Discharge (15:13-15) ... 210
B. FOR THE MAN IN SPECIFIC (15:16-18) 210
   1. Of the Man (15:16-17) 210
   2. Of the Man with a Woman (15:18) 211
C. FOR THE WOMAN IN GENERAL (15:19-30) 212
   1. The Person of the Woman with a Discharge (15:19-20) 212
   2. The Man of the Woman with a Discharge (15:21-24) 213
   3. The Illness of the Woman with a Discharge (15:25-26) 213
   4. The Nurse of the Woman with a Discharge (15:27) 214
   5. The Atonement of the Woman with a Discharge (15:28-30) 214
D. FOR THE CEREMONY IN GENERAL (15:31) 215
E. FOR THE MAN AND WOMAN IN GENERAL (15:32-33) 215

CHAPTER 16 217

XI. THE LAW CONCERNING THE DAY OF ATONEMENT (16:1-34) ... 217

A. THE TIME OF THE GIVING OF THE LAW FOR THE DAY OF ATONEMENT (16:1-28). 217

        1.   The Prohibition of Entry into the Holy of Holies (16:1-2)....217
        2.   The Permission of Entry into the Holy of Holies (16:3-5). ...218
        3.   The Program of Entry into the Holy of Holies (16:28)..........219
   B.   THE DAY OF THE DAY OF ATONEMENT (16:29). 227
        1.   A Statute for Cessation (16:30-31)...227
        2.   A Statute for Succession (16:32-33)..228
        3.   A Statute for Expiation (16:34)..229

CHAPTER 17..**230**

XII.   **THE LAW FORBIDDING THE EGYPTIAN AND CANAANITE WAYS (17:1-18:30)**..**230**

   A.   THE FORBIDDEN WORSHIP (17:1-9)..233
        1.   The Sacrifice (17:1-7)..233
        2.   The Burnt (17:8-9)...239
   B.   THE FORBIDDEN BLOOD (17:10-16)..240
        1.   The Animal's Life Taken by Man (17:10-16)..........................240
        2.   The Animal's Life Taken by Nature (17:15-16)....................242

CHAPTER 18..**244**

   C.   THE FORBIDDEN RELATIONSHIPS (18:1-30)..244
        1.   When Israel Enters Canaan Land (18:1-5)............................244
        2.   When Israel Sees Canaan Land (18:24-30)..........................253

CHAPTER 19..**255**

XIII.   **THE LAW OF THE WAYS OF LIFE (19:1-37)**....................................**255**

   A.   THE WAYS OF THE LORD'S HOLINESS (19:1-18)...................................255
        1.   You Shall (19:1-10)..255
        2.   You Shall Not (19:11-18)..258
   B.   THE WAYS OF THE LORD'S STATUTES (19:19-37)................................261
        1.   Concerning the Different Kinds of Things (19:19)...............261
        2.   Concerning the Carnal Kinds of Things (19:20-22)............262
        3.   Concerning the Planting Kinds of Things (19:23-25).........263
        4.   Concerning the Cultic Kinds of Things (19:26)....................264
        5.   Concerning the Grooming Kinds of Things (19:27)............264
        6.   Concerning the Body Marking Kinds of Things (19:28)......264
        7.   Concerning the Trafficking Kinds of Things (19:29)............264
        8.   Concerning the Worship Kinds of Things (19:30)................265
        9.   Concerning the Defiling Kinds of Things (19:31).................265
       10.   Concerning the Elderly Kinds of Things (19:32)..................265
       11.   Concerning the Foreigner Kind of Things (19:33-34).........266
       12.   Concerning the Commerce Kinds of Things (19:35-36)......266
       13.   Concerning the LORD's Kind of Things (19:37)...................266

CHAPTER 20..**267**

XIV. THE LAW OF THE SIN PENALTY (20:1-27). 267

    A.   The Idolatry Sins (20:1-8)...267
        1.   By Playing the Harlot with Molech (20:1-5). 267
        2.   By Playing the Harlot with Mediums (20:6-8). 268
    B.   The Relationship Sins (20:9-26). 269
        1.   The Profanity in Family Relationships (20:9). 269
        2.   The Penalty in Sexual Relationships 270
        3.   The Purpose in Godly Relationships (20:26). 273
    C.   The Mediums Sin (20:27). 274

CHAPTER 21 276

XV. THE LAW FOR THE LIFE OF A PRIEST (21:1-22:14). 276

    A.   To Keep the Priestly Line Holy (21:1-8)..276
        1.   From Defiling Himself by Touching the Dead (21:1)...........276
        2.   From Defiling Himself by the Blood Relationships (21:4)...277
        3.   From Defiling Himself by Altering the Flesh (21:5).............277
        4.   From Defiling Himself by Profaning the LORD (21:6). 278
        5.   From Defiling Himself by Women Relationships (21:7)......278
        6.   From Defiling Himself by His Consecration (21:8). 279
    B.   To Keep the Priestly Family Holy (21:9). 279
    C.   To Keep the Highest Priest Holy (21:10-15)..................................280
        1.   His Garments (21:10). 280
        2.   His Actions (21:11). 280
        3.   His Wife (21:13-15). 281
    D.   To Keep the Priesthood Holy (21:16-24). 281
        1.   The Man with a Physical Defect Cannot Offer the LORD's Food (21:16-21)...281
        2.   The Man with a Physical Defect Can Eat the LORD's Food (21:24).   282

CHAPTER 22 284

    E.   To Keep the Gifts of Israel Holy (22:1-14).....................................284
        1.   The Purpose of the Holy Gifts (22:1-2). 284
        2.   The Prohibited of the Holy Gifts 284
        3.   The Punishment of the Holy Gifts (22:14). 287

XVI. THE LAW OF THE ANIMAL OFFERINGS (22:17-33).................... 288

    A.   The Offering Must Be without Defect (22:17-25)........................288
        1.   The Burnt Offering (22:17-20)..288
        2.   The Sacrifice of Peace Offering (22:21-25)........................289
    B.   The Offering Must Meet Requirements (22:27-33).....................289
        1.   The Age of the Animal (22:27). 289
        2.   The Restriction of the Animal (22:28)...............................290
        3.   The Presentation of the Animal (22:29). 290

| | | 4. | The Eating of the Animal (22:33)..290 |

CHAPTER 23 292

XVII.		**THE LAW OF THE APPOINTED TIMES AND SEASONS (23:1-44).** 292
	A.	THE SABBATH DAY (23:1-4)..292
	B.	THE PASSOVER (23:5)..292
	C.	THE FEAST OF UNLEAVENED BREAD (23:4-8). 293
	D.	THE FIRST FRUITS (23:9-14). 294
	E.	THE DAY OF PENTECOST (23:15)..296
	1.	The Offering for Pentecost (23:16-22)....................................296
	F.	THE DAY OF THE NEW YEAR (23:23-25). 299
	G.	THE DAY OF ATONEMENT (23:26-28). 300
	1.	The Restriction (23:29-32)..301
	H.	THE FEAST OF BOOTHS (23:33-24). 302
	1.	The First of the Seven Days (23:35). 302
	2.	The Days of the Seven Days (23:36). 302
	3.	The Eighth Day after the Seven Days (23:37-38). 302
	4.	The Events of the Seven Days (23:39)...................................303

CHAPTER 24 306

XVIII.		**THE LAW FOR THE TABERNACLE OBJECTS (24:1-9)**...............306
	A.	THE MENORAH (24:1-4). 306
	B.	THE TABLE OF SHOWBREAD (24:5-9)..307

XIX.		**THE LAW FOR THOSE WHO FIGHT (24:10-23).** 308
	A.	THE EXAMPLE OF THE ISRAELITE WHO BLASPHEMES (24:10-12)..........308
	1.	The Consequence (24:13). 309
	2.	The Communication (24:16)...309
	B.	THE EXAMPLE OF THE DIFFERENCE BETWEEN MAN AND BEAST (24:17-23). 310
	1.	The Story (24:17-21)...310
	2.	The Standard (24:22)..310
	3.	The Stoning (24:23). 311

CHAPTER 25 312

XX.		**THE LAW OF THE YEARS OF REST (25:1-22).** 312
	A.	THE REST OF THE FIELDS IN THE SEVENTH YEAR (25:1-7). 312
	B.	THE REST OF THE JUBILEE IN THE FIFTIETH YEAR (25:8-13)..................313
	C.	THE REST OF THE PROPERTY IN THE SEVENTH YEAR............................315
	1.	Establish the Value of the Crops (25:14-17). 315
	2.	Establish the Blessing of the Crops (25:18-21). 316
	3.	Establish the Consumption of the Crops (25:22). 317

XXI.		**THE LAW OF THE REDEMPTION (25:23-26:46).**	**317**
	A.	THE LAND (25:23-34).	317
	1.	Redemption Rights of the Land (25:23).	317
	2.	Redemption Rights of Sold Land (25:25-28).	319
	3.	Redemption Rights in Walled Cities (25:29-30).	319
	4.	Redemption Rights in Unwalled Villages (25:31).	320
	5.	Redemption Rights for Levite Cities (25:32-34).	320
	B.	THE PEOPLE (25:35-55).	322
	1.	Provisions for the Poor (25:35-44).	322
	2.	Provisions for the Slaves (25:44-55).	323

CHAPTER 26 .... **326**

	C.	THE LAW OF THE SERVANTS OF THE LORD (26:1-46).	326
	1.	Laws for the Faithful Servants (26:1-13).	326
	2.	Laws for the Unfaithful Servants (26:14-39).	330
	3.	Laws for the Repentant Servants (26:40-46).	337

CHAPTER 27 .... **340**

XXII.		**THE LAW OF THE VALUATION (27:1-33).**	**340**
	A.	THE VALUATION OF PERSONS FOR REDEMPTION (27:1-2).	340
	1.	The Male Twenty to Sixty (27:3).	340
	2.	The Female Twenty to Sixty (27:4).	340
	3.	The Male Five to Twenty (27:5a).	341
	4.	The Female Five to Twenty (27:5b).	341
	5.	The Male One Month to Five (27:6a).	341
	6.	The Female One Month to Five (27:6b).	341
	7.	The Male Sixty and Upward (27:7a).	341
	8.	The Female Sixty and Upward (27:7b).	341
	9.	The Poor (27:8).	341
	B.	THE VALUATION OF ANIMAL FOR REDEMPTION (27:9-13).	342
	1.	The Clean Animals (27:9-10).	342
	2.	The Unclean Animals (27:11-13).	342
	C.	THE VALUATION OF PROPERTY FOR REDEMPTION (27:14-24).	343
	1.	The Consecrated Home (27:14-15).	343
	2.	The Consecrated Fields (27:16-18).	343
	3.	The Redeemed Fields (27:19-21).	344
	4.	The Purchased Fields (27:22-24).	345
	D.	THE VALUE OF THE VALUATIONS FOR REDEMPTION (27:25-33).	345
	1.	The Shekel (27:25).	345
	2.	The Tithe (27:30-33).	347
XXIII.		**THE LAW OF THE CONCLUSION (27:34)**	**349**

Preface

Here in America, we basically know the laws of the land. But most of us really do not know the laws that are on our nation's books. The one set of laws that we do know are those that we were forced to learn to obtain our driver's license. Do this, do that, turn like this, turn like that, park here, park there, we all know those laws whether we observe them. After the Exodus of the Nation of Israel out of Egypt, under the direction of Moses, the LORD gave His divine laws to His chosen, select, and even as Paul and Peter called them "elect" people. Those laws did not apply to all the people on the earth; they were specifically for the guidance of the bloodline of the Nation of Israel all the way to the arrival of their Messiah, Who, during His ministry here on earth, would fill up those laws with additional instructions. Those changes by Jesus were for the Israelites, but, as prophesied, Israel's leadership would reject Jesus and lead the people astray from their true Messiah. Jesus then, as prophesied, opened the doors to the Gentiles of the world in the prophesied mystery called the Church. The fulfilled Laws would then apply to all people of all nations who would believe in Him as the Messiah and Savior for all generations.

Living in America, several thousand years after the giving of those Levitical laws to people of the Nation of Israel, enlightened by Israel's Messiah Whom we know as Jesus, the One Whom they rejected, and Whom we serve in His Church with a new direction and enhanced message, we struggle with information found in this third book of the Bible. It seems so foreign to us. So unnecessary. So confusing. Yet, to the Israelites, as they would soon leave Mount Sinai to claim the Promised Land, it was not foreign, unnecessary, or confusing. It was the foundation of their legal system as the Nation of Israel. Whether or not they liked it, it was still their laws to obey or disobey. What we miss by not knowing the laws in this book is its importance in the context of every passage that follows in the Bible. Because we have all sixty-six, independent witnesses in the Holy Bible, we have the fortunate ability to see in its pages the examples of the fulfillment of each letter and intent of those laws. The Jews knew those laws because they lived by them and they understood why certain stories in the Bible turned out the way they did. For example, there was a young man born of the priestly line of Aaron who was set to be the high priest in his father's place one day. His father was the current high priest at the time. But in his teenage years he disqualified himself from ever serving as a priest at any level and he ended up as the commander of the body guard of King David. The text in 2 Samuel 11 tells us what he had done in his early years; the text in Leviticus 21:1-4 tells us why his teenage deeds had forfeited eternally his right to be the high priest one day. You see, anyone in the priestly line could not become the high priest if he had touched a dead human, except for his mother, father, wife, male son or unmarried daughter or anything with paws. The young man had disqualified himself in his teenage years by killing two Moabite men, and Egyptian man and a lion. Not knowing the law, we miss that point when reading through 2 Samuel. Knowing the law sheds great light on the true context of the passage. And so it is with every story in the rest of the Bible that comes after this book. We will find many classic examples in the Bible as we study together this interesting book of Israel's laws and discover the reasons the Israelites did what they did and will do what they do throughout all the generations.

What is the purpose of this study? It is to make this seemingly difficult book easy to understand so that its content will open the true context and intent found in the rest of God's Word.

Jim Hastings

Chapter 1

I. **The Timing of the Law (1:1)**

The book begins with, *"Then the LORD called to Moses and spoke to him from the tent of meeting, saying,"* (1:1).

In those words, we have the timing, and, yet, how many of us have missed it as we pass by this written real estate in our yearly read through the Bible. The book of Numbers sets the stage for this first verse to be written. You see, Moses had pitched a tent a little distance outside the camp at Mount Sinai and called it the "tent of meeting." Anyone who wanted to seek the LORD could go there. It was there that the LORD spoke these words to Moses. The Tabernacle was constructed in the last half of the first year and that Tabernacle sat inside "the tent of meeting." The construction of the Tabernacle took some time to complete. It was after the tent was complete but before the Tabernacle was erected within the tent that the LORD began to give to Moses the laws recorded in this book. These words were not given to Moses on Mount Sinai but in the tent of meeting. As the instructions of this book began to be implemented, at the erection and consecration of the Tabernacle complex coupled with the ordination of the priests, the LORD then moved from the top of the mount to live within the tent of meeting or Tabernacle where He rested above the Mercy Seat on top of the Ark of the Covenant behind the Veil. Most of the information in this book was totally new to the Jewish people who had just left four hundred and thirty years of life in the Egyptian culture. Just after the first anniversary of leaving Egypt, on Nisan 15th, the whole nation would pack up and leave Mount Sinai and arrive at Kadesh-barnea about three months later where twelve spies would be sent to investigate the Promised Land and bring back a report. But before leaving Mount Sinai for Kadesh-barnea, the books of Genesis, Exodus and Leviticus would be completed and in the care of the nation, to be carried along with the Tabernacle and all its furniture and fixtures.

II. The Requirements of the Offerings (1:2-6:7)
A. The Source of the Offering (1:2)

Continuing in verse 2 of chapter 1, the LORD said to Moses, *"Speak to the sons of Israel and say to them, 'When any man of you brings an offering to the LORD, you shall bring your offering of animals from the herd or the flock..."* (1:2).

In this second verse we hit head on the first reason for the book of Leviticus but we also hit on a point that has been difficult to understand for many generations in the past caused by its translation into the English language. In this version we read *"your offering of animals from the herd or the flock...."* Unbeknown to most readers, there are four words in that phrase that might cause confusion in rendering a true interpretation of the intended meaning.

Throughout this commentary, four English Bible translations will be mentioned often to bring clarity to the interpretation and understanding of the LORD's intent. Here is an overview of the four English Bibles that will be mentioned often.

The Wycliffe Bible – AD 1380: Most of you have heard of the Wycliffe Bible Translation organization. Its name is drawn from John Wycliffe who was an English theologian and a seminary professor at University of Oxford who was the first to produce a translation of the Bible for English speaking people. His translation was produced in Middle English. His translation was not from the original Hebrew but from Jerome's Latin Vulgate that was commissioned by the Church in 382 AD. Wycliffe was a master of the English and Latin languages at the time and used his Middle English words that most closely matched the meaning of the Latin words. Nevertheless, it was a very good translation and has been found to be extremely faithful to the original Hebrew even though Wycliffe was not a master of the Hebrew language. This faithfulness was in part because Jerome was a master of the Hebrew as well as the Latin; therefore, because his translation of the Vulgate was faithful to the original meaning of the text, so, too, Wycliffe's translation was faithful to the original text. He began the translation in August of 1380 and completed it in the summer of 1381. His English version caused a great riff with the Catholic Church which did not accept his translation. It was his desire to provide a translation that the poor preachers could use to take the Bible truth to the English people. Wycliffe suffered a stroke while saying Mass on December 28th, 1384 and died on December 31,1384 in Lutterworth, Leicestershire. In the years after his death, Wycliffe's followers were persecuted by the Church. In 1408, the "Constitutions of Oxford" banned some of Wycliffe's writings and proclaimed that his Bible translation was unlicensed by the Church and a crime punishable by the charges of heresy. On May 4, 1415, the Council of Constance declared Wycliffe a heretic and banned all his writings as well as posthumously excommunicating him and his dead remains from the Church. The council also decreed that his remains should be removed from the consecrated ground in which he was buried and be burned. In 1428, Pope Martin V agreed. Wycliffe's bones were exhumed, burned and the ashes cast into the River Swift. Nonetheless, Wycliffe's Middle English work has stood the test of time being found faithful to the original Word of God.

The Tyndale's Bible – AD 1526: William Tyndale, also known as William Hychyns, completed his BA in 1496 and his MA in 1512 at Oxford University. He then went on to study at the University of Cambridge where Erasmus had been the teacher of Greek from August 1511 to January 1512. Even though Erasmus left the university the year Tyndale arrived, Erasmus was a great influence on Tyndale. Tyndale was a fluent linguist in English, Latin, Spanish, German, Italian, Hebrew, French and Greek. As you might tell from the dates of Tyndale's life, the reformation from the Catholic church was in full swing and at one point Tyndale had a great argument with the leaders of the Church in Gloucestershire. He felt that the church leaders were blasphemous in regards to the Scripture and according to John Foxe, Tyndale said, "I defy the Pope, and all his laws; and if God spares my life, ere many years, I will cause the boy that driveth the plow to know more of the Scriptures than thou dost!"[1] In 1523, Tyndale arrived in London expecting to secure approval to translate the Greek and Hebrew Bible into English. Permission was not granted. In the spring of 1524, Tyndale traveled to Europe and registered at the University of Wittenberg under the name "Guilleimus Daitici ex Anglia" which is accepted to be "William Tyndale from England." By 1525, Tyndale had completed the translation of the Greek New Testament into English with the help of William Roy. It was published in 1526 but condemned by the Catholic Church in October 1526 by Bishop Tunstall who ordered all copies to be

---

[1] *Foxe, John* (1926) [1563]. "Ch. XII". In Forbush, William Byron (ed.). *The Book of Martyrs*. New York: Holt, Rinehart And Winston.

burned in public. After that, Tyndale moved to Hamburg where he began translating the Hebrew Old Testament into English. He published Genesis, Exodus, Leviticus, Numbers, Deuteronomy in 1530 and Jonah in 1531. His work continued with the help of Miles Coverdale and John Rogers; however, in 1536, Tyndale was condemned for his heresy under the king of England's command. In the early days of October 1536, Tyndale was strangled to death while tied to a stake and his death body was burned. It is interesting that by 1540, just four years after his death, Tyndale's translation, including the completed Bible under the work of Coverdale and Rogers was published in England under the order of the new king. King Henry's official Great Bible was based on Tyndale's work. Just about 84% of every modern translation today relies on Tyndale's work. It, like Wycliffe's work, is faithful to the original Scripture. Tyndale's work was in Modern English and helps show the progression of English words and definitions that faithfully reflect the original meanings. It is for that reason that we want and need to look at the words he used in his translation as we search for the true meaning of God's Word in our study.

The King James Version – AD 1611: King James VI was the king of Scotland. In 1601 he attended a general assembly of the Church of Scotland in Burnisland, Fife where he heard a proposal to produce a new English Bible that followed the rhyme and cadence of the popular Shakespearean English of the Day. By 1604, King James had become the King of England and he ordered a conference called the *Hampton Court* in that year for the purpose of commissioning a new translation for the Church to answer the problems put forth by the Puritans in the Church of England with some of the words used in previous English Bibles. A committee of fifty-four scholars were tasked with the job and these men were divided into six committees, two committees each based at Westminster, Cambridge, and Oxford. The text for their work was based on the Bishop's Bible which was a revised version of previous English works by Tyndale, Coverdale, Matthew's Bible, the Great Bible, and the Geneva Bible. It was not an original translation. Forty-two copies of the Bishop's Bible were produced and given to the committees to use and make changes and notes in the margins. Their work was completed by January 1609 and a committee began to review all the changes and produced one harmonized copy of the entire Bible. The Bible was not originally called the King James Version, it was called the Authorized Version because it was authorized by King James, not God. Robert Barker was the king's printer and he began printing and selling the version in 1611. You could buy the entire Bible loose-leaf for ten shillings or bound together for twelve.

The original King James Version is hard to read because the English alphabet and spellings were not yet standardized in the move from Middle English. A "v" was used for a "u" and in other places a "u" was used for a "v." An example is the name *David* which was spelled *Dauid*. The "ff" was used for the "s" sound. All of this was corrected by 1769 when the Modern English alphabet and spellings were standardized. Here is an example from 1 Corinthians 13.

KJV 1611 - [1] Though I speake with the tongues of men & of Angels, and haue not charity, I am become as sounding brasse or a tinkling cymbal. [2] And though I haue the gift of prophesie, and vnderstand all mysteries and all knowledge: and though I haue all faith, so that I could remooue mountaines, and haue no charitie, I am nothing.

KJV 1769 - [1] Though I speak with the tongues of men and of angels, and have not charity, I am become *as* sounding brass, or a tinkling cymbal. [2] And though I have *the gift of* prophecy, and understand all mysteries, and all knowledge; and though I have all faith, so that I could remove mountains, and have not charity, I am nothing.

Note that in the second verse of the KJV 1769 example the words *the gift of* is in italics. This change was to indicate that these three words were not found in the original text of the Greek but added by the scholars to help with the translation interpretation. It is a grave mistake because it interjects the theology of the revision scholars on the committee rather than allowing the original text to speak. For example, prophecy is not a gift. This prophecy is not the ability to tell the future, it is the ability to speak, if nothing more than to read aloud the Word of God and let it speak to the heart of the hearer. It is the telling of what has been said previously and record in God's Word, not speaking some new Word from God that is not already in His Holy Writ.

The New American Standard Version – AD 1963 New Testament, AD 1971 Old Testament: By the middle 1900's, it was evident that American English was different from England English. Although we used many of the same words in America and England, the definitions of those words were different. The King James Version of England was becoming extremely difficult to use and to grasp the true intent of God's Word. Here is a quick example.

KJV 1769: 1 Thessalonians 4:15 - For this we say unto you by the word of the Lord, that we which are alive *and* remain unto the coming of the Lord <u>shall not prevent them</u> which are asleep

NASV 1963: 1 Thessalonians 4:15 - For this we say to you by the word of the Lord, that we who are alive and remain until the coming of the Lord, <u>will not precede those</u> who have fallen asleep.

Note that in England in 1769, the word "prevent" meant pre – event or go – before. In other words, the KJV 1769 was saying "we which are alive and remain unto the coming of the Lord shall not go before them which are asleep. The NASV 1963 corrected that for Americans by saying "will not precede those."

Throughout this commentary you will hear me reference these four English Bibles from time to time because the understanding of the history of our English word development will greatly help in understanding the words, we need to use to thoroughly understand what words we should be using in translating the Hebrew text to English.

In our NASB version we read *"your offering of animals from the herd or the flock...."*

Wycliffe reads *"... a sacrifice of beasts, that is, of oxen and of sheep ...."*

Tyndale reads *"...bringe it of the **catell**: euen of the oxen and of the shepe."* (... bring it of the cattel: even of the oxen and of the sheep...).

The KJV reads *"...your offering of the cattle, even of the herd, and of the flock."*

Wycliffe used the words "beasts, oxen, sheep." The NASV used the words "animals, herd, flock." Tyndale used "cattle, oxen, sheep." KJV used "cattle, herd, flock." At first glance it seems that these are very different words with very different meanings – but are they?

Two groups of animals will be accepted by the LORD for His offering, those from the herd and the flock. But do not rush past these two groups too fast. To the Israelite living in the wilderness below Mount Sinai, these two groups of animals had great meaning. Why? Because the herd and the flock could mean only the animals that the Israelites took with them when they left Egypt just months before. Here we must ask the question, "What kind of animals did the Egyptians allow the Israelites to take with them when they left Egypt and why?"

First, the herd is a reference to the large bovine cows or oxen animals which are said to be kept in herds. The Smith Bible Dictionary says,

> Throughout Bible history the oxen were clearly the most precious animal for the LORD's people next to horse and mule. But the herd oxen provided the honored sacrifice in worship besides being the main stay used in daily life to plough the fields, and yield milk, butter, and cheese. also flesh meat, and milk, chiefly converted, probably, into butter and cheese (Num. 7:3; Ps. 69:31; Isa. 66:3; Deut. 32:14; 2 Sam. 17:2). The agricultural and general usefulness of the ox in ploughing, threshing, and as a beast of burden, 1 Chron. 12:40; Isa. 46:1, made a slaughtering of him seem wasteful. Herdsmen, etc., in Egypt were a low, perhaps the lowest, caste; but of the abundance of cattle in Egypt, and of the care there bestowed on them, there is no doubt. Gen. 47:6, 17; Ex. 9:4, 20. So the plague of hail was sent to smite especially the cattle, Ps. 78:48, the first-born of which also were smitten. Ex. 12:29. The Israelites departing stipulated for, Ex. 10:26, and took "much cattle" with them. ch. 12:38. Cattle formed thus one of the traditions of the Israelitish nation in its greatest period, and became

almost a part of that greatness. The occupation of herdsman was honorable in early times. Gen. 47:6; 1 Sam. 11:5; 1 Chron. 27:29; 28:1. Saul himself resumed it in the interval of his cares as king; also Doeg was certainly high in his confidence. 1 Sam. 21:7. Pharaoh made some of Joseph's brethren "rulers over his cattle." David's herdmasters were among his chief officers of state. The prophet Amos at first followed this occupation.[2]

The oxen from the herd were the great offering that meant much when given because it was so vital to the occupation of sustaining life for every Jewish family.

Second, the flock. Sheep, goats, and birds were raised in flocks and considered small animals. They were not raised in herds although, in the late 1500s, the English language began to refer to sheep and goats being kept in herds, but this was not the original mean of the Bible text. Flocks of doves were raised by the Jews for the meat, as well as fowl.

This initial introduction to the *burnt offering* means the oxen from the herd and the sheep, goat or dove from the flock was to be used. Let us look on in the text for the specific instruction for the *burnt offering*.

B. The Burnt Offering (1:1-2:16)
  1. From the Herd (1:1-9)
    a) Only a Male Bull Without Defect (1:3)

The LORD speaks, *"If his offering is a burnt offering from the herd, he shall offer it, a male without defect; he shall offer it at the doorway of the tent of meeting, that he may be accepted before the LORD"* (1:3).

---

[2] Smith, W. (1986). In *Smith's Bible Dictionary*. Nashville: Thomas Nelson.

(1) The Animal

First, at this point in the text, the LORD does not qualify the reason for the difference between the offering from the herd or the flock. He only says, *"If his offering is a burnt offering from the herd, ..."* Therefore, the person making the offering has some say in what is to be offered and the LORD will accept it. However, there are two restrictions on this animal. It must be a male and it must be without defect.

(2) The Place

Second, the animal was to be led to the doorway of the tent of meeting. This was a very solemn and restricted place; only the priests were allowed in this area at any time of the day or night. Nevertheless, when a person brought a *burnt offering*, he was allowed into this area to make his atonement for sin. The doorway curtain to the tent of meeting always faced east. At a safe distance further east, the Altar sat which burned with fire continuously. A large wash basin was near the Altar. The person would bring his offering into the area between the front curtain door of the tent and the Altar. That was the only place the offering would be accepted by the LORD. The person was not allowed to go into the tent of meeting, that was the place for the priests. The person would stand with his offering outside the door.

(3) The Transfer (1:4)

The LORD continues, *"He shall lay his hand on the head of the burnt offering, that it may be accepted for him to make atonement on his behalf"* (1:4). It is not the priest doing this, it is the person bringing the offering.

(4) The Sacrifice (1:5)

The LORD says, *"He shall slay the young bull before the LORD; and Aaron's sons the priests shall offer up the blood and sprinkle the blood around on the altar that is at the doorway of the tent of meeting"* (1:5). It is not the priest killing the animal, it is the person bringing the offering. The priest is there to catch some of the blood from the neck wound. The priest will then use his fingers to sprinkle some of that blood around the four sides of the Altar.

(5) The Process (1:6)

The LORD instructed the offeror to do the following. *"He shall then skin the burnt offering and cut it into its pieces"* (1:6). It is not the priest who skins and quarters the animal, it is the person who brings the animal. This process is done while the priest is sprinkling the blood around the Altar.

(6) The Fire (1:7)

The LORD then says, *"The sons of Aaron the priest shall put fire on the altar and arrange wood on the fire"* (1:7). The fire at the Altar was continuous, but it was not always raging as was needed for the *burnt offering*. While the offeror skinned and quartered the animal, the priest stoked the fire in preparation for the animal parts to be placed on the grill of the Altar.

(7) The Placement (1:8)

"Then Aaron's sons the priests shall arrange the pieces, the head and the suet over the wood which is on the fire that is on the altar" (1:8). The whole animal, except the skin would be place on the Altar to burn. The word "suet" used in this verse means the pure fat of the animal. At this point, no restrictions are placed on the use of the suet; it is to be burned. Later we will see a restriction placed on the suet in Leviticus chapter 3.

(8) The Particular (1:9)

But the LORD was particular about the handling of certain parts of the animal that were to be offered on the Altar. That is where the basin of water came into the ceremony. The LORD states, *"Its entrails, however, and its legs he shall wash with water. And the priest shall offer up in smoke all of it on the altar for a burnt offering, an offering by fire of a soothing aroma to the LORD"* (1:9).

With the presentation of the animal, the person making the offering placed his hand on the head of the animal to transfer the sins which he had committed to the animal as he was seeking forgiveness. He then killed the animal in a symbolic act of killing the old sin that was transferred in the act of worship. The washing of the inward parts of the animal as well of the legs was extremely important. It symbolized the washing of the inward parts of the person who offered the animal so that he could live forgiven of the sin that was once within him. The washing of the legs represented the way the person who offered the animal would continue to walk after the ceremony, washed to walk in a newness of life from that day on.

2. From the Flock (1:10-17)
a) A Male Sheep or Goat Without Defect (1:10-13)

Not everyone could afford to offer a large ox for a burnt offering. In that case, the LORD allowed a smaller animal from the flock, specifically the sheep and the goat. Notice that the animal had to meet the same requirement as the oxen being a male sheep or goat without defect. The rest of the instruction from the LORD is the same as for the oxen. *"But if his offering is from the flock, of the sheep or of the goats, for a burnt offering, he shall offer it a male without defect. He shall slay it on the side of the altar northward before the LORD, and Aaron's sons the priests shall sprinkle its blood around on the altar. He shall then cut it into its pieces with its head and its suet, and the priest shall arrange them on the wood which is on the fire that is on the altar. The entrails, however, and the legs he shall wash with water. And the priest shall offer all of it, and offer it up in smoke on the altar; it is a burnt offering, an offering by fire of a soothing aroma to the LORD"* (1:10-13).

b) From the Birds (1:14-17)

But the LORD changed the plan when the offering was a bird. He says, *"But if his offering to the LORD is a burnt offering of birds, then he shall bring his offering from the turtledoves or from young pigeons"* (1:14). The turtle dove is a very innocent and beautiful bird. It is a clean bird, easy to keep in flocks at the home. The age of the turtle does not matter, it is always accepted by the LORD. The turtle dove is one kind of animal, the pigeon is another; although, both are in the dove family of animals. Pigeons grow much larger than turtle doves, but both are tasty and raise for their meat in the Jewish families. Young pigeons were wholly acceptable for the burnt offering of the poor person. Surely the poorest of the poor could afford a dove or pigeon for his offering.

(1) The Priest (1:15-17)

But with the offering of a turtle dove or young pigeon, it was not the person who brought the bird who killed it, it was the priest. The LORD instructed the priest as follows. *"The priest shall bring it to the altar, and wring off its head and offer it up in smoke on the altar; and its blood is to be drained out on the side of the altar. He shall also take away its crop with its feathers and cast it beside the altar eastward, to the place of the ashes. Then he shall tear it by its wings, but shall not sever it. And the priest shall offer it up in smoke on the altar on the wood which is on the fire; it is a burnt offering, an offering by fire of a soothing aroma to the LORD"* (1:15-17).

The priest was to wring the head off the animal and its was offered with the body on the Altar. However, the priest had to first cast away the "crop," filled with grain, found under the neck of the bird as well as all its feathers. These were cast on the east side of the Altar, far away from the tent of meeting. The wings were torn, not cut, but place on the Altar with the rest.

(2) The Aroma (1:17)

In all cases, with the animal from the herd or the flock, the animal was totally consumed by the fire, save for the skin of the oxen, sheep, or goat which we will later learn will be given to the priest on duty. The LORD says about this total consumption of the animal, *"it is a burnt offering, an offering by fire of a soothing aroma to the LORD"* (1:9, 13,17). It was a sweet aroma, an acceptable odor, a sweet-smelling savor that pleased the LORD. A total sacrifice to the LORD for the atonement of sin.

In Chapter 2 we will discover the introduction to the grain offering found in Leviticus.

Law Review – Chapter One – The Burnt Offering

In Chapter One we learned about the law of the *burnt offering*. The offering could be from either the herd or the flock. If it was from the herd, it was a bull without defect offered at the door of the Tent of Meeting. If it was from the flock, it could be a sheep or goat offered at the north side of the Brazen Altar. If it was a turtle dove or a young pigeon, it was offered on the west side of the Brazen Altar. With the bull, sheep and goat, the giver placed his hand on the head of the animal to transfer his sin to the animal and then he would cut its neck. The priest would catch some of the blood to sprinkle around the Brazen Altar. While the priest was sprinkling the blood and stoking the fire, the giver would skin and quarter the animal. The inner organs and the legs of the animal were washed in the water from the Basin nearby. The priest would place all the parts of the animal on the Brazen Altar and burn them until they were completely consumed. The offering of the turtle dove or young pigeon was different. The giver gave the bird to the priest who wrung its neck and placed the head on the Brazen Altar. The crop was emptied and thrown on the east side of the

Altar along with all the feathers smolder and burned in the ashes. The blood was poured out on the west side of the Altar, the wings were torn off and the body was placed on the Brazen Altar to be totally consumed. Two types of animals could be given for the *burnt offering*, four choices of animals were allowed and all were to be burnt until they were nothing but ashes. The smell of the smoke from the animals was a sweet aroma to the LORD, holy and acceptable to Him.

In Chapter 2 we come to the Law of the Grain Offering.

Law Review – Chapter One – The Burnt Offering

In Chapter One we learned about the law of the *burnt offering*. The offering could be from either the herd or the flock. If it was from the herd, it was a bull without defect offered at the door of the Tent of Meeting. If it was from the flock, it could be a sheep or goat offered at the north side of the Brazen Altar. If it was a turtle dove or a young pigeon, it was offered on the west side of the Brazen Altar. With the bull, sheep and goat, the giver placed his hand on the head of the animal to transfer his sin to the animal and then he would cut its neck. The priest would catch some of the blood to sprinkle around the Brazen Altar. While the priest was sprinkling the blood and stoking the fire, the giver would skin and quarter the animal. The inner organs and the legs of the animal were washed in the water from the Basin nearby. The priest would place all the parts of the animal on the Brazen Altar and burn them until they were completely consumed. The offering of the turtle dove or young pigeon was different. The giver gave the bird to the priest who wrung its neck and placed the head on the Brazen Altar. The crop was emptied and thrown on the east side of the Altar along with all the feathers smolder and burned in the ashes. The blood was poured out on the west side of the

Altar, the wings were torn off and the body was placed on the Brazen Altar to be totally consumed. Two types of animals could be given for the *burnt offering*, four choices of animals were allowed and all were to be burnt until they were nothing but ashes. The smell of the smoke from the animals was a sweet aroma to the LORD, holy and acceptable to Him.

Chapter 2

In Chapter 2 we come to the Law of the Grain Offering. The Grain Offering

3. The Raw-Ingredient Grain Offering (2:1-2:16)
a) The Ingredients (2:1)

In Chapter 2 verse 1 we find the raw ingredients of the grain offering. *"Now when anyone presents a grain offering as an offering to the LORD, his offering shall be of fine flour, and he shall pour oil on it and put frankincense on it"* (2:1). We might note here that some English translations use the words *cereal offering* instead of *grain offering* in this verse. Either is correct. The English word *cereal* comes from the Latin word which means the edible grain portions of various grasses. All grains come from some variety of a grass plant. We should also mention here that in some old versions of the English Bibles, the *grain offering* is called a *meat-offering*. Most scholars agreed that the word *meat* is a misprint for the word *meal* which would surely be an appropriate ancient alternative for the words *grain or cereal*.

Three ingredients are given for the grain offering – fine flour, oil, and frankincense. These raw ingredients were all mixed together. We do not know if these ingredients were combined before arriving at the Brazen Altar or mixed at the Altar; nevertheless, they were mixed for the offering. The exact measurements of each ingredient is not given here.

(1) Fine Flour

In the ancient world as also today, flours were ground from a variety of grains. The most common were wheat, barley, and corn. Any of these would work for the *fine flour* grain offering if the product was *fine*. That is an interesting word. In our western world we tend to think of grains being ground to a course texture or pulverized to a dust texture. But that is not the meaning of this word. The word *fine* indicates the quality of the flour rather than the ground texture. The flour was to be of a superior quality – high grade, from the most perfect seeds.

(2) Oil

The kind of oil is not mentioned here, but no doubt it is a reference to olive oil. Although, oils have been extracted since ancient times from all sorts of seeds and used as ingredients in cooking and as a carrier liquid for incense. Olive, flaxseed, hemp, coconut, sesame, grapeseed, canola, corn, sunflower, peanut, palm, and avocado are all used to produce oils and were available to the Israelite people. Nonetheless, olive oil was the most widely used and meant in the Scripture. Oil was extracted from all these options in the same way, by pressing the product in a press until the oils were squeezed out. Ancient oil presses are not rare and many styles have been discovered.

In ancient times, oil was comparable to butter that we use today in the sense that it was added to grain or meal products to make them more palatable to the taste. In certain cultures, olive oil, as well as other flavorful oils are used extensively in food preparation.

(3) Frankincense

We think of *frankincense* as a incense or perfume used for the smell it produces. We know of its uses in the preparation of a body for burial to help cover up the smell of the rotting flesh. But *frankincense* is the resin from a vegetable plant that can be consumed by humans. We find it in the supplement sections of our drug stores under the name Boswellia and it is consumed to help with osteoarthritis, rheumatoid arthritis, asthma, and inflammatory bowel disease. It is called *frank* because of the freeness with which the odor goes forth when burned. It burns for a long time with a steady flame. The tree that it comes from is cut and the first resin which comes forth is the purest and whitest. With each successive cut, the resin becomes spotted with yellow. As frankincense becomes old, it loses its white color. In ancient days, the finest of the frankincense in the world was found in Arabia, the very area where Mount Sinai was located.

b) The Act of Worship (2:2)

The LORD instructed the act of worship for the grain offering when He says, *"He shall then bring it to Aaron's sons the priests; and shall take from it his handful of its fine flour and of its oil with all of its frankincense. And the priest shall offer it up in smoke as its memorial portion on the altar, an offering by fire of a soothing aroma to the LORD"* (2:2).

At the Brazen Altar, the giver would hold out the bowl where the ingredients were mixed and the priest on duty would reach in and grab a handful of the mixture and place it on the fire. Notice that the handful of the mixture was called the *"memorial portion."* The English word *memorial* is our attempt to translate the Hebrew word that means *to remember*. The whole mixture of the raw ingredients was not offered on the Altar, only a portion, only a handful, just a little of the mixture to use as a reminder of the purpose of the grain offering. What was the purpose of the gain offering? The burnt offering was for the remission of sin. For that the sacrifice of an living animal was the only remedy. The grain offering could never take the place of the burnt offering. Rather, the grain offering is a memorial, a reminder. Of what? It was a reminder of the graciousness of the LORD Who provides generously for the needs of each individual, according to each need. The smell of the cooking bread on the Brazen Altar was a sweet aroma to the LORD, a reminder of His goodness to His people.

c) The Remainder of the Mixture (2:3)

Not all the mixture was placed on the Brazen Altar. That which remained in the bowl after the handful was removed was given to the priest. Verse 2:3 says, *"The remainder of the grain offering belongs to Aaron and his sons: a thing most holy, of the offerings to the LORD by fire"* (2:3). For the priest it was a ready-made dough mix to take and cook. The left-over portion was a *thing most holy* because it was the provision for the daily needs of the ministers of the LORD. Priests were not allowed to own land, herds, flocks or raise crops. The *burnt offering* provided them with animal hides for clothing, water bags and whatnot. The grain offering provided them with their daily bread.

4. The Oven-Baked Grain Product (2:4)

But the LORD did not require the grain offering to be only raw ingredients mixed together. The grain could be cooked in the oven and brought to the Altar as cakes or wafers. The Scripture says, *"Now when you bring an offering of a grain offering baked in an oven, it shall be unleavened cakes of fine flour mixed with oil, or unleavened wafers spread with oil"* (2:4).

The baked goods could be cakes or wafers. But notice the one restriction, they had to be unleavened. We know of leaven today as *yeast*. It is a product produced by the fermentation process which cause the bread dough to rise. Any dough, allowed to sit for a while, will begin to ferment and produce leaven or yeast. If you wanted leavened bread, a small amount of old fermented dough would be added to new dough which would cause the whole lump of new dough to expand and rise into a large loaf filled with small air pockets. The LORD will condemn the use of leaven or yeast and use it as an example of sin, how it puffs up the person, making him or her seem bigger or better than they really are. Bread cakes or flat wafers that were cooked in the oven and brought to the LORD could not contain leaven or yeast. That meant that the dough had to be fresh with no old left-over dough mixed in. In other words, the nature of the old dough could not be included with the nature of the new life in the LORD.

5. The Griddle-Cooked Grain Offering (2:5-6)

Baking the grain was not the only method by which a cooked offering could be brought to the LORD. He allowed the grain mixture to the cooked on a griddle. The Scripture says, *"If your offering is a grain offering made on the griddle, it shall be of fine flour, unleavened, mixed with oil; you shall break it into bits and pour oil on it; it is a grain offering"* (2:5-6).

Some English versions of the Bible use the words *frying pan* instead of *griddle* in this verse. The Hebrew word is *marhesheth* and it means a *pan that is used to boil* foods. Instead of filling the pan with vegetables, meat, and water to boil, the pan was left dry and the dough was cooked like we would cook a pancake or tortilla. Oil was used to hold the flour together in the pan, but after the fried bread was removed from the pan, it was divided into smaller pieces and more oil was poured over the bread. Notice also that the bread could not contain leaven for the same reason as mentioned before.

6. The Pan-Cooked Grain Offering (2:7-10)

The grain offering could also be cooked in a pan rather than quickly fried or baked in an oven. Cooking in the pan was a slower process that provided a different textured product. The Bible says in verse 7-9, *"Now if your offering is a grain offering made in a pan, it shall be made of fine flour with oil.*

Chapter 2

When you bring in the grain offering which is made of these things to the LORD, it shall be presented to the priest and he shall bring it to the altar. The priest then shall take up from the grain offering its memorial portion, and shall offer it up in smoke on the altar as an offering by fire of a soothing aroma to the LORD" (2:7-9).

The pan cooked bread had a different amount of oil included that allowed the product to be moist yet cooked inside. This bread was brought to the Brazen Altar where the priest on duty would tear off a *memorial portion* and burn it on the Altar for a sweet-smelling aroma to the LORD. It is the same as with all the means of grain offerings that the LORD would allow. Not mentioned here, but mentioned with the first option of the raw ingredient offering, the leftover cooked bread was surely given to the priest on duty that day to be shared with the other priests' families. We know that because the Scripture says in verse 10, *"The remainder of the grain offering belongs to Aaron and his sons: a thing most holy of the offerings to the LORD by fire"* (2:10). The people would give their offerings to the LORD and the LORD would give a portion of His gifts to the priests to provide for their daily needs.

7. **The Forbidden Ingredients (2:11)**
   a) Offerings without Leaven and Honey (2:11)

The LORD has already mentioned the one restriction for the grain offering by using the word *unleavened*. But, knowing the nature of mankind, He makes sure that the people understand His restriction. Verse 11 says, *"No grain offering, which you bring to the LORD, shall be made with leaven, for you shall not offer up in smoke any leaven or any honey as an offering by fire to the LORD"* (2:11).

We have already discussed in the study the restriction of leaven in the grain offerings. However, the LORD includes honey in this verse. Why? The process of fermentation always uses some kind of sugar. Fermentation is a chemical process where sugar, or glucose is broken down anaerobically. In the process, a foaming or frothing occurs in the process of breaking down the sugars growing microorganisms in the absence of air producing carbon dioxide and alcohol. Modern societies use sugar every day, yet in ancient times, sugar was rare save for the sweet sugar known as honey, a special treat in the ancient world. When honey was added to the dough mixture, the fermentation process was jump started and occurred rapidly in the pre-refrigeration world. Therefore, the LORD knowing that honey would cause the acceleration of leaven or yeast to occur, long before it was finally understood and explained by Louis Pasteur in 19th century, it was forbidden from being included in any grain offering presented at the Brazen Altar.

b) Offerings with Leaven and Honey (2:12)

But leaven and honey was not restricted from all offerings given to the LORD. Verse 12 says, *"As an offering of first fruits you shall bring them to the LORD, but they shall not ascend for a soothing aroma on the altar"* (2:12).

The offering of *first fruits* is mentioned for the first time in the book of Leviticus and it is associated with the grain offering. First fruits is the initial tithe of the grain field given to the LORD at the Tabernacle or Tent of Meeting. Those grains could be raw, cooked in the oven, griddle or in the pan and they could include leaven and honey. However, when they were brought to the LORD as an offering, no portion of the first fruits offering containing leaven or honey could be placed on the Brazen Altar. What was the purpose of bringing a grain offering containing leaven or honey to the LORD? It was a gift to the LORD that the LORD would give to the priests for their families. Leaven and honey were not forbidden from the Tabernacle property, it was only restricted from being offered on the Brazen Altar as a grain offering, but not as a first fruit offering.

8. Seasoned with Salt (2:13)

Salt has always been used in the diets of almost all people of all lands. It is a chemical compound primarily of sodium chloride used as a preservative, purifier, or seasoning. In this passage the LORD required it on grain offerings as seasoning. Verse 13 says, *"Every grain offering of yours, moreover, you shall season with salt, so that the salt of the covenant of your God shall not be lacking from your grain offering; with all your offerings you shall offer salt"* (2:13).

Whether or not the grain offering is for the Brazen Altar or simply a first fruits offering for the priests, salt was to be added for seasoning. The verse says that it is the *salt of the covenant of your God*. What does that mean? To capture the understanding of this phrase we need to include its reference to the Mosaic covenant in Numbers 18:19, the Davidic Covenant in 2 Chronicles 13:5 and the sacrifices in Ezekiel 43:24. In each case, the *salt of the covenant* emphasizes the enduring nature, the everlasting agreement, of the LORD in His covenants with His people.

9. The Roasted Grain Offering (2:14-16)

Finally, the LORD allows for a roasted or parched grain offering. The LORD says, *"Also, if you bring a grain offering of early ripened things to the LORD, you shall bring fresh heads of grain roasted in the fire, grits of new growth, for the grain offering of your early ripened things. You shall then put oil on it and lay incense on it; it is a grain offering. The priest shall offer up in smoke its memorial portion, part of its grits and its oil with all its incense as an offering by fire to the LORD"* (2:14-16).

The LORD calls for the *fresh heads of grain* to be *roasted in the fire*. Think of it this way, an ear of corn on the stalk in the field is a *fresh head of grain*. You can roast that ear of corn in its husk in a fire or you can roast it in a pan or on a griddle without the need for oil or grease of any kind. The head of grain is not taken apart, it is roasted just as it comes cut off the plant. The same is true for wheat, barley, maze, etc. In the case of the latter, the roasted grains will begin to fall off the stalks as they are roasted and the pan or griddle was needed to keep the grains from falling into the fire.

The LORD also calls them the *grits of new growth*. Here in America, we think of *grits* as the coarsely ground hominy that is cooked into a mush. But that is not the meaning of the word *grits* in this passage. Here it means the uncrushed, unground, unbeaten, grain cornel seeds. They may be separated from each other, but each *grit* is a totally intact cornel of wheat, barley, corn seed, etc. They are to be roasted whole, cooked intact.

After being roasted in some method over the fire, oil and incense was to be aπdded to them before they were given to the priest to place on the Brazen Altar. As with all the other options for the grain offerings, only a *memorial portion* of the offering was placed on the Altar. The rest of the offering was given to the priests on duty to feed their families. As always, the roasted offering on the Brazen Altar provided a sweet and pleasing aroma to the LORD.

This roasted offering was to be presented to the LORD as soon as the first, early heads of grain, of whatever kind of plant, were ripened and ready to consume. The LORD required the offering to be given to Him, but, in turn, He had priests and their families that needed to be fed.

With that, the grain offering is easy to grasp. Next, we will study the peace offering.

Chapter 2

You you may have noticed that I did not follow my usually opening remarks concerning the beginning of a new book study. I did not tell you the origin of the name of the book as we call it in our English language. That omission was purposeful. The book of Leviticus is one of the least used but most vital content in the whole Scripture. When reading through the many commentaries of old, most scholars will indicate that the Old Testament Book of Leviticus is vital mainly to the understanding of the New Testament Book of Hebrews. I disagree with that position. It is important to the understanding of the Book of Hebrews but it is much more important to the understanding of the entire Old and New Testaments down to the Book of Hebrews and on to the last verse of the Revelation. Why do I say that? The genesis of that belief comes from the name of this book as it was called in the Jewish Word of God. Let us explore that point for a moment.

If you were to pick up a Jewish Tanakh, the equivalent of our Old Testament, and turn to the third book, it would not say Leviticus. It would say *Torath Kohanim*. Torath means *book of the,* and Kohanim means *priests*. So, in the Jewish Bible, this book is called the *Book of the Priests*. Now we must make a distinction. Which priests? The name *Kohanim* tells it all.

In my book study of Deuteronomy, I provided you with a chart that revealed the order that the camp was to caravan from place to place following the cloud by day or the fire by night after leaving Mount Sinai. It is profitable to insert that chart here. Look at the chart carefully.

Order of the March of the Camp

First	Judah
Second	Issachar
Third	Zebulun
Fourth	Tabernacle Complex taken down and follows Zebulun – Gershon and Merari
	The Tabernacle Complex to be completely erected before Holy objects arrive.
Fifth	Reuben
Sixth	Simeon
Seventh	Gad
Eighth	Holy Objects - Kohath
Ninth	Ephraim
Tenth	Manasseh
Eleventh	Benjamin
Twelth	Dan
Thirteenth	Asher
Fourteenth	Naphtali

In the chart, we notice that fourth in the order of the caravan, the descendants of Gershon and Merari were tasked with transporting the Tabernacle Complex except for the Holy objects which would be the Ark of the Covenant, the Table of Show Bread, the Altar of Incense, the Menorah, and the rest. The Holy objects were to be eighth in the caravan and carried by the Kohaths.

The Gershons, Meraris and Kohaths were all descendants of Jacob's son named Levi. Therefore, all these descendants from these three men were Levites and they were designated by the LORD as the perpetual religious leaders of the Nation of Israel. Aaron, the first high priest was from the tribe of Levi and were therefore Levites by birth. Gershon was the eldest son of Levi. Merari was the youngest son of Levi. Kohath was the middle son and the grandfather of Moses and Aaron (Genesis 46:11; Exodus 6:16; Numbers 3:17; 26:57–58; 1 Chronicles 6:1; 23:12).

All three sons would be enlisted as the perpetual religious leaders of the Nation of Israel; however, the sons of Kohath held the most important role in the LORD's Levitical organization. The descendants of Kohath held the distinct privilege that they could be the priests among the nation. Some would be honored to hold the position of the High Priest. No descendant of Gershon or Merari could

Chapter 2

ever do that. They would have the honor of receiving the offerings, as we are learning about this new book study of Leviticus. They could touch and carry the most Holy objects of the Tabernacle complex; no descendant of Gershon or Merari could ever do that.

With that as the background, this third book of the Bible is the *book of the Kohanim* or instructions for the most important Levitical duties in the worship of the LORD, the Kohaths. If this book is for the Kohath priests, why is it important to us? Let me give an example of why this book is important.

As a teenager, when I would get in trouble and be punished by my parents, for some reason, I would pick up my Bible and begin to read it. Being honest, I only read my Bible when I was in trouble or if some tragedy occurred in my family. At the age of eleven, when my father died in March of that year, I clung to my Bible and *read it religiously!* How could life go on without dad? How could we pay the bills? I understood that because my mother procured me a job throwing the Waxahachie Daily Light in my neighborhood and told me I had to go to work to pay for my own things. She was desperate to hold on to house, the car, put food on the table and simply pay the utility bills. I would find her reading her Bible late at night and sometimes all night. I, too, knowing how hard it was, picked up a second job that year working honey bees for Stroope's Honey. For the Fourth of July and the New Years, I picked up a third job selling fireworks at a stand on the side of the road just outside of the city limits. I struggle with that because money was too hard to come by and I never understood why someone would spend hard earned money to blow away in a flash. As I grew older, I noticed that as my friends whose relationships with girlfriends were breaking up, they, too, broke open the Word of God and searched for answers. In my ministry of almost thirty years, I was in a unique position called Helping Hands at Sagemont Church. Weekly, people would make appointments with me for guidance. In almost every case, something had gone terribly wrong in their life either by their own making, the making of others, or the fall of the economy. In almost every case they were looking for a spiritual answer to their real and personal dilemma. They had poured through their Bibles. They knew the answer was there. But because they did not know where to look, they were weary and came to me to show them where to find their answer. They came to me with a load of bricks filled with trouble that they could not carry any longer on their own and they asked me to help carry their load until they could get their strength back. They, in essence, were looking for an answer from God and a remedy for their mess.

The *book of the Kohanim,* given the Greek name *Leuitikon Biblion* (Levite Bible) in the Septuagint in 250 BC when the Old Testament was translated into Greek for the Greek speaking Jews, was not a good retitling of the book. Our name *Leviticus* come from a rendering of the Greek into English from *Leuitikon* (the "u" being pronounces as a "v"). This book was properly written for the Kohaths as an instruction manual to give answers to the other tribes of Israel when life had gone wrong and they were filled with sin before the LORD. He provided a way for that remedy for the Jews when they came to the Tabernacle to seek the LORD in worship for the remission of sins. Nothing is new about human nature as the LORD created it. People in trouble will instinctively seek Him, their Creator. He provided ministers to give those answers by providing the elements of His laws.

Chapter 2

As my daughter made her journey through three years of law school, her mother and I became her faithful and constant students. As she studied her notes, we would listen for hours on end as she would teach us what she was learning. The one thing that we learned early is that the laws on the books all have specific elements that must be present for the law to be used. That is exactly what the LORD is doing in these first required offerings found in the first seven chapters of the book. He is teaching the priests, the Kohaths, the elements of each law. As the book develops, more laws are attached to these first laws based on how the elements appear. But, be that as it may, the reason the LORD is being so detailed in these basic offerings is because the elements must be known and followed faithfully. They will be the ingredients in the foundation of the process for the eternal salvation for each person – individually. They will also the be ingredients in the foundation set by the LORD when He came to earth and took on the human flesh and blood to be the ultimate sacrifice for our sins.

This book rightfully should be called the *book of the priests* because it is their handbook from the LORD for helping those in need. With that as the background, let us do a little law review of Chapters 1 and 2 and a variant of the *burnt offering* called the *peace offering*.

Law Review – Chapter One and Two – The Burnt and Grain Offerings

The first two required offerings were simple and easy to understand. The burnt offering could be from two kinds of animals, those kept in herds or those kept in flocks. For the Nation of Israel, one year out of Egypt and at the foot of Mount Sinai, that meant the animals that were taken from Egypt. Herds of oxen were taken. Flocks of sheep, goats, turtle dove and pigeons were taken. A male ox without blemish was offered at the door of the tent of meeting. A sheep or goat without blemish was offered at the north side of the Brazen Altar. The turtle dove or young pigeon was given to the priest at the west side of the Altar. The giver would place his hand on the head of the ox, sheep or goat and then cut its neck. The priest would catch some of the blood and sprinkle it around the Altar and then stoke the fire. While the priest stoked the fire, the giver would skin and quarter the animal so the priest could place it on the Altar. The inner parts and legs would be washed in the basin of water before being placed on the Altar and completely consumed in the fire and rendered to ash. The neck of the turtle dove or young pigeon was wrung by the priest on the west side of the Altar and the blood was drained there. The feathers were removed as well as the contents of the crop and cast to the east side of the Altar where the ashes were gathered. The wings were torn off and the bird was placed on the Altar to be totally consumed in the fire and rendered to ash.

The grain offering used fine flour, oil and incense (spice). The simplest and first way to make the offering was to place all the raw ingredients in a bowl and present it to the priest. The priest would take a handful and cast it onto the Altar to be totally consumed. The rest of the raw mixture was given to the priest for use by the other priest or their families. The grain offering could also be baked in an oven, fried on a griddle, pan cooked or roasted. However, the mixture could not include leaven or honey. No matter how this offering was brought to the Altar, a small amount was placed on the Altar and burned until it was ash. The leftover portions of the offering were given to the priest for the other priests or their families to consume. Grain offerings that contained leaven and/or honey could be brought to the priests and their families, but could never be offered on the Brazen Altar.

Chapter 3

Now we come to the third offering, the peace offering.

C. The Peace Offering (3:1-17)
1. From the Herd (3:1-2)
a) Male or Female (3:1-2)

The peace offering is like the burnt offering, but not the same. The LORD said in Chapter 3 verse 1, *"Now if his offering is a sacrifice of peace offerings, if he is going to offer out of the herd, whether male or female, he shall offer it without defect before the LORD. He shall lay his hand on the head of his offering and slay it at the doorway of the tent of meeting, and Aaron's sons the priests shall sprinkle the blood around on the altar."* (3:1-2).

Like the *burnt offering*, the *peace offering* could be an animal from the herd of oxen. But in this case, it could be a male or female ox without blemish. Like in the burnt offering, the giver would lay his hand on the head of the animal and kill it at the door of the tent of meeting. In the same way as the *burnt offering*, the priest would catch some of the blood and sprinkle it around the Brazen Altar.

Before moving on to discover the steps in the rest of the peace offering ceremony, let us consider the word "peace" as it is used here. In his 1525 translation, Tyndale used the words "peace offering" in his translation and rightfully so. In his 1380 translation, Wycliffe used the words "peaceable things," and rightfully so. In 1380, the best translation of the Hebrew word *selemime* was "peaceable things." It meant a happiness for things such as safety, welfare, or prosperity. By 1525, the word "peace" by itself meant the same except it included the idea of the happiness of a friendly

Chapter 3

relationship between people. But now we must deal with the word "happiness" used to define the translation of the word *selemime.*" In 1380 and 1525, the word "happiness" was used the way we use the word "thankfulness" today. Tyndale's use of the words "peace offering" have been carried through in most English translations to today, but the newer versions that use the words "fellowship offering (NIV, Holman, CSB)" or "thank offering," are closer to the original intent of the LORD's meaning. This *peace offering* is not for sin, but for gratitude. It is a thank you gift to the LORD for safety, wellbeing, or prosperity. Of course, all of this has to do with the fellowship of one with another in a right relationship. Between relatives and friends, there is a happiness that fills the souls and the offering is a thanks to the LORD for that time of life.

With the *burnt offering*, the word "sacrifice" was not used, but it is used here with this *peace offering.* We must never confuse the word "sacrifice" with the word "offering." The two are different and have different meanings in Scripture. In our definition of words today, the term "sacrifice" is most often used to mean *doing without something.* By 1805, the term *self-sacrifice* was developed and it meant to *do without so someone else could have something.* Through the years, we have dropped the *self* from the term and we used the word *sacrifice* to mean *self-sacrifice.* That is not the intent of the word anywhere in the Bible. The LORD never asks you to give something that you need, He never asks you to do without, so anyone else can have. The LORD gives you the provisions for life. He asks for a tithe or an offering from what He has given you but He never asks you to give something you cannot afford to give. He never gives you something that you need for you to give it to someone else. In the Scripture, the word "sacrifice" always means *to take the life – to kill.* In the peace offering, the life of an animal was taken so that the body of the animal could be offered as a gift to the LORD. Without a death, there is no sacrifice being offered. Nothing died in a grain offering, so there is no sacrifice associated with that offering. In addition, the grain offering is just a small gift from the massive harvest that the LORD gave to you. With the burnt offering, it, too, is but a tenth of what the LORD gave to you. For example, the LORD will give you ten animals and he ask you to give one back to Him in a sacrifice peace offering. You are never giving all that He gave you and placing you in a position of doing without.

Be that as it may, the peace offering of the oxen was sacrificed at the door of the tent of meeting. With the animal skinned and quartered, the procedures for the remaining part of the offering changed from that of the burnt offering.

b) The Fat (3:3-4)

Concerning the fat on the organs of the animals, the LORD says, *"From the sacrifice of the peace offerings he shall present an offering by fire to the LORD, the fat that covers the entrails and all the fat that is on the entrails, and the two kidneys with the fat that is on them, which is on the loins, and the lobe of the liver, which he shall remove with the kidneys."* (3:3-4).

Notice that the whole skinned oxen were not placed on the Brazen Altar. Only the fat attached to the inner organs, the loins, the two kidneys, with their fat, and the liver were placed on the Altar and burnt to ashes. At this point, the Scripture does not tell us what was done with the rest of the animal, but we will find out that it was given to the priest to cook for the other priests or their families.

c) The Aroma (3:5)

When fat is cooked on an open fire, it melts into grease drops in the fire and smokes is formed. The priests are the ones to place the animal on the Altar for that to happen.

The LORD says, *"Then Aaron's sons shall offer it up in smoke on the altar on the burnt offering, which is on the wood that is on the fire; it is an offering by fire of a soothing aroma to the LORD."* (3:5). We have studied the phrase "soothing aroma to the LORD" and it means the same here.

   2.   From the Flock (3:6-7)
       a)   Male or Female (3:6-8)

As with the burnt offering, the peace offering could be taken from the flock. The LORD says this about lamb being offered. *"But if his offering for a sacrifice of peace offerings to the LORD is from the flock, he shall offer it, male or female, without defect. If he is going to offer a lamb for his offering, then he shall offer it before the LORD, and he shall lay his hand on the head of his offering and slay it before the tent of meeting, and Aaron's sons shall sprinkle its blood around on the altar."* (3:6-8). This part of the ceremony is the same as with the oxen in the burnt offering and the peace offering. However, unlike the burnt offering, the peace offering can be a male or female lamb without defect.

       b)   The Fat (3:9-11)

Reading on we find that the fat of the lamb is to be offered in the same manner as the fat of the oxen with one added exception, the fat of the tail. The Scripture says, *"From the sacrifice of peace offerings he shall bring as an offering by fire to the LORD, its fat, the entire fat tail which he shall remove close to the backbone, and the fat that covers the entrails and all the fat that is on the entrails, and the two kidneys with the fat that is on them, which is on the loins, and the lobe of the liver, which he shall remove with the kidneys. Then the priest shall offer it up in smoke on the altar as food, an offering by fire to the LORD."* (3:9-11). It is not shown here, but the rest of the meat was given to the priests and their families to eat. We will learn that later in Chapter 7.

c) The Goat (3:12-16)

As with the burnt offering, the instructions for the lamb and the goat were together. With this peace offering, the two were separated. Concerning the goat, which has no fatty tail, a separate instruction must be given. The LORD says for the goat, *"Moreover, if his offering is a goat, then he shall offer it before the LORD, and he shall lay his hand on its head and slay it before the tent of meeting, and the sons of Aaron shall sprinkle its blood around on the altar. From it he shall present his offering as an offering by fire to the LORD, the fat that covers the entrails and all the fat that is on the entrails, and the two kidneys with the fat that is on them, which is on the loins, and the lobe of the liver, which he shall remove with the kidneys priest shall offer them up in smoke on the altar as food, an offering by fire for a soothing aroma; all fat is the LORD'S."* (3:12-16).

Another difference between the burnt and peace offerings is quickly noticed. The LORD did not allow the turtle doves or young pigeons to be used in the peace offering.

d) The Perpetual Statute (3:17)

Attached to the peace offering regulations is an interesting perpetual statute. The LORD says, *"It is a perpetual statute throughout your generations in all your dwellings: you shall not eat any fat or any blood."* (3:17).

Wycliffe 1380 translated "perpetual statute" as *everlasting right*. Tyndale 1525 translated it as a *law forever*. Both are correct. By the mid 14th century, as Wycliffe was doing his work, the word perpetual had garnered the meaning of *everlasting, unceasing, existing indefinitely, and continuing forever in the future*. That definition of the word has lasted to this day and is clearly understood.

Chapter 3

The word "statute" meant *law or decree*. It means the same today, but it is not used as commonly in the home; however, it is still used extensively in the legal world.

Other versions of the English Bible will translate the two words as *lasting ordinance, permanent law, statute forever, rule kept forever, everlasting statute and statute age-during*. All these translations are perfectly acceptable for a correct understanding of the length of this law from the LORD, *"you shall not eat any fat or any blood."* The question we must ask here is, "Is this a statute for just the priest or is it for all the Nation of Israel?"

As we know, if you are going to eat meat, it is impossible to remove all the fat before cooking. Additionally, the fat acts as a seasoning for the meat while cooking. We can bleed an animal, but it, too, is impossible to remove all the blood before cooking.

Concerning the fat, back in Chapter 1, in the instructions for the burnt offering, the *suet* of the animal was placed on the fire. In that chapter we learned that the *suet* was the *purest fat* found on an animal. It was the best fat found on the animal and highly prized. Here in verse 17, the LORD does not use the word *suet* but the word *fat*. What is the difference?

When we arrive at Leviticus Chapter 17, we are going to learn that *blood,* is the bearer of life. Another place in the Scripture we learn that *life is in the blood*. Therefore, it is easy to understand that the blood belongs to the LORD because He is the giver of life. He required the blood to be shed from the offerings that were offered to Him. As for the fat, according to Smith,

> The Hebrews distinguished between the suet or pure fat of an animal and the fat which was intermixed with the

lean (Neh. 8:10). Certain restrictions were imposed upon them in reference to the former: some parts of the suet, viz., about the stomach, the entrails, the kidneys, and the tail of a sheep, which grows to an excessive size ... produces a large quantity of rich fat, were forbidden to be eaten in the case of animals offered to Jehovah in sacrifice (Lev. 3:3, 9, 17; 7:3, 23). The ground of the prohibition was that the fat was the richest part of the animal, and therefore belonged to God (3:16).[3]

As for the perpetual statute found here in 3:17, with the peace offering, the blood was spilt and the richest parts of the fat were offered on the Brazen Altar. The rest of the meat of the offering was given to the priest and their families to eat. That meat included fat that was not cut away and put on the Altar. Therefore, verse 3:17 most probably means that the priests were never to eat of the fat that was placed on the Altar or the blood that was spilt from the sacrifice. It is a perpetual statute for the Levites found her in the Levitical Law.

In Chapter 4, we will learn about the sin offering.

---

[3] Unger, M. F., Harrison, R. K., Vos, H. F., Barber, C. J., & Unger, M. F. (1988). In *The new Unger's Bible dictionary* (Rev. and updated ed.). Chicago: Moody Press.

Chapter 4

Chapter 4 of Leviticus introduces the requirements of the *sin offering*. Before we dive into that offering, I want to give you a snapshot of how it is outlined in the text. In order, we will discover the required offering for the following.

- The unintentional sin of a priest that brings guilt on the people.
- The unintentional sin of the whole nation that brings guilt on the people.
- The unintentional sin of a leader that brings guilt on himself.
- The unintentional sin of a common person that brings guilt on himself.

We will also be moving through chapter 5 and the first part of chapter 6 which introduces the requirements for the *guilt offering*. A snapshot of how it is outlined is as follows.

- The intentional sin of failing to come forth as a witness against sin.
- The intentional sin of touching unclean things.
- The intentional sin of speaking thoughtlessly through the lips.
- The intentional sin of unfaithful act against Holy things.
- The intentional sin of acts unaware.

We have already covered the step-by-step process of the offerings in the last three chapters. In this chapter which covers the *sin and guilt offerings,* we will notice that the ordered step by step process of the *burnt, peace, sin and guilt offerings* are always the same as follows even though the details may be slightly different in each step.

- The offering of the animal.
- The slaying of the animal.
- The work of the priest.
- The offering of the fat.
- The disposition of the remains.

The *burnt offering* was the most basic of all the animal offerings. The *peace offering* was built on the burnt offering with a few changes. The *sin and guilt offerings* are built on the first two animal offerings. With this information in mind, in conjunction with the law training we have already covered in the first three chapters, we will be able to move quickly through these two offerings in this chapter and hopefully find them easy to grasp and understand.

D. The Sin Offerings (4:1-35)
  1. For the Unintentional Sin of the Person of a Priest – a Bull (4:1-12)
     a) The Offering of the Bull (4:1)

Everyone sins! Most of our sins are intentional. We lie on purpose. We take something because there are a bunch of them laying around – we are stealing. We say something hurtful because something hurtful has been said to us. And so, the sins go, intentional sins. But everyone also sins unintentionally and that is the context the LORD's instructions for the *sin offering* – unintentional sin. Doing wrongful things, we would not do on purpose. Doing things that are wrong and we never knew it was wrong. The wrong was unintentional. It was still wrong. As you have heard the saying, "there is no excuse for the ignorance of the Law," the same is true with the LORD. But when it was the priest who committed the unintentional sin, it brought guilt on the people under his guidance. Verse 1 says, *"Then the LORD spoke to Moses, saying, 'Speak to the sons of Israel, saying, If a person sins unintentionally in any of the things which the LORD has commanded not to be done, and commits any of them, if the anointed priest sins so as to bring guilt on the people, then let him offer to the LORD a bull without defect as a sin offering for the sin he has committed.'"* (4:1-3).

The priest would have to offer a bull without defect for the remission of his unintentional sin. Unlike the other offerings we have studied, the giver, who was not a priest, offered the animal for the sin. But in this case, it was the priest who needed redemption offered the animal and the high priest handled the ceremony.

b) The Slaying of the Bull (4:4)

We find the next step for the sinful priest in verse 4. *"He shall bring the bull to the doorway of the tent of meeting before the LORD, and he shall lay his hand on the head of the bull and slay the bull before the LORD."* (4:4). This part is just like the burnt offering accept that it is the priest killing the bull.

c) The Work of the Priest (4:5-7)

But then, a different priest, the anointed priest must help with the ceremony. Verse 5. *"Then the anointed priest is to take some of the blood of the bull and bring it to the tent of meeting, and the priest shall dip his finger in the blood and sprinkle some of the blood seven times before the LORD, in front of the veil of the sanctuary. The priest shall also put some of the blood on the horns of the altar of fragrant incense which is before the LORD in the tent of meeting; and all the blood of the bull he shall pour out at the base of the altar of burnt offering which is at the doorway of the tent of meeting."* (4:5-7).

With the offering for the priest's unintentional sin, the details are different. Instead of sprinkling the blood around the Brazen Altar, the anointed priest, that being the High

Priest, will take the blood of the bull into the Tent of Meeting, the Tabernacle, and sprinkle the blood seven times in front of the Veil.

Going through the door of the Tent of Meeting, the first room was called the *Holy Place*. It was a rectangle twenty cubits long and ten cubits wide and tall (The Hebrew cubit was 17.5 inches. Therefore, the Holy Place was about 30 feet long, 15 feet wide and tall.) The back wall of that room was a Veil. It was made of blue, purple, scarlet, and fine twisted linen (Exodus 26:31). Just in front of that Veil, at the back of the first room, the Altar of Incense stood. There, the anointed priest would rub blood on the four horns of the table. At each of the four corners on the top of the table, a horn was carved that protruded up. The rest of the blood that the anointed priest caught from the bull was poured out at the base of the Brazen Altar where all the other blood for all the other offerings was poured.

d) The Offering of the Fat (4:8-10)

At this point, the fat of the bull was offered exactly like the fat of the burnt offering was offered. Verse 8. *"He shall remove from it all the fat of the bull of the sin offering: the fat that covers the entrails, and all the fat which is on the entrails, and the two kidneys with the fat that is on them, which is on the loins, and the lobe of the liver, which he shall remove with the kidneys (just as it is removed from the ox of the sacrifice of peace offerings), and the priest is to offer them up in smoke on the altar of burnt offering."* (4:8-10).

e) The Disposal of the Remains (4:11-12)

The priest was not allowed to keep the hide of this bull. In fact, nothing of this bull could be kept by anyone. Verse 11. *"But the hide of the bull and all its flesh with its head and its legs and its entrails and its refuse, that is, all the rest of the bull, he is to bring out to a clean place outside the camp where the ashes are poured out, and burn it on wood with fire; where the ashes are poured out it shall be burned."* (4:11-12).

The fire on the Brazen Altar never went out. For that reason, a great deal of ash and coal were formed. The ash had to be disposed of in an appropriate way. Do not rush past what the instruction is in verse 12. The ash was carried outside the camp to a place where a fire was burning. The ash was then burnt in the fire. Even the ashes from the Brazen Altar went through the fire. There, where the ashes were burned anew, the hide and all the remains of the bull were burned to ashes.

2. For the Unintentional Sin of the Nation – A Bull (4:13-21)
a) The Offering of the Bull (4:13-14)

Not only can a priest sin, but a whole nation can sin also. For that kind of sin, a bull with no defect was required also. *"Now if the whole congregation of Israel commits error and the matter escapes the notice of the assembly, and they commit any of the things which the LORD has commanded not to be done, and they become guilty; when the sin which they have committed becomes known, then the assembly shall offer a bull of the herd for a sin offering and bring it before the tent of meeting"* (4:13-14).

So far, this was the same as the *burnt offering* that we studied first and the *sin offering* we are studying now. Now, who will slay the bull.

b) The Slaying of the Bull (4:15)

It would be the elders who would stand there and slay the bull. Verse 15. *"Then the elders of the congregation shall lay their hands on the head of the bull before the LORD, and the bull shall be slain before the LORD"* (4:15).

c) The Work of the Priest (4:16-18)

And as with the *sin offering* for the priest who sinned, this offering for the sin of the nation found the anointed priest taking the lead in the ceremony. Verse 16. *"Then the anointed priest is to bring some of the blood of the bull to the tent of meeting; and the priest shall dip his finger in the blood and sprinkle it seven times before the* LORD, *in front of the veil. He shall put some of the blood on the horns of the altar which is before the* LORD *in the tent of meeting; and all the blood he shall pour out at the base of the altar of burnt offering which is at the doorway of the tent of meeting."* (4:16-18).

This work of the anointed priest was the same as that with the *sin offering* for the priest who had sinned. Then comes the fat.

d) The Offering of the Fat (4:19-20)

Verse 19. *"He shall remove all its fat from it and offer it up in smoke on the altar. He shall also do with the bull just as he did with the bull of the sin offering; thus he shall do with it. So the priest shall make atonement for them, and they will be forgiven."* (4:19-20).

The fat was consumed on the Brazen Altar the same as with the *burnt offering* and the *sin offering* of the priest as we covered above in this chapter.

e) The Disposal of the Remains (4:21)

Then, just as the remains of the offering for the unintentional sins of the priest were burned outside the camp, so, too, the remains of this offering for the sins of the nation were burned outside the camp. *"Then he is to bring out the bull to a place outside the camp and burn it as he burned the first bull; it is the sin offering for the assembly."* (4:21).

3. For the Unintentional Sin of a Leader – A Male Goat (4:22-26)

a) The Offering of the Male Goat (4:22-23)

The *sin offering* was required for the unintentional sins of the priests and the nation, but it was also required for the leaders of the tribes. Verse 22. *"When a leader sins and unintentionally does any one of all the things which the* LORD *his God has commanded not to be done, and he becomes guilty, if his sin*

Chapter 4

which he has committed is made known to him, he shall bring for his offering a goat, a male without defect." (4:22-23).

For the unintentional sin of the leaders, the offering is a male goat without defect.

b) The Slaying of the Male Goat (4:24)

It was the leader who brought the goat and made the offering. Verse 24. *"He shall lay his hand on the head of the male goat and slay it in the place where they slay the burnt offering before the LORD; it is a sin offering."* (4:24).

Notice that the verse says, "slay it in the place where they slay the burnt offering." When we go back to the *burnt offering* in chapter one, the goat and the lamb were slain on the northside of the Brazen Altar, not at the door of the Tent of Meeting like the bull. Therefore, the goat of this sin offering was slain in the same place that the goat of the *burnt offering* was slain. But instead of being a *burnt offering*, the verse make it clear at the end when it says, "it is a sin offering."

It is at times like this passage where Leviticus becomes difficult to understand because the LORD and Moses are beginning to refer us back to previous examples already given in the book as examples of how to do the new thing that is being presented. In this case, the goat was to be slain in the *sin offering* exactly where the goat was slain in the *burnt offering*.

c) The Work of the Priest (4:25)

After the slaying of the goat, the priest proceeded with his work. Verse 25. *"Then the priest is to take some of the blood of the sin offering with his finger and put it on the horns of the altar of burnt offering; and the rest of its blood he shall pour out at the base of the altar of burnt offering."* (4:25).

We must be careful to catch the change that has happened with the blood of this male goat offering. The priest did not take it into the Tent of Meeting as with the bull offerings before. Here the priest rubs the blood on the four horns of the Brazen Altar, not the Altar of Incense as before. He did not sprinkle the blood around the Brazen Altar, but simply pours it out at the base of the Altar as with all the previous *sin offerings.*

d) The Offering of the Fat (4:26)

Then comes the offering of the fat. Verse 26. *"All its fat he shall offer up in smoke on the altar as in the case of the fat of the sacrifice of peace offerings. Thus the priest shall make atonement for him in regard to his sin, and he will be forgiven."* (4:26).

It seems that the LORD and Moses are beginning to deliver the instructions in shorthand. Rather, the information is being presented in such a way that a simple reference to a previously detailed offering can be the example. In this case it is the *fat of the goat sacrifice of the peace offering.* How was that explained? Chapter 3:16 says this, *"the fat that covers the entrails and all the fat that is on the entrails, and the two kidneys with the fat that is on them, which is on the loins, and the lobe of the liver, which he shall remove with the kidneys priest shall offer them up in smoke on the altar as food, an offering by fire for a soothing aroma; all fat is the LORD'S."*

It is not mentioned here so we must ask the question, what is to be done with all the remains of the goat after the fat was offered? The answer is not found here in these details about the ceremony; however, when we arrive in Chapter 7, the LORD will give a law that tells us the answer to this question. We will have to wait to see what the LORD says about the disposition of the remains of the goat.

Chapter 4

4. **For the Unintentional Sin of the Common People (4:27-35)**
   a) **An Offering of the Female Goat (4:27-31)**

Common, everyday people, commit unintentional sins too. The LORD addressed that in verse 27. *"Now if anyone of the common people sins unintentionally in doing any of the things which the LORD has commanded not to be done, and becomes guilty, if his sin which he has committed is made known to him, then he shall bring for his offering a goat, a female without defect, for his sin which he has committed."* (4:27-28).

   b) **The Slaying of the Female Goat (4:29)**

This time, with the common people, the animal was to be a female goat. Verse 29. *"He shall lay his hand on the head of the sin offering and slay the sin offering at the place of the burnt offering."* (4:29).

The instruction has become even shorter. Where was the goat slain in the *burnt offering?* At the north side of the Brazen Altar. Goats and lambs (sheep) were always slain at the north side of the Brazen Altar.

   c) **The Work of the Priest (4:30)**

Then, the priest would go to work. Verse 30. *"The priest shall take some of its blood with his finger and put it on the horns of the altar of burnt offering; and all the rest of its blood he shall pour out at the base of the altar."* (4:30).

Crisp and clean, blood of the female goat was placed on the horns of the Brazen Altar, just as with the male goat, and the blood was poured at the its base.

   d) **The Offering of the Fat (4:31)**

Moving on, we find the fat of the female goat was handled the same as the male goat before. *"Then he shall remove all its fat, just as the fat was removed from the sacrifice of peace offerings; and the priest shall offer it up in smoke on the altar for a soothing aroma to the LORD. Thus the priest shall make atonement for him, and he will be forgiven."* (4:31). How do we know what portions of fat were to be placed on the Brazen Altar? The instructions tell us here that it was the same fat portions as *"was removed from the sacrifice of peace offering."* We read that above with the male goat.

e) An Offering of the Female Lamb (4:32-35)

But in the case of the common people, the LORD was always gracious, kind and understanding. If the person who did not own a female goat, a female lamb could be offered. Verse 32. *"But if he brings a lamb as his offering for a sin offering, he shall bring it, a female without defect."* (4:32).

f) The Slaying of the Female Lamb (4:33)

Where was the lamb to be slain? Verse 33. *"He shall lay his hand on the head of the sin offering and slay it for a sin offering in the place where they slay the burnt offering."* (4:33).

Nothing new here. The female lamb was to be slain in the same place as the lamb was slain for the *burnt offering* – the north side of the Brazen Altar.

g) The Work of the Priest (4:34)

Then the priest went to work. Verse 34. *"The priest is to take some of the blood of the sin offering with his finger and put it on the horns of the altar of burnt offering, and all the rest of its blood he shall pour out at the base of the altar."* (4:34).

All is the same.

h) The Offering of the Fat (4:35)

Then the fat was offered. Verse 35. *"Then he shall remove all its fat, just as the fat of the lamb is removed from the sacrifice of the peace offerings, and the priest shall offer them up in smoke on the altar, on the offerings by fire to the LORD. Thus the priest shall make atonement for him in regard to his sin which he has committed, and he will be forgiven."* (4:35).

All was the same as with the male and female goat offerings before. But once again, what was to be done with all the remains of the lamb after the fat was offered? We will have to wait until Chapter 7 to find that answer too.

In the first *burnt offering,* the detail of the instruction was extensive. But each new offering that came after, the new offering was based on the details of a previous offering. A with this offering for the common people, the ceremony is the same as the previous ones, but the details of the steps could be shortened by simply referencing a previous offering.

Chapter 5

E. The Guilt Offerings (5:1-19)
1. Examples of Intentional Sins (5:1-4)

The difference between the *sin offering and the guilt offering* is the intentionality of the act. *Sin offerings* are for the unintentional sins; *guilt offerings* are for the intentional sins. Here are the examples the LORD listed for this chapter.

- The intentional sin of failing to come forth as a witness against sin.
- The intentional sin of touching unclean things.
- The intentional sin of speaking thoughtlessly through the lips.
- The unintentional sin of unfaithful act against Holy things.
- The unintentional sin of acts unaware.

Let us look at the first example.

a) A Person Who Does Not Come Forth as a Witness (5:1)

A guilt offering was required when a person did not come forth as a witness. Chapter 5, verse 1. *"Now if a person sins after he hears a public adjuration to testify when he is a witness, whether he has seen or otherwise known, if he does not tell it, then he will bear his guilt."* (5:1).

What is an *adjuration to testify?* It is a formal promise that binds an individual to do as pledged under the threat of some penalty. For example, a man saw a crime or heard first-hand information about the crime that would help assist in apprehending the criminal. After hearing the officials call for witnesses, he remains silent and does not

Chapter 5

speak, he is guilty of his intentional sin to withhold information and must bear the guilt of his sin.

b) A Person Who Touches an Unclean Things (5:2-3)

The guilt offering was also required when a person touched an unclean thing. Verse 2. *"Or if a person touches any unclean thing, whether a carcass of an unclean beast or the carcass of unclean cattle or a carcass of unclean swarming things, though it is hidden from him and he is unclean, then he will be guilty. Or if he touches human uncleanness, of whatever sort his uncleanness may be with which he becomes unclean, and it is hidden from him, and then he comes to know it, he will be guilty."* (5:2-3).

We touch everything today and think nothing of it. Oh, there are the things that are disgusting to us and we refuse to touch them, but that is not what is meant in this passage. The LORD decreed the certain things were clean and holy and certain things were unclean. Unclean animals included pigs and birds of prey. We will see the LORD's list on this in chapter 11.

c) A Person Who Swears Thoughtlessly with His Lips (5:4)

The guilt offering was required of the person who swore thoughtlessly with his lips. Verse 4. *"Or if a person swears thoughtlessly with his lips to do evil or to do good, in whatever matter a man may speak thoughtlessly with an oath, and it is hidden from him, and then he comes to know it, he will be guilty in one of these."* (5:4).

This example is about the rash person who will say anything and swear to anything without considering the consequences – caring not for what it hurts or who it hurts. These are the first three and they are grave. The fourth in this chapter is worse and must be dealt with separately.

2. Remedies for Intentional Sins (5:5-13)
a) Confession (5:5)

For the first three sins, what can a person do that to remedy the guilt of an intentional sin? Verse 5. *"So it shall be when he becomes guilty in one of these, that he shall confess that in which he has sinned."* (5:5).

Confession is the answer. For the first step, he must admit that he has sinned.

b) The Offering of the Female Lamb or Goat (5:6)

The guilty person must then bring an offering of a female lamb or goat. Verse 6. *"He shall also bring his guilt offering to the LORD for his sin which he has committed, a female from the flock, a lamb or a goat as a sin offering. So the priest shall make atonement on his behalf for his sin."* (5:6).

Notice that this *guilt offering* of the lamb or goat was presented in the same manner as a *sin offering*. That was the underlying ceremony for this guilt offering.

c) The Offering of the Two Turtle Doves or Two Young Pigeons (5:7-11)

But if the guilty person was too poor to bring a lamb or a goat, he could bring two turtle doves or two young pigeons. Verse 7. *"But if he cannot afford a lamb, then he shall bring to the LORD his guilt offering for that in which he has sinned, two turtledoves or two young pigeons, one for a sin offering and the other for a burnt offering.* (5:7).

The poorest must bring two birds. One will be offered like a *sin offering;* the other will be offered like a *burnt offering.*

(1) The Work of the Priest for the Sin Offering (5:8-9)

The two birds were brought and presented to the priest at the west side of the Brazen Altar. Then, the priest took birds and began his work with one of the birds as a *sin offering.* Verse 8. *"He shall bring them to the priest, who shall offer first that which is for the sin offering and shall nip its head at the front*

Chapter 5

of its neck, but he shall not sever it. He shall also sprinkle some of the blood of the sin offering on the side of the altar, while the rest of the blood shall be drained out at the base of the altar: it is a sin offering." (5:8-9).

We must stop right here to notice something very important. Birds were not part of the *sin offerings* as described in chapter four. Making birds available as a sin offering in only here when a person has committed an intentional sin and it is part of the *guilt offering*. Therefore, the LORD allowed a bird to be offered as a *sin offering* by the poorest of the people as part of the *guilt offering*.

In the *burnt offering*, the neck of the bird was wrung, the head removed and the crop was discarded (1:15). Here the head of the bird is nipped at the front but not severed (5:8). The problem is, in both verses, the same Hebrew word was used for *wring and nip*. Why was it translated different? Hebrew is hard to translate because the words are word pictures. One word can take several words to translate into English. In Leviticus 1:15, the head of the bird was completely snatched from the body. Here in Leviticus 5:8, the head was pinched and bent backward sharply to kill the bird but not separated from the body. We think of *nip* to mean *to cut*, but in the days of Wycliffe and Tyndale, it meant to pinch and twist sharply. We can rest assured that the word *nip* in this passage means to pinch and bend back sharply. As with the *burnt offering*, the blood was sprinkled on the west side of the Brazen Altar and the rest was poured at the base of the Altar.

(2) The Work of the Priest for the Guilt Offering (5:10)

As for the second bird, verse 10 says, *"The second he shall then prepare as a burnt offering according to the ordinance. So the priest shall make atonement on his behalf for his sin which he has committed, and it will be forgiven him."* (5:10).

Because it was an offering like the birds of the *burnt offering*, this second birds neck was wrung completely from its body in the beginning of the ceremony.

d) The Offering of the Ephah of Fine Flour (5:11)

But the poorest of the poorest of the poor might not be able to afford the birds when an intentional sin was committed. The LORD provided for those people too. Verse 11. *"But if his means are insufficient for two turtledoves or two young pigeons, then for his offering for that which he has sinned, he shall bring the tenth of an ephah of fine flour for a sin offering; he shall not put oil on it or place incense on it, for it is a sin offering."* (5:11).

How much is a *"tenth of an ephah"*? An ephah is an Egyptian unit measurement of dry grains.[4] You might think that odd that the Nation of Israel would be using and Egyptian term and an Egyptian unit of measurement, but when you stop to think about it, all the Israelites had known for the last four hundred and thirty years was the Egyptian way of life. When this book was given to Israel, the nation has only been out of Egypt for about eleven months and they had just completed the building of the Tabernacle complex.

As a unit of measure, an ephah was just about equal to ten pints. Therefore, a *tenth of an ephah* is just about equal to one pint of grain or sixteen ounces. It is to be *fine* flour, meaning the best and most perfect grain seeds. Also notice that the offering was dry, no oil, no incense (spice).

e) The Work of the Priest with the Ephah of Fine Flour (5:12-13)

The poor man would bring his *tenth of an ephah*, the pint of flour, and give it to the priest at the west side of the Brazen Altar, the same location that the *grain offering* was

---

[4] Smith, W. (1986). In *Smith's Bible Dictionary*. Nashville: Thomas Nelson.

presented, verse 12 tells us the work of the priest with the flour. *"He shall bring it to the priest, and the priest shall take his handful of it as its memorial portion and offer it up in smoke on the altar, with the offerings of the LORD by fire: it is a sin offering. So the priest shall make atonement for him concerning his sin which he has committed from one of these, and it will be forgiven him; then the rest shall become the priest's, like the grain offering.'"* (5:12-13).

Just a handful of the pint would be thrown on the Brazen Altar as a *sin offering* for the guilt of that person's intentional sin. The remaining fine flour belonged to the priest. It was not an official *grain offering*, but it was like a *grain offering* in that the priest would use the fine flour later to make bread.

3. Offering for Unfaithful Acts Against Holy Things (5:14-16)
a) The Offering of the Ram and the Silver Shekels (5:14-15)

Then the LORD addressed the necessity for a *guilt offering* for sins against the LORD's holy things. Verse 14. *"Then the LORD spoke to Moses, saying, 'If a person acts unfaithfully and sins unintentionally against the LORD'S holy things, then he shall bring his guilt offering to the LORD: a ram without defect from the flock, according to your valuation in silver by shekels, in terms of the shekel of the sanctuary, for a guilt offering.'"* (5:14-15)

What were the "LORD's holy things"? The part of the grain offering that was given to the priest was a "thing most holy" (2:3; 2:10). All the offerings by fire to the LORD were "most holy" (6:17). The *sin offering* was "most holy" (10:17). The sons of Aaron who were priests were "most holy" (Numbers 4:4). The land that the Levites were to live on was "most holy" (Ezekiel 48:12). The Tabernacle complex with all its furniture, fixtures and utensils was surely most holy too. The LORD had a law, a statute, or an ordinance about all of these and breaking those orders constituted a sin, intentional or not.

For this sin, a ram was required. The ram was a male sheep. The Hebrew word for *ram* means *exalted or royal*. This ram was not only perfect in every way, without physical scares or defects, it was to be of a ram of the genetic line whose ancestors were the best of the best *rams* in the nation in shape, wool, healthiness, and offspring. The sacrifice of a ram of this nature was the costliest offering of them all. The exalted ram. Sinning against the LORD's most holy was costly and still is today. It was sacrilege.

But when the ram was presented at the door of the Tent of Meeting, the priest was to put a value on the animal according to the shekels used in bringing tithes to the sanctuary. The Hebrew word translated here as *sanctuary* simply means the "holy" ground of the Tabernacle complex. The word is *qodesh* and it means *holy*.

b) The Restitution (5:16)

The priest made the valuation of the ram and verse 16 tells us, *"He shall make restitution for that which he has sinned against the holy thing, and shall add to it a fifth part of it and give it to the priest. The priest shall then make atonement for him with the ram of the guilt offering, and it will be forgiven him."* (5:16).

We do not know what valuation the priests would normally place on a ram but we can give an example. It the priest valued the ram at five shekels, the offender would have to give one shekel in restitution for his sin. Then the ram was slain and the fat was offered as a *guilt offering* on the Brazen Altar. What happened to the rest of the animal? The LORD will tell us that in chapter 7.

4. Offering for any Intentional Acts of Sin Unaware (5:17-19)

The LORD also demanded a *guilt offering* for intentionally breaking any of His commands unaware. Verse 17. *"Now if a person sins and does any of the things which the LORD has*

Chapter 5

commanded not to be done, though he was unaware, still he is guilty and shall bear his punishment." (5:17).

This required offering may seem strange to most. How can a person intentionally do something unaware? It is quite easy. We do such things regularly. Here is a very simple example. You have just exited off the freeway and you entered downtown Houston for the first time in your life. At the third street you make a right turn. Unbeknown to you, you just turned right on a one-way street going the wrong way. You intentionally turned right; you were unaware that you broke the law. The police in front of you stopped you to render a penalty for your sin. You sinned intentionally unaware.

a) The Offering of the Ram (5:18a)

When it came to the commands of the LORD, ignorance was no excuse. Intentionally doing something that broke one of the LORD's laws, even though you did not know the LORD's law, it was still a sin and it carried a heavy penalty. Verse 18a. *"He is then to bring to the priest a ram without defect from the flock, according to your valuation, for a guilt offering."* (5:18a).

As with the sin against the holy things of the LORD, the perfect and valuable ram was to be valued in shekels. The shekels were given to the priest.

b) The Work of the Priest (5:18b-19)

Then, once the value was paid, the priest would do his work. Verse 18b. *"So the priest shall make atonement for him concerning his error in which he sinned unintentionally and did not know it, and it will be forgiven him. It is a guilt offering; he was certainly guilty before the LORD."* (5:18b-19). But what was done with the remains of the ram? We will find that out in the next chapter. But we are not through with the guilt offerings. Chapter 6 continues with the topic.

Chapter 6

5. Offering for Sins Against the LORD Through Sins Against Others (6:1-7)

   a) The Sin Against Others (6:1-5)

Sins against others was just as serious a transgression as sins against the LORD. In fact, you cannot sin against another without sinning against the LORD. The LORD addressed the *guilt offering* here in Chapter 6 verse 1. Listen to the whole story. *"Then the LORD spoke to Moses, saying, When a person sins and acts unfaithfully against the LORD, and deceives his companion in regard to a deposit or a security entrusted to him, or through robbery, or if he has extorted from his companion, or has found what was lost and lied about it and sworn falsely, so that he sins in regard to any one of the things a man may do; then it shall be, when he sins and becomes guilty, that he shall restore what he took by robbery or what he got by extortion, or the deposit which was entrusted to him or the lost thing which he found, or anything about which he swore falsely; he shall make restitution for it in full and add to it one-fifth more. He shall give it to the one to whom it belongs on the day he presents his guilt offering."* (6:1-5).

These were strong words used by the LORD. Robbery, extortion, lies, sworn falsely, mistrust. The guilty party was required to make restitution in full to the victim. A value was to be placed on the sin and one-fifth of that value was to be given to the victim in addition to the full restitution. When was it to be given to the victim? "... on the day he presents his guilt offering." The priest was the witness that the debt had been paid in full.

b) The Offering of the Ram (6:6)

The offering was again a ram. Verse 6. *"Then he shall bring to the priest his guilt offering to the LORD, a ram without defect from the flock, according to your valuation, for a guilt offering..."* (6:6).

And again, the ram was to be valued and a fifth part of the valuation in shekels was to be brought to the priest as a *guilt offering*.

c) The Work of the Priest (6:7)

And, as in the proper order of the ceremony for all the offerings, the work of the priest came next. Verse 7. *"... and the priest shall make atonement for him before the LORD, and he will be forgiven for any one of the things which he may have done to incur guilt."* (6:7).

This ceremony seems very short, but it is built exactly as the ram offerings for *guilt offering* stated above. All the same elements of the *guilt offering* are involved. However, we still must ask, "What happened to the remains of the animals that were not burned outside the camp?" We will discover that answer next.

III. The Law of the Offerings
A. The Law of the Burnt Offering (6:8-14)
1. Cooking Time (6:8-9)

From the first verse and on through the book of Leviticus, the LORD presented five important offerings that He was going to require His Nation of Israel to observe. These offerings and these details were completely new to the nation. Even though we can find similar offerings by the same names in the book of Genesis, those offerings did not conform to the restrictions and guidance found in these instructions. I want to note here as a point of theological correctness, when we see those offerings mentioned in Genesis, we should never apply any of these details to those offerings. Able, Cain, Noah, Abraham, Isaac, nor Jacob followed these instructions when making their offerings to the LORD in the book of Genesis because the LORD had not revealed these instructions to them.

We should also mention that at this point in the book of Leviticus, there were no priests in the Nation of Israel. Aaron and his sons had not been ordained as priests. All of this was just the preliminary information, instructions, and laws that the LORD wanted the priests to abide by when and after they were ordained.

With chapter 6, verse 8, the LORD began to apply laws to the five offerings that He had just detailed. In general, these were laws for the priesthood to follow. The is the Book of the Priests as the Hebrew Bible rightly states. The first was the law of the cooking time for the burnt offering. Verse 8. *"Then the LORD spoke to Moses, saying, 'Command Aaron and his sons, saying, This is the law for the burnt offering: the burnt offering itself shall remain on the hearth on the altar all night until the morning, and the fire on the altar is to be kept burning on it'"* (6:8-9).

The fire on the Brazen Altar was to rage all night and render the burnt offering to ash.

2. Collecting Ash (6:10 – 11)
a) The Dress of the Priest at the Altar (6:10)

The next morning, the priest was to discard the ashes of the burnt offering, but there was a law about that too. It had to do with the formal dress of the priest when he was at the Altar. Verse 10. *"The priest is to put on his linen robe, and he shall put on undergarments next to his flesh; and he shall take up the ashes to which the fire reduces the burnt offering on the altar and place them beside the altar."* (6:10).

When it was time to collect the ashes from the burnt offering which have fallen through the grate of the hearth into in the fire below, the priest was to collect them in his formal priestly dress with his linen robe and proper undergarments.

b) The Dress of the Priest Away from the Altar (6:11)

After the priest had collected the ashes from the Brazen Altar in a container, he was to change his dress. Verse 11. *"Then he shall take off his garments and put on other garments, and carry the ashes outside the camp to a clean place."* (6:11).

The dress garments of the priest were to be worn when he was doing the priestly duties in the Tabernacle complex. But when he left his duties, he was to change his garments and put on regular common clothing when he left the complex. To dispose of the ashes outside the camp in a clean place, he had to put on his common clothing.

3. Continuous Fire (6:12-13)

After the law concerning the disposal of the ashes, the LORD gave the law of the continuous fire. Verse 12. *"The fire on the altar shall be kept burning on it. It shall not go out, but the priest shall burn wood on it every morning; and he shall lay out the burnt offering on it, and offer up in smoke the fat portions of the peace offerings on it. Fire shall be kept burning continually on the altar; it is not to go out"* (6:12-13).

No doubt, this law assumed that in the morning, the fire that had raged through the night would have burned down to where the ashes could be collected, but some of the burning wood would still be alive because under the LORD's orders, the fire could not be allowed to go out. Then, as soon as the ashes were collected, the fire was stoked anew and began to rage again for the burnt and fat of the peace offerings of the new day.

B. The Law of the Grain Offering (6:14-18)
1. Presentation of Offering (6:14)

We now come to the law of the grain offering. It tells us the person who was to present the offering to the LORD and the place of the offering. Verse 14. *"Now this is the law of the grain offering: the sons of Aaron shall present it before the LORD in front of the altar."* (6:14).

When the LORD said, *"that the sons of Aaron shall present"* it indicated that once the giver handed the parts of his offering to the priest, the priest placed them on the Brazen Altar, not the giver. Then the LORD told the priest to present the offering *"in front of the altar."* The word "front" means on the east side. The goat, sheep and ram offerings were presented to the priest on the north side of the Altar. The birds were presented to the priest on the west side of the Altar. The bulls were presented to the priest at the door of the Tent of Meeting. But once the grain offering was in the hands of the priest, he was to place it on the Altar from the east side.

2. Amount of the Offering (6:15)

The amount of the grain offering was to be a handful. Verse 15. *"Then one of them shall lift up from it a handful of the fine flour of the grain offering, with its oil and all the incense that is on the grain offering, and he shall offer it up in smoke on the altar, a soothing aroma, as its memorial offering to the LORD."* (6:15).

The words *"Then one of them"* was a reference to the priest who was on duty at the time of the grain offering. The handful of grain with the oil and incense was placed on the Altar by the priest at the east side.

3. Remainder of the Offering (6:16)

The remainder of the grain offering, the leftover portion, was given to Aaron and his sons to eat. Verse 16. *"What is left of it Aaron and his sons are to eat. It shall be eaten as unleavened cakes in a holy place; they are to eat it in the court of the tent of meeting."* (6:16).

Tabernacle Complex showing the Tent of Meeting. The "court" is anywhere inside the curtain that is around the complex.

The leftover portion of the grain offering was to be made into cakes and as the passage says, it was to be eaten in *"a holy place ... in the court of the Tent of Meeting."* Where was the "court of the Tent of Meeting?" Surrounding the entire Tabernacle complex was a screen fence. Anywhere inside that screen fence was a holy place. In other words, the cakes made from the leftover grain offering were to be eaten inside the screened area of the complex.

4. Restriction of the Offering (6:17)

The LORD wanted the priest to remember that He put a restriction on the cakes made from the leftover grain offering. Verse 17. *"It shall not be baked with leaven. I have given it as their share from My offerings by fire; it is most holy, like the sin offering and the guilt offering."* (6:17).

No leaven was allowed because the grain offering was "most holy" like the *sin* and *guilt offerings*. The LORD said about the leftovers from the *grain offering* in Leviticus 2:3,

"The remainder of the grain offering belongs to Aaron and his sons: a thing most holy, of the offerings to the LORD by fire."

Here, the LORD indicated for the first time that the *sin* and *guilt* offerings were *most holy*. Why? I am telling you this now because as the LORD continues with these laws for these offerings in the following verses, we are going to learn the answer to the reoccurring question, "What was done with the meat of the animals after the fat was removed from the *sin* and *guilt offerings* and offered on the Brazen Altar?" The answer, as we will discover was the same as the leftovers of the *grain offering*, the meat was given to the priest. What for?

5. Ingestion of the Offering (6:18)

The leftover portions of the *grain offering*, as well as the leftover portions of the sin and guilt offerings were to be ingested by the priests. Verse 18. *"Every male among the sons of Aaron may eat it; it is a permanent ordinance throughout your generations, from the offerings by fire to the LORD. Whoever touches them will become consecrated."* (6:18).

The leftover portions of the offerings were given to the priest for them to eat as a permanent ordinance. They were *most holy* because they were part of a person's offering to the LORD for sin. Because it was part of the holy offering, the leftover portions themselves were *consecrated*.

To *consecrate* means to *set apart for the service of the LORD*. The offerings that were set apart for the priests from the grain, peace, sin, and guilt offerings were set apart for a holy purpose, to feed the priest, the LORD's servants. Only the priests were to consume their portions because they were the ones set aside by the LORD to be His priests. They were the only ones who legally could eat the leftovers set aside for them. By eating the leftover offering portions each day, the priest was essentially being consecrated anew.

Chapter 6

C. The Law of the Grain Ordination Offering (6:19-23)
1. Amount of the Offering (6:19-20)

After speaking about the consecration of the leftovers of the *grain, sin and guilt offerings,* the LORD introduced the law of the *ordination offering.* This offering was not one of the five original offerings. It was new. It had to do with the offering required by the LORD for the ordination of Aaron and his sons as anointed priests. It was a grain offering but and it had a slight change but an important change. Verse 19. *"Then the LORD spoke to Moses, saying, "This is the offering which Aaron and his sons are to present to the LORD on the day when he is anointed; the tenth of an ephah of fine flour as a regular grain offering, half of it in the morning and half of it in the evening."* (6:19-20).

The amount of the grain offering for each priest for the ordination day was the same as the amount of the ordinary grain offering of each individual as introduced in the second required offering. It was a tenth of an ephah of fine flour and it was to be presented by the priest being anointed. It was about a pint of fine flour. Half a pint was offered on the Brazen Altar in the morning of the ordination and the other half a pint was to be offered in the evening. It would have been better if our translators used the word "afternoon" instead of "evening" in our English language. In the Jewish world, the new day began about 6:00 PM with "night". In our western world, that is the beginning of our evening. In the Jewish world, evening begins when the sun reaches its highest point at high noon and begins to go down. In our western world we call that "afternoon." In the Jewish world, the word *day* means the daylight hours. The *night* means the dark hours. In our world, the day is bookend with dark to start the day and dark to end the day. In the Jewish world, the day starts with dark and end with light. In the Jewish world the daylight hours have two parts, the *morning,* (before noon) and the *evening* (after noon). Half of the pint of the grain offering was to be offered on the Brazen Altar in the *morning* and half in the *afternoon.*

2. Preparation of the Offering (6:21)

What recipe was followed in the preparation of this ordination offering? Verse 21. *"It shall be prepared with oil on a griddle. When it is well stirred, you shall bring it. You shall present the grain offering in baked pieces as a soothing aroma to the LORD."* (6:21).

The offering was to be cooked on a griddle with oil and then broken into pieces. That is how the ordination offering was to be prepared. It was to be divided in half and half was offered in the morning and the other half was to be offered in the evening on the Brazen Altar as a sweet aroma to the LORD.

3. Giver of the Offering (6:22)

Who was the giver of the ordination offering? Verse. 22. *"The anointed priest who will be in his place among his sons shall offer it. By a permanent ordinance it shall be entirely offered up in smoke to the LORD."* (6:22).

The giver was the priest who was being ordained. All of it grain and oil was to be offered.

4. Restriction of the Offering (6:23)

Just to be sure the priest understood this ordination offering, the LORD said in verse 23, *"So every grain offering of the priest shall be burned entirely. It shall not be eaten."* (6:23).

Unlike the grain offering presented as the second of the five offerings, nothing of this ordination offering was to be eaten by the priest. It all belonged to the LORD as a sweet aroma.

Chapter 6

D. The Law of the Sin Offering (6:24-30)
  1. Place of the Offering (6:24-25)

Next, the LORD gave the law for the sin offering. Verse 24. *"Then the LORD spoke to Moses, saying, 'Speak to Aaron and to his sons, saying, 'This is the law of the sin offering: in the place where the burnt offering is slain the sin offering shall be slain before the LORD; it is most holy.'"* (6:24-25).

The key in this verse concerning the *sin offering* is found in the phrase telling us that it was to be slain in the *"same place where the burnt offering is slain."* In review, offering from the herd, the bull, was slain at the door of the Tent of Meeting. The ram, sheep or goat was slain at the north side of the Brazen Altar. The two turtle doves or two young pigeon was slain at the west side of the Brazen Altar. All the offerings to the LORD were placed on the Brazen Altar from the east side.

  2. Ingestion of the Offering (6:26)

With this *sin offering*, we come to the ingestion of the offering. Who can eat the leftover portions of the meat that were not offered on the Brazen Altar? Verse 26. *"The priest who offers it for sin shall eat it. It shall be eaten in a holy place, in the court of the tent of meeting."* (6:26).

Here we find that the meat not offered on the Brazen Altar, the leftovers, as we might say, were to be eaten by the priest who was performing the ceremony *"in the court of the tent of meeting,"* just as the *grain offering* was eaten. The whole area inside the curtain that surrounded the Tabernacle complex was holy. The priest could find a spot to sit or stand to eat the meat anywhere within that curtain area.

  3. Restrictions of the Offering (6:27a-28b)
    a) Touching the Flesh (6:27a)

Now we come to the restrictions of the offering. First, the *sin offerings* had restrictions on who could touch the offering just as that of the *burnt and grain offerings*. Verse 27a. *"Anyone who touches its flesh will become consecrated;"* (6:27a). As a reminder, the meat eaten by the priest was *"consecrated,"* meaning it was set aside for holy purposes. It was the priest who was that holy purpose. The offering was made to the LORD and only the priest was designated to partake of the meat.

b) Splashing the Blood (6:27b)

Second, the LORD gave instructions if blood was splashed on the holy garments of the priest. Verse 27b. *"...and when any of its blood splashes on a garment, in a holy place you shall wash what was splashed on."* (6:27b).

Based on the previous instructions concerning the *"holy place"* for eating the meat within the curtain boundary around the Tabernacle complex, we can safely say that the soiled garments could be washed clean only within the confines of the complex.

c) Breaking of the Pot (6:28a)

Third we come to the breaking of the pot. Verse 28a. *"Also the earthenware vessel in which it was boiled shall be broken;"* (6:28a). The leftover meat that was not placed on the Brazen Altar was boiled. In this verse, it mentions the meat being boiled in an *"earthenware vessel."* We would say a *clay pot*. This verse tells us how the meat was cooked for the priest to eat. It was boiled. But it also tells us that when a clay pot was used to cook this holy meat, the pot was to be destroyed afterwards. Why? We are about to learn in the next part of this verse that if the pot was metal, specifically made of bronze, the pot was to be scoured and rinsed in water. Based on the difference between the two, as we look at the instruction for the clay pot, its composition was porous. The clay was molded and then fired in the furnace. However, the pot was rough and porous with pits that would hold the residue from boiling the meat. Glazes were not used as we do today to make the pots slick with a hard surface that can be cleaned. Therefore, this instruction from the LORD had to be for health sanitary reasons. A clay pot that had meat boiled in it would not be clean enough to cook another pot of meat later. In that case, if new meat would be been put in a dirty pot, unclean, unholy, the meat would be dirty, unclean, unholy.

d) Washing of the Pot (6:28b)

Lastly, as we just mentioned, we come to the washing of the metal pot. Not all pots had to be broken. Verse 6:28b. *"... and if it was boiled in a bronze vessel, then it shall be scoured and rinsed in water."* (6:28b).

Metal pots could be cleaned. As in this case, the LORD wanted them to be *"scoured and rinsed in water"* before they were reused. In other words, the dirty pot could be made clean for holy purposes again.

4. Ingestion of Offering (6:29)

But who could eat the meat of the *sin offering*? Verse 29. *"Every male among the priests may eat of it; it is most holy"* (6:29).

There we have it, the priest who offered the meat was not the only one to eat the meat. All of the male priests could eat of the *sin offering* meat boiled in a pot.

5. Blood of the Offering (6:30)

Still again, the LORD gave a warning about the blood of the offering. Verse 30. *"But no sin offering of which any of the blood is brought into the tent of meeting to make atonement in the holy place shall be eaten; it shall be burned with fire."* (6:30).

With the *sin offering*, the blood was taken by the priest and sprinkled seven times in front of the Veil. Also, some of the blood was rubbed on the four horns of the Altar of Incense. It was forbidden for any of that blood to be eaten.

The leftover blood that was caught by the priest and not used to sprinkle before the Veil or rub on the horns had to be poured in the coals and ashes on the east side of the Brazen Altar where they would be burn and then taken outside the camp to a clean place and burned again.

Chapter 7

E. The Law of the Guilt Offering (7:1-2a-10)
   1. Place of the Offering (7:1-2a)

As chapter 7 opens, the LORD gave His law for the *guilt offering*. Verse 1. *"Now this is the law of the guilt offering; it is most holy. In the place where they slay the burnt offering they are to slay the guilt offering, ..."* (7:1-2a).

Here we find that the guilt offerings were to be slain in the same place as the *burnt offering*. All is the same.

   2. Blood of the Offering (7:2b)

Then the LORD speaks to the blood of the offering. Verse 2b. *"... and he shall sprinkle its blood around on the altar."* (7:2b)

Unlike the *sin offering*, the blood associated with the *guilt offering* was to be sprinkled around the Brazen Altar just like the blood of the *burnt and peace offerings*. As a reminder, the blood of the *sin offering was sprinkled* inside the Tent of Meeting. The blood of the *guilt offering* was sprinkled around the Brazen Altar.

   3. Fat of the Offering (7:3-5)

On to the fat of the offering the LORD speaks. Verse 3. *"Then he shall offer from it all its fat: the fat tail and the fat that covers the entrails, and the two kidneys with the fat that is on them, which is on the loins, and the lobe on the liver he shall remove with the kidneys. The priest shall offer them up in smoke on the altar as an offering by fire to the LORD; it is a guilt offering."* (7:3-5)

The fat of each offering was to be totally consumed on the Brazen Altar. Nothing new here.

4. Ingestion of the Offering (7:6-7)

After offering the fat on the altar, the LORD addressed the ingestion of the offering. Verse 6. *"Every male among the priests may eat of it. It shall be eaten in a holy place; it is most holy. The guilt offering is like the sin offering, there is one law for them; the priest who makes atonement with it shall have it."* (7:6-7).

We must be careful when reading *"Every male among the priests may eat of it ...."* The LORD had just addressed the offering of the fat and then He said this. The LORD has repeatedly made it clear that the fat of the offering was not to be eaten by anyone, including the priest. The fat belonged to the LORD and was burnt for a soothing aroma. Verses 6 and 7 must means the leftover meat not offered on the Brazen Altar. It belonged to the priest who officiated the ceremony. The LORD said, *"the priest who makes atonement with it shall have it."*

Notice that the LORD does not instruct the priest to eat the meat in the holy place as He instructed with the *sin offering*. Each priest had a family and the leftovers from the *guilt offerings* could surely be taken home to the family.

5. Hide of the Offering (7:8)

Furthermore, the LORD gave the law for the hide of the *guilt offering*. Verse 8. *"Also the priest who presents any man's burnt offering, that priest shall have for himself the skin of the burnt offering which he has presented."* (7:8).

Just as the priest who officiated the ceremony received the meat; he also received the hide of the animal for his own. It could be used by his family.

6. Grain of the Offering (7:9)

If you remember, if the person could not afford an animal for the *guilt offering*, a tenth of an ephah of fine flour without oil or incense could be offered. Verse 9. *"Likewise, every grain offering that is baked in the oven and everything prepared in a pan or on a griddle shall belong to the priest who presents it.:"* (7:9).

In the original instruction for the *grain offering* as part of the *guilt offering*, a handful of the flour was thrown on the Altar but the rest was given to the priest presenting the offering to be his own. It was the same in this instruction.

7. Owner of the Offering (7:10)

But then the LORD addressed who was the owner of the leftover grain of the *guilt offerings*. Verse 10. *"Every grain offering, mixed with oil or dry, shall belong to all the sons of Aaron, to all alike."* (7:10).

The offering of the grain was part of the *guilt offering* and it did not include oil or incense. However, this verse says about the grain, *"mixed with oil or dry."* This is the key to understanding the intent of the LORD here. It must mean that with any of the *grain offerings* including those of the priests making a *grain offering*, the offerings belonged to the sons of Aaron. To them, the leftover ingredients not offered on the Brazen Altars were given to them. That is specific. The leftover grain offerings belonged to those who were ordained as priests and their families.

F. The Law of the Sacrifice of Peace Offering (7:11-21)
1. When it is for a Thanksgiving (7:11-12)

The LORD then addressed the law of the *sacrifice of peace offering* and made an addition to that ceremony in this instruction. Verse 11. *"Now this is the law of the sacrifice of peace offerings which shall be presented to the LORD. If he offers it by way of thanksgiving, then along with the sacrifice of thanksgiving he shall offer unleavened cakes mixed with oil, and unleavened wafers spread with oil, and cakes of well stirred fine flour mixed with oil."* (7:11-12).

The normal *sacrifice of peace offering* was to be offered exactly as it was presented in chapter three. However, here, the LORD added the phrase, *"If he offers it by way of thanksgiving...."* What does that mean? The Hebrew word for *thanksgiving* is *towdah* and it means to *give praise with an extension of the hand in adoration.*

If you will remember, when we discussed the original instruction for the *sacrifice of peace offering,* it was not for sin, but for gratitude. It was a thank you gift to the LORD for safety, wellbeing, or prosperity on the part of the one bringing the offering to the LORD. Of course, all of this had to do with the fellowship of one with another in a right relationship. Between relatives and friends, there was a happiness that filled the soul and the offering was a thanks to the LORD for that time of life. It seems like the two are still the same. What is the difference?

The original *sacrifice of peace offering* given in chapter 3 was for the common man's offering. Here in chapter 7, this law was for the priests. When a person brought a *sacrifice of peace offering* for the purpose of thanksgiving, the priests was to add to that offering *"unleavened cakes mixed with oil, and unleavened wafers spread with oil, and cakes of well stirred fine flour mixed with oil."* Think of it this way, it was the other items the priest would add to complete the meal.

a) Additions to the Offering for the Priests (7:13)

Verse 13, *"With the sacrifice of his peace offerings for thanksgiving, he shall present his offering with cakes of leavened bread."* (7:13).

The LORD did not expect the priest to eat only meat for his meal; He allowed the priest to eat cakes and wafers with the meat.

b) Presentation of the Cakes and Wafers (7:14)

But the LORD did not allow the cakes and wafers to be simply added to the meat at the time of the eating. Rather, a portion of the cakes and the wafers used by the priest had to be offered on the Brazen Altar also. Verse 14. *"Of this he shall present one of every offering as a contribution to the LORD; it shall belong to the priest who sprinkles the blood of the peace offerings."* (7:14)

Here we discover that a sample of the cakes and the wafers provided by the priest to complete the meal was also offered on the Brazen Altar. The leftover cakes and wafers belonged to the priest who performed the ceremony.

c) Ingestion of the Peace Offering (7:15)

As far as the ingestion of the *sacrifice of peace offering* with the cakes, wafers, and oil by the priest, when was he allowed to eat these offerings. Verse 15. *"Now as for the flesh of the sacrifice of his thanksgiving peace offerings, it shall be eaten on the day of his offering; he shall not leave any of it over until morning."* (7:15).

The priest was allowed by the LORD to eat the offering on the day it was brought before the LORD. It could not be eaten the through the night or the next morning.

2. When it is for a Votive or Freewill (7:16-17)

Then the LORD added another twist that we have not seen so far. The *sacrifice of peace offering* could also be a votive or freewill offering. Verse 16. *"But if the sacrifice of his offering is a votive or a freewill offering, it shall be eaten on the day that he offers his sacrifice, and on the next day what is left of it may be eaten; but what is left over from the flesh of the sacrifice on the third day shall be burned with fire."* (7:16-17).

The word "votive" means *vow*. Both "votive" and "vow" mean "a binding promises made to God, often as part of a plea for safety, military victory, or a family.[5]

---

[5] Crocker, L. K. (2016). <u>Vows, Religious in the Ancient World</u>. In J. D. Barry, D. Bomar, D. R. Brown, R. Klippenstein, D.

The word "freewill" offering means "a spontaneous gift (Ex. 35:29), a voluntary sacrifice (Lev. 22:23; Ezra 3:5), as opposed to one in consequence of a vow, or in expiation of some offence."[6]

So, if a common person brought a *sacrifice of peace offering* as a *vow* to the LORD based on something, he was asking the LORD to do, it was a votive or vow offering. The leftovers of a *sacrifice of peace offering* attached to a votive or vow could be eaten by the priest the day of the offering and the following day but not on the third day. If there were any leftovers left on the third day, those leftovers must be burned instead of consumed.

If a common person brought a *freewill* offering as a voluntary or spontaneous *sacrifice of peace offering* as well, it could be eaten by the priest the day of the offering and the following day but not on the third day. On the third day, any leftovers had to be burned.

a) Restriction for Third Day Ingestion (7:18)

The penalty for the restriction of the third day ingestion was severe. Verse 18. *"So if any of the flesh of the sacrifice of his peace offerings should ever be eaten on the third day, he who offers it will not be accepted, and it will not be reckoned to his benefit. It shall be an offensive thing, and the person who eats of it will bear his own iniquity."* (7:18).

This verse might bring some confusion because it says, *"So if any of the flesh of the sacrifice of his peace offerings should ever be eaten on the third day, ..."* The pronoun *"his"* does not tell

---

Mangum, C. Sinclair Wolcott, ... W. Widder (Eds.), *The Lexham Bible Dictionary*. Bellingham, WA: Lexham Press.

[6] Easton, M. G. (1893). In *Easton's Bible dictionary*. New York: Harper & Brothers.

us if it is speaking of the common person or the priest. In addition, it says, *"he who offers it will not be accepted, ..."* Who is the "he"?

Here is our answer. After the common person handed the offering to the priest, the offering belonged to the priest. It no longer belonged to the common person who gave the gift originally. It belonged to the priests to eat because he was the one who presented it on the Brazen Altar, not the common person. Common people could not eat of the offerings on the Brazen Altar. Therefore, these pronouns are pointing to the priest who presided over the ceremony and made the presentation.

b) Restriction for Contaminating with the Unclean (7:19)

But even though the priest presented the offering and it was his to eat, that did not mean that he could be careless. He had to keep everything clean in the process. Verse 19. *"Also the flesh that touches anything unclean shall not be eaten; it shall be burned with fire. As for other flesh, anyone who is clean may eat such flesh."* (7:19).

Two things are addressed by the LORD in this verse, the things that the meat touches and the cleanliness of the priest eating the meat. Considering these two things that the LORD has already told us, a clay pot that had been used to boil the meat could not be used a second time. That pot had to be crushed because it was considered unclean. If the pot was used a second time, the meat would be considered unclean and could not be eaten by the priest. If a metal pot was used to boil the meat, it had to be scoured and rinsed to be considered clean. If it was not, then the priest could not eat the meat. Next, a priest, who was not properly clean, (in his priestly garments), would be considered unclean and could not eat the meat. In other words, if the priest was dressed in his common clothes, he could not eat the meat because he would have been considered unclean.

(1) Penalty for Eating While Unclean (7:20)

With that, we find that the LORD imposed a penalty for eating while unclean. Verse 20. *"But the person who eats the flesh of the sacrifice of peace offerings which belong to the LORD, in his uncleanness, that person shall be cut off from his people."* (7:20).

This penalty was strict. It was mandatory that any priest who ate the meat of an offering while being unclean himself was to be excommunicated from the Nation of Israel.

(2) Penalty for Touching the Unclean (7:21)

The LORD continued to detail this penalty in verse 21. *"When anyone touches anything unclean, whether human uncleanness, or an unclean animal, or any unclean detestable thing, and eats of the flesh of the sacrifice of peace offerings which belong to the LORD, that person shall be cut off from his people."* (7:21).

Here the LORD covered all the possible bases for how a priest could become unclean before he ate the meat of the offering. Let us examine the simplest example from the first phrase, *"When anyone touches anything unclean...."* Here is an example of that. If a priest touched his common clothing while still in his priestly garments, he was unclean. If he then ate the meat of the offering, he was to be put out of the Nation of Israel. Simply, that could excommunicate the priest from his work, his ordination, and his people. A strong penalty.

G. The Law of the Fat (7:22-27)
1. Restriction on the Fat Offering (7:22-23)

The LORD then turned to the law of the fat and told of its restrictions. Verse 22. *"Then the LORD spoke to Moses, saying, 'Speak to the sons of Israel, saying, 'You shall not eat any fat from an ox, a sheep or a goat.'"* (7:22-23).

Here we need to remind ourselves of what the LORD considered as the fat of the ox, sheep, and goat. It was the fat attached to the entrails, two kidneys, loins, lobe of the liver, and with the sheep, its tail. The sons of Israel were instructed to never eat these portions of the ox, sheep, or goat.

2. Uses for Non-Offering Fat (7:24)

But the restriction of not eating the fat of the ox, sheep and goat did not mean that the fat could not be used for other purposes. Verse 24. *"Also the fat of an animal which dies and the fat of an animal torn by beasts may be put to any other use, but you must certainly not eat it."* (7:24).

What other purposes could the fat be used for? Making soap, greasing wheels and more.

3. Penalty for Eating the Fat Offering (7:25)

This law was directed to all the sons of Israel (7:22). As such, all the descendants of Jacob were subject to it, including the priest but also every one of the nations. Everyone could face a terrible penalty for eating the specific fat identified by the LORD that was His of the ox, sheep, or goat. Verse 25. *"For whoever eats the fat of the animal from which an offering by fire is offered to the LORD, even the person who eats shall be cut off from his people."* (7:25).

As we can tell, the LORD was serious about this law. Eating the specific fat identified by the LORD demanded that a person be excommunicated from the nation.

4. Penalty for Eating the Blood Offering (7:26-27)

But the LORD extended the same penalty to the eating of blood from any animal. Verse 26. *"You are not to eat any blood, either of bird or animal, in any of your dwellings. Any person who eats any blood, even that person shall be cut off from his people."* (7:26-27).

H. The Law of the Sacrifice of Peace Offering for the Common Person (7:28-34)

1. The Giver of the Sacrifice of Peace (7:28-29)

In verse 28, the LORD gave the law concerning the duties of the common person who brought the *sacrifice of peace offering*. Verse 28. *"Then the LORD spoke to Moses, saying, 'Speak to the sons of Israel, saying, 'He who offers the sacrifice of his peace offerings to the LORD shall bring his offering to the LORD from the sacrifice of his peace offerings.'"* (7:28-29).

No one could be a stand-in or substitute for the giver. Only the giver could bring the *sacrifice of peace offering* to the LORD at the Tent of Meeting and the Brazen Altar. If you wanted to send an offering, you had to be the one to bring it.

2. The Slayer of the Sacrifice of Peace (7:30a-34)

   a) Brought to the Fire (7:30a)

Once you brought the offering to the Tabernacle complex, you had to be the one who handed it over to the priest who would place it on the fire. Verse 30a. *"His own hands are to bring offerings by fire to the LORD."* (7:30a).

   b) Breast a Wave Offering (7:30b)

The giver was to carve away the fat from the breast of the animal and present the breast as a wave offering. Verse 30b. *"He shall bring the fat with the breast, that the breast may be presented as a wave offering before the LORD."* (7:30b).

What was a wave offering? In this case, the breast was lifted toward the heavens in front of the Brazen Altar and it was waved back and forth, but it was not placed on the Brazen Altar. It was a portion of what we have been calling the leftover meat that was not offered on the Altar but was given to the priests to eat.

c) Fat Offered by the Priest (7:31)

Verse 31 tells us what happened to the fat of the breast and the breast itself. *"The priest shall offer up the fat in smoke on the altar, but the breast shall belong to Aaron and his sons."* (7:31).

The fat was placed on the Altar. From the past passages, the breast would have been boiled to feed any of the sons of Aaron who were present.

d) Right Thigh Given to the Priest (7:32)

But the breast was not the only portion handed to the priest by the giver. Verse 32. *"You shall give the right thigh to the priest as a contribution from the sacrifices of your peace offerings. The one among the sons of Aaron who offers the blood of the peace offerings and the fat, the right thigh shall be his as his portion."* (7:33).

The breast was given for all the sons of Aaron to eat. The right thigh was given to the priest who was officiating the ceremony to be his alone.

e) Owner of the Breast and Thigh (7:34)

The LORD had a name for both parts given to the priest. One was the *breast of the wave* offering. The other was the *thigh of the contribution*. Verse 34. *"For I have taken the breast of the wave offering and the thigh of the contribution from the sons of Israel from the sacrifices of their peace offerings, and have given them to Aaron the priest and to his sons as their due forever from the sons of Israel."* (7:34).

The breast and the right thigh of every *sacrifice of peace offering* were to always belong to the Aaron and his sons.

I. The Portions for the Priests (7:35-38)

1. Consecrated to Aaron and His Sons (7:35)

To conclude this section concerning the law of the offerings, Moses said in verse 35, *"This is that which is consecrated to Aaron and that which is consecrated to his sons from the offerings by fire to the LORD, in that day when he presented them to serve as priests to the LORD."* (7:35).

To say it simply in our everyday language, all the leftovers of the offerings that were not to be burnt totally on the Brazen Altar belonged to the priest.

2. Given to Aaron and His Sons (7:36)

To this point in the story line, Aaron and his sons had not been ordained or anointed as priests. Nevertheless, in this section concerning the law of the offerings, the LORD told all the people that these laws would begin with the anointing of Aaron and his sons as priest and would continue throughout the generations. Verse 36. *"These the LORD had commanded to be given them from the sons of Israel in the day that He anointed them. It is their due forever throughout their generations."* (7:36).

3. Law of the Offerings (7:37-38)

Finally, Moses signed these instructions as law. Verse 37. *"This is the law of the burnt offering, the grain offering and the sin offering and the guilt offering and the ordination offering and the sacrifice of peace offerings, which the LORD commanded Moses at Mount Sinai in the day that He commanded the sons of Israel to present their offerings to the LORD in the wilderness of Sinai."* (7:37-38).

These laws were not given when Moses was on Mount Sinai, rather they were given when Moses and Israel were camped at the foot of Mount Sinai. The LORD delivered these instructions to Moses at the Tent of Meeting (1:1). To this point in the story, not one of these offerings had been observed. But now, with the guidelines and instructions in place, it was time to have a high priest anointed along with his sons. It was Moses who officiated the ordination service and anointed Aaron and his sons as the priests.

Finally, we will put everything we have learned in this book to use. With all the details and laws in place concerning the *burnt, grain, sacrifice of peace, sin and guilt offerings,*

it was then time for the ordination of Aaron and his sons as the first priests of the Nation of Israel. All the details and laws were important and the first time the nation would experience them was during the consecration of the Tabernacle complex and the ordination of the priests. Moses oversaw all of this. He would be the one to consecrate the Tabernacle and preside over the ceremony of the anointing of the priests. The date of this consecration and ordination was recorded by Moses in the book of Exodus. It would be worthwhile for us to hear that record again to set the stage for the details in our study for today. Exodus 40, starting in verse 17. (*Words in parenthesis are mine in the following passage.*)

Instructions for Setting Up the Tabernacle of the Tent of Meeting

¹Then the LORD spoke to Moses, saying, ² "On the first day of the first month (*Nisan*) you shall set up the tabernacle of the tent of meeting (*the Tabernacle stood inside the Tent of Meeting*). ³ You shall place the ark of the testimony *(Ark of the Covenant)* there, and you shall screen the ark with the veil. ⁴ You shall bring in the table and arrange what belongs on it; and you shall bring in the lampstand and mount its lamps. ⁵ Moreover, you shall set the gold altar of incense before the ark of the testimony, and set up the veil for the doorway to the tabernacle. ⁶ You shall set the altar of burnt offering in front of the doorway of the tabernacle of the tent of meeting. ⁷ You shall set the laver (*basin with water*) between the tent of meeting and the altar and put water in it. ⁸ You shall set up the court all around and hang up the veil for the gateway of the court.

Instructions for Anointing the Tabernacle in the Tent of Meeting

⁹Then you shall take the anointing oil and anoint the tabernacle and all that is in it, and shall consecrate it and all its furnishings; and it shall be holy. ¹⁰ You shall anoint the altar of burnt offering and all its utensils, and consecrate the altar, and the altar shall be most holy. ¹¹ You shall anoint the laver and its stand, and consecrate it.

Instructions for Anointing the Priests

¹² Then you shall bring Aaron and his sons to the doorway of the tent of meeting and wash them with water. ¹³ You shall put the holy garments on Aaron and anoint him and consecrate him, that he may minister as a priest to Me. ¹⁴ You shall bring his sons and put tunics on them; ¹⁵ and you shall anoint them even as you have anointed their father, that they may minister as priests to Me; and their anointing will qualify them for a perpetual priesthood throughout their generations." ¹⁶ Thus Moses did; according to all that the LORD had commanded him, so he did.[7] (Exodus 40:1-16).

In the rest of Exodus chapter 40, we can read about each step Moses took to fulfill the instructions we just read. On the first day of Nisan, 1464 BC, Moses led the erection of the Tabernacle complex with the material that had been prepared. He then anointed the complex to consecrate it in preparation for the ordination ceremony. He then brought Aaron and his sons to the complex and performed the ceremony just as he was instructed.

---

[7] *New American Standard Bible, 1995 Edition: Paragraph Version*. (1995). (Ex 40:1–16). La Habra, CA: The Lockman Foundation.

Chapter 8

IV. The Ordination and Offerings for Aaron and His Sons by Moses (8:1-9:24)
   A. Day One of the Ordination (8:1-36)
      1. The Priest and the Offerings (8:1-4a)

Here in Leviticus chapter 8, the mystery writer introduces the LORD's instruction to Moses for the ordination ceremony of Aaron and his sons on the same day as the erection and consecration of the Tabernacle complex Verse 1. *"Then the LORD spoke to Moses, saying, "Take Aaron and his sons with him, and the garments and the anointing oil and the bull of the sin offering, and the two rams and the basket of unleavened bread, and assemble all the congregation at the doorway of the tent of meeting. So Moses did just as the LORD commanded him."* (8:1-4a).

Day one of the ordination of Aaron and his sons included the garments, anointing oil, a bull for the sin offering, two rams and unleavened bread which will be used as a *grain offering.* The men and the items were gathered at the doorway of the Tent of Meeting which covered the holy Tabernacle.

   2. The Announcement to the Nation (8:4b – 5)

When everything was ready and the congregation was assembled, verse 4b says the following. *"When the congregation was assembled at the doorway of the tent of meeting, Moses said to the congregation, 'This is the thing which the LORD has commanded to do.'"* (8:4b – 5).

The announcement to the nation is not too surprising. What I find surprising is what is not said or explained in this verse. The curtains that surrounded the courtyard of the complex were high enough that no one outside the curtains could have seen in. The courtyard was 175 feet long and 87 ½ feet wide. It would have been impossible for 601,730 men, age twenty and over to gather inside the curtains in the courtyard of the Tabernacle complex to watch. The whole square footage of the courtyard was 15,313 ½ feet. That means that on every square foot, 39 people would have to be standing, not sitting, on each other's shoulders – 39 people high. Impossible. But the clue to this problem is found in the passage we read a few minutes ago in Exodus 40:8. *"You shall set up the court all around and hang up the veil for the gateway of the court."* The LORD did not instruct Moses to hang the curtain that surrounded the court. He told him to set up the court, which included the Tabernacle, the Basin, Altar of Incense, Table of Show Bread, the Candlestick, and Brazen Altar, but says nothing about the curtain. Further, He told Moses to hang the veil that acted like the door of the curtain boundary on the east side. Because of the way Moses was told to have the poles and braces for the veil door constructed, the veil could be hung without relying on the curtain screen that surrounded the complex. Therefore, when the assembly gathered at the "doorway of the tent of meeting, it must have meant that they gathered all around the complex and out as far as needed for everyone to be present without the barrier of the curtain screen being present.

   3. **The Washing of Aaron and His Sons (8:6)**

With everyone present, Moses followed the instructions. Verse 6. *"Then Moses had Aaron and his sons come near and washed them with water."* (8:6).

The Basin of water for washing was located about halfway between the door of the Tent of Meeting and the

Brazen Altar. Its first use was to wash the feet and hands of Moses and Aaron and Aaron's sons. Going back to Exodus chapter 40 and starting in verse 30 we find the following.

> Exodus 40:30 He placed the laver between the tent of meeting and the altar and put water in it for washing. [31] From it Moses and Aaron and his sons washed their hands and their feet. [32] When they entered the tent of meeting, and when they approached the altar, they washed, just as the LORD had commanded Moses.[8]

4. The Dressing of Aaron (8:7-9)

Moses dressed Aaron first. Verse 7. *"He put the tunic on him and girded him with the sash, and clothed him with the robe and put the ephod on him; and he girded him with the artistic band of the ephod, with which he tied it to him. He then placed the breastpiece on him, and in the breastpiece he put the Urim and the Thummim. He also placed the turban on his head, and on the turban, at its front, he placed the golden plate, the holy crown, just as the LORD had commanded Moses."* (8:7-9).

Moses did not stop here in Leviticus to explain the meaning of all these pieces that made up the High Priest's garments. He did not need to do that in this book because the people had just finished making them a short time before and all of that was recorded in the book of Exodus. For our purposes here, we will create a chart with the items and a short description.

---

[8] Exodus 40:30–32

Item	Description
Tunic, Turban and Sash	You shall weave the tunic of checkered work of fine linen, and shall make a turban of fine linen, and you shall make a sash, the work of a weaver.[9]
Robe	You shall make the robe of the ephod all of blue. [32] There shall be an opening at its top in the middle of it; around its opening there shall be a binding of woven work, like the opening of a coat of mail, so that it will not be torn. [33] You shall make on its hem pomegranates of blue and purple and scarlet *material,* all around on its hem, and bells of gold between them all around: [34] a golden bell and a pomegranate, a golden bell and a pomegranate, all around on the hem of the robe. [35] It shall be on Aaron when he ministers; and its tinkling shall be heard when he enters and leaves the holy place before the LORD, so that he will not die.[10]
Ephod with artistic band	They shall also make the ephod of gold, of blue and purple *and* scarlet *material* and fine twisted linen, the work of the skillful workman. [7] It shall have two shoulder pieces joined to its two ends, that it may be joined. [8] The skillfully woven band, which is on it, shall be like its workmanship,

---

[9] Exodus 28:39

[10] Exodus 28:31–35

	of the same material: of gold, of blue and purple and scarlet *material* and fine twisted linen. ⁹ You shall take two onyx stones and engrave on them the names of the sons of Israel, ¹⁰ six of their names on the one stone and the names of the remaining six on the other stone, according to their birth. ¹¹ As a jeweler engraves a signet, you shall engrave the two stones according to the names of the sons of Israel; you shall set them in filigree *settings* of gold. ¹² You shall put the two stones on the shoulder pieces of the ephod, *as* stones of memorial for the sons of Israel, and Aaron shall bear their names before the LORD on his two shoulders for a memorial. ¹³ You shall make filigree *settings* of gold, ¹⁴ and two chains of pure gold; you shall make them of twisted cordage work, and you shall put the corded chains on the filigree *settings*.¹¹ ⁶ They made the onyx stones, set in gold filigree *settings*; they were engraved *like* the engravings of a signet, according to the names of the sons of Israel. ⁷ And he placed them on the shoulder pieces of the ephod, *as* memorial stones for the sons of Israel, just as the LORD had commanded Moses.¹²
Breastpiece	You shall make a breastpiece of judgment, the work of a skillful workman; like the work of the ephod you shall make it: of gold, of blue and purple and scarlet *material* and fine twisted linen you shall make it. ¹⁶ It shall be square *and* folded double, a span in length and a span in width. ¹⁷ You shall mount on it four rows of stones; the

---

[11] Exodus 28:6–14

[12] Exodus 39:2–7

first row *shall be* a row of ruby, topaz and emerald; ¹⁸ and the second row a turquoise, a sapphire and a diamond; ¹⁹ and the third row a jacinth, an agate and an amethyst; ²⁰ and the fourth row a beryl and an onyx and a jasper; they shall be set in gold filigree. ²¹ The stones shall be according to the names of the sons of Israel: twelve, according to their names; they shall be *like* the engravings of a seal, each according to his name for the twelve tribes. ²² You shall make on the breastpiece chains of twisted cordage work in pure gold. ²³ You shall make on the breastpiece two rings of gold, and shall put the two rings on the two ends of the breastpiece. ²⁴ You shall put the two cords of gold on the two rings at the ends of the breastpiece. ²⁵ You shall put the *other* two ends of the two cords on the two filigree *settings*, and put them on the shoulder pieces of the ephod, at the front of it. ²⁶ You shall make two rings of gold and shall place them on the two ends of the breastpiece, on the edge of it, which is toward the inner side of the ephod. ²⁷ You shall make two rings of gold and put them on the bottom of the two shoulder pieces of the ephod, on the front of it close to the place where it is joined, above the skillfully woven band of the ephod. ²⁸ They shall bind the breastpiece by its rings to the rings of the ephod with a blue cord, so that it will be on the skillfully woven band of the ephod, and that the breastpiece will not come loose from the ephod. ²⁹ Aaron shall carry the names of the sons of Israel in the breastpiece of judgment over his heart when he enters the holy place, for a memorial before the LORD continually. ³⁰ You shall put in the breastpiece of judgment the ᵇUrim and the

Chapter 8

	Thummim, and they shall be over Aaron's heart when he goes in before the LORD; and Aaron shall carry the judgment of the sons of Israel over his heart before the LORD continually.[13]
Urim Thummin	You shall put in the breastpiece of judgment the ᵇUrim and the Thummim, and they shall be over Aaron's heart when he goes in before the LORD; and Aaron shall carry the judgment of the sons of Israel over his heart before the LORD continually.[14]
Golden Plate and Holy Crown	They made the plate of the holy crown of pure gold, and inscribed it like the engravings of a signet, "Holy to the LORD." ³¹ They fastened a blue cord to it, to fasten it on the turban above, just as the LORD had commanded Moses.[15]

As far as what these six items looked like, we are helpless. Long have they been gone, perhaps since the destruction of the Temple by Titus in 70 AD. Nevertheless, thankful to Josephus (born 30 AD in Jerusalem, died 100 AD in Rome), a Jewish historian of the first century who was writing for the Romans, we have written descriptions of the various items which he had the privilege of seeing. For further details about these items of the priestly garments, I have described them in detail in my Exodus Chapters 28:2-4 study.

---

[13] Exodus 28:15–30

[14] Exodus 28:30

[15] Exodus 39:30–31

5. The Anointing of the Tabernacle (8:10-11)

After dressing Aaron, Moses anointed the Tabernacle. Verse 10. *"Moses then took the anointing oil and anointed the tabernacle and all that was in it, and consecrated them. He sprinkled some of it on the altar seven times and anointed the altar and all its utensils, and the basin and its stand, to consecrate them."* (8:10-11).

We find this story in Exodus chapter 40.

"Then you shall take the anointing oil and anoint the tabernacle and all that is in it, and shall consecrate it and all its furnishings; and it shall be holy. ¹⁰ You shall anoint the altar of burnt offering and all its utensils, and consecrate the altar, and the altar shall be most holy. ¹¹ You shall anoint the laver and its stand, and consecrate it." (Exodus 40:9-11).

6. The Anointing of Aaron (8:12)

Then Moses anointed Aaron. Verse 12. *"Then he poured some of the anointing oil on Aaron's head and anointed him, to consecrate him."* (8:12).

Exodus 40:13 says, *"You shall put the holy garments on Aaron and anoint him and consecrate him, that he may minister as a priest to Me."*

The process of anointing Aaron fulfilled the purpose of consecrating him, meaning it set him apart from all others to be the first high priest of the Nation of Israel. From that moment on, he was in a different class from all the other people of the nation.

7. The Dressing of Aaron's Sons (8:13)

Next, Moses dressed Aaron's sons. Verse 13. *"Next Moses had Aaron's sons come near and clothed them with tunics, and girded them with sashes and bound caps on them, just as the LORD had commanded Moses."* (8:13).

It is not mentioned here in Leviticus, but after dressing Aaron's sons, Moses anointed them too. We find that in

Chapter 8   111

Exodus 40:14-15. *"You shall bring his sons and put tunics on them; and you shall anoint them even as you have anointed their father, that they may minister as priests to Me; and their anointing will qualify them for a perpetual priesthood throughout their generations."*

8. The Bull of the Sin Offering (8:14-17)

Following the anointing of Aaron and his sons as priests, Moses offered a bull as a sin offering. The LORD gave that instruction first so Moses would know how to perform it properly. It was time for the first sin offering to be experienced and Moses would be the one to demonstrate it to Aaron and his sons who would perform it many times in their office duties as priests. The order of the ceremony was always the same.

- The animal was offered.
- The laying of the hands occurred to transfer the sin.
- The animal was slain, skinned, and cut up.
- The blood was sprinkled around the Brazen Altar and rubbed on its four horns.
- The rest of the blood was poured out at the base of the Altar.
- The fat was offered.
- All the rest of the animal, including the hide, was burned to ashes outside the camp.

Here is the record for this bull sin offering in Leviticus chapter 8 starting with verse 14. *"Then he brought the bull of the sin offering, and Aaron and his sons laid their hands on the head of the bull of the sin offering. Next Moses slaughtered it and took the blood and with his finger put some of it around on the horns of the altar, and purified the altar. Then he poured out the rest of the blood at the base of the altar and consecrated it, to make atonement for it. He also took all the fat that was on the entrails and the lobe of the liver, and the two kidneys and their fat; and Moses offered it up in smoke on the altar. But the bull and its hide and its flesh and its refuse he burned in the fire outside the camp, just as the LORD had commanded Moses."* (8:14-17).

All sin offerings followed this same order.

9. The First Ram of the Burnt Offering (8:18-21)

Then Moses offered a ram, a male sheep, for a burnt offering. We studied in detail the order of the ceremony for a burnt offering in chapter 1. This ram was the first burnt offering following the giving of the LORD's guidelines for it. The order of the ceremony was always the same.

- The animal, if it was a sheep was offered on the northside of the Brazen Altar.
- The laying of the hands occurred to transfer the sin.
- The animal was slain, skinned, and cut up.
- The blood was sprinkled around the Brazen Altar (not rubbed on the four horns).
- The legs and entrails were washed and placed on the Brazen Altar.
- All the rest of the animal was burned to ashes on the Brazen Altar except the hide.
- The hide was given to the priest.

Here is the record for this ram sin offering in Leviticus chapter 8 starting with verse 18.

"Then he presented the ram of the burnt offering, and Aaron and his sons laid their hands on the head of the ram. Moses slaughtered it and sprinkled the blood around on the altar. When he had cut the ram into its pieces, Moses offered up the head and the pieces and the suet in smoke. After he had washed the entrails and the legs with water, Moses

offered up the whole ram in smoke on the altar. It was a burnt offering for a soothing aroma; it was an offering by fire to the LORD, just as the LORD had commanded Moses." (8:18-21).

10. The Second Ram of the Ordination Offering (8:22-36)

The second ram, (male sheep), was brought to the northside of the Brazen Altar where, as before with the first ram, Aaron and his sons placed their hands on the ram to transfer their sin. This was the ordination offering and it had to do with consecrating Aaron and his sons. Therefore, we see a few new details in this offering that, in the future, would only apply to the ordination of the priests. It would never apply to the offerings of common people. Here is a snap shot of the order of the ceremony.

- The animal, if it was a sheep was offered at the door of the Northside of the Brazen Altar.
- The laying of the hands occurred to transfer the sin.
- The animal was slain, skinned, and cut up.
- The blood was placed on the right ear lobe, right thumb and right big toe of the priests being ordained and the rest of the blood was sprinkled around the Brazen Altar (not rubbed on the four horns).
- The fat, including the fat tail because this was a sheep, and the right thigh were presented.
- The grain offering of the ordination, which was introduced in chapter 6 verses 19-23, was presented. One cake, one cake with oil and one wafer was placed on both the fat and thigh. Aaron and his sons offered the fat and thigh as wave offerings. Moses then took them back and placed them on the Brazen Altar.
- The breast was presented as a wave offering.

- All the rest of the animal was burned to ashes on the Brazen Altar except the hide.
- The garments of Aaron and his sons were sprinkled with blood and anointing oil.
- The breast was boiled.
- All the rest of the meat, cakes and wafers were burned.
- Aaron and his sons entered the Tent of Meeting and stayed inside for seven days.

Here is the whole story in the book of Leviticus chapter 8 starting in verse 22. "Then he presented the second ram, the ram of ordination, and Aaron and his sons laid their hands on the head of the ram. Moses slaughtered it and took some of its blood and put it on the lobe of Aaron's right ear, and on the thumb of his right hand and on the big toe of his right foot. He also had Aaron's sons come near; and Moses put some of the blood on the lobe of their right ear, and on the thumb of their right hand and on the big toe of their right foot. Moses then sprinkled the rest of the blood around on the altar. He took the fat, and the fat tail, and all the fat that was on the entrails, and the lobe of the liver and the two kidneys and their fat and the right thigh. From the basket of unleavened bread that was before the LORD, he took one unleavened cake and one cake of bread mixed with oil and one wafer, and placed them on the portions of fat and on the right thigh. He then put all these on the hands of Aaron and on the hands of his sons and presented them as a wave offering before the LORD. Then Moses took them from their hands and offered them up in smoke on the altar with the burnt offering. They were an ordination offering for a soothing aroma; it was an offering by fire to the LORD. Moses also took the breast and presented it for a wave offering before the LORD; it was Moses' portion of

Chapter 8

the ram of ordination, just as the LORD had commanded Moses. So Moses took some of the anointing oil and some of the blood which was on the altar and sprinkled it on Aaron, on his garments, on his sons, and on the garments of his sons with him; and he consecrated Aaron, his garments, and his sons, and the garments of his sons with him. Then Moses said to Aaron and to his sons, "Boil the flesh at the doorway of the tent of meeting, and eat it there together with the bread which is in the basket of the ordination offering, just as I commanded, saying, 'Aaron and his sons shall eat it. The remainder of the flesh and of the bread you shall burn in the fire. You shall not go outside the doorway of the tent of meeting for seven days, until the day that the period of your ordination is fulfilled; for he will ordain you through seven days. The LORD has commanded to do as has been done this day, to make atonement on your behalf. At the doorway of the tent of meeting, moreover, you shall remain day and night for seven days and keep the charge of the LORD, so that you will not die, for so I have been commanded." Thus Aaron and his sons did all the things which the LORD had commanded through Moses." (8:22-36).

Chapter 9

B. Day Eight of the Ordination (9:1-24)
 1. The Calling of Aaron, His Sons, and the Elders (9:1-6)
   a) Words to Aaron and His Sons – Sin and Burnt Offerings (9:1-2)

On day eight after the ordination, Moses came to the Tent of Meeting and call Aaron and his sons out of the tent. Moses also called the elders to join them. Chapter 9 verse 1 tells us what Moses said next. *"Now it came about on the eighth day that Moses called Aaron and his sons and the elders of Israel; and he said to Aaron, Take for yourself a calf, a bull, for a sin offering and a ram for a burnt offering, both without defect, and offer them before the LORD.'"* (9:1-2).

   b) Words to the Elders - Sin, Burnt, Sacrifice of Peace, Grain Offerings (9:3-4)

At the same time, Moses gave the elders instructions for their offerings. Verse 3. *"Then to the sons of Israel you shall speak, saying, 'Take a male goat for a sin offering, and a calf and a lamb, both one year old, without defect, for a burnt offering, and an ox and a ram for peace offerings, to sacrifice before the LORD, and a grain offering mixed with oil; for today the LORD will appear to you.'"* (9:3-4).

Aaron and his sons would make two offerings on the last day of their ordination ceremony, the elders would make four.

   c) Words of Moses to Aaron, His Sons, and the Elders (9:5-6)

At Moses' calling, the men complied with Moses' command. Verse 5. *"So they took what Moses had commanded to the front of the tent of meeting, and the whole congregation came near and stood before the LORD. Moses said, "This is the thing which the*

LORD *has commanded you to do, that the glory of the* LORD *may appear to you.'"* (9:5-6).

2. Aaron's Offerings (9:7-8)

Aaron's bull calf sin offering would be first. Verse 7. *"Moses then said to Aaron, 'Come near to the altar and offer your sin offering and your burnt offering, that you may make atonement for yourself and for the people; then make the offering for the people, that you may make atonement for them, just as the* LORD *has commanded.' So Aaron came near to the altar and slaughtered the calf of the sin offering which was for himself."* (9:7-8).

Aaron's offerings were for two purposes as listed in this passage. First, it was to make atonement for Aaron himself. Second, it was to make atonement for the people of the nation. The word *atonement* means the "reconciliation between God and a person or group of people."[16] Aaron brought his bull calf sin offering first to reconcile himself to God.

a) Aaron's Sin Offering (9:9-11)

The order of this sin offering was the same as the order of the sin offering eight days before. A sin offering is a sin offering and the LORD detailed the order in chapter 4. We presented the order earlier. May we do it again here for review.

- The animal was offered at its proper place at the Tent of Meeting. In this case, because it is a bull, it is offered where all bulls in all offerings are offered, at the door to the Tent of Meeting.

---

[16] Brockway, D. (2016). Atonement. In J. D. Barry, D. Bomar, D. R. Brown, R. Klippenstein, D. Mangum, C. Sinclair Wolcott, ... W. Widder (Eds.), *The Lexham Bible Dictionary*. Bellingham, WA: Lexham Press.

- The laying of the hands occurred to transfer the sin.
- The animal was slain, skinned, and cut up.
- The blood was sprinkled around the Brazen Altar and rubbed on its four horns.
- The fat was offered.
- All the rest of the animal, including the hide, was burned to ashes outside the camp.

Now we will read the Scripture to see that the order was followed by Moses. Aaron would bring the bull and slay it. The blood was given to Moses. Verse 9. *"Aaron's sons presented the blood to him; and he dipped his finger in the blood and put some on the horns of the altar, and poured out the rest of the blood at the base of the altar. The fat and the kidneys and the lobe of the liver of the sin offering, he then offered up in smoke on the altar just as the LORD had commanded Moses. The flesh and the skin, however, he burned with fire outside the camp."* (9:9-11).

3. Aaron's Ram Burnt Offering (9:12-14)

Aaron's ram burnt offering would be second. In this case, the offering was for the people of the nation. Once again, the order of the burnt offering ceremony was always the same. The only change would depend on the kind of animal being slain and where it was to be slain. Here is that order.

- The animal, if it was a sheep was offered on the northside of the Brazen Altar.
- The laying of the hands occurred to transfer the sin.
- The animal was slain, skinned, and cut up.
- The blood was sprinkled around the Brazen Altar (not rubbed on the four horns).
- The legs and entrails were washed.

- All the rest of the animal was burned to ashes on the Brazen Altar except the hide.
- The hide was given to the priest.

Now we will read the record and see that Aaron's second offering matched the order of the burnt offering. *"Then he slaughtered the burnt offering; and Aaron's sons handed the blood to him and he sprinkled it around on the altar. They handed the burnt offering to him in pieces, with the head, and he offered them up in smoke on the altar. He also washed the entrails and the legs, and offered them up in smoke with the burnt offering on the altar."* (9:12-14).

The record matched the LORD's details from chapter 1 perfectly.

4. Elder's Offering (9:15-24)
a) The Goat Sin Offering (9:15)

On that same day, Moses offered the six offerings presented by the elders of the Nation of Israel. Each of the offering ceremonies were presented exactly in accordance with the guidelines presented by the LORD in the first six chapters of this book. So, here, we come to the first of the six offerings for the people. Verse 15. *"Then he presented the people's offering, and took the goat of the sin offering which was for the people, and slaughtered it and offered it for sin, like the first."* (9:15).

That is all Moses recorded about this goat sin offering. Yet, because we have learned the details of the sin offering, we know exactly what took place that day. The ceremony followed the order for the sin offering as follows.

- The animal was offered at its proper place at the Tent of Meeting. In this case, because it was a goat, it was offered at the northside of the Brazen Altar.

- The laying of the hands occurred to transfer the sin.
- The animal was slain, skinned, and cut up.
- The blood was sprinkled around the Brazen Altar and rubbed on the four horns.
- The fat was offered.
- All the rest of the animal, including the hide, was burned to ashes outside the camp.

b) The Calf and Lamb Burnt Offering (9:16)

All Moses said about this calf and lamb burnt offering was in one sentence. Verse 16. *"He also presented the burnt offering, and offered it according to the ordinance."* (9:16).

In verses 3 – 4 of this chapter, Moses had told the elders what to bring for the burnt offering. There we find that the animals were to be a calf and a lamb, both in their first year of life. It is a burnt offering; therefore, it was to follow the instructions given by the LORD for a burnt offering found in chapter one. Here is a snapshot of the order of worship.

- The animal, if it was a calf, it was offered at the door to the Tent of Meeting. If it was a sheep it was offered on the northside of the Brazen Altar.
- The laying of the hands occurred to transfer the sin.
- The animal was slain, skinned, and cut up.
- The blood was sprinkled around the Brazen Altar (not rubbed on the four horns).
- The legs and entrails were washed.
- All the rest of the animal was burned to ashes on the Brazen Altar except the hide.
- The hide was given to the priest.

There were two animals offered that day. The first was a calf and the second was a lamb. Except for their hides, their entire bodies were burnt on the Brazen Altar.

5. The Grain Offering (9:17)

With the sin and burnt offering completed, the grain offering was brought to the Altar. Verse 17. *"Next he presented the grain offering, and filled his hand with some of it and offered it up in smoke on the altar, besides the burnt offering of the morning."* (9:17).

No details here, but we know the details because we know the instruction the LORD gave concerning the ceremony of this offering. Here is a snapshot of the offering.

- The ingredients of fine flour, oil and incense were mixed. It could be raw, baked, pan fried on a griddle, cooked in a pot, or roasted. No leaven or honey could be used.
- The offering was handed to Moses on the westside of the Brazen Altar.
- Moses took a handful of the grain offering and placed it on the Brazen Altar as a memorial portion.
- The rest of the grain offering was given to the priest to eat.

6. Ox and Ram Sacrifice of Peace Offering (9:18-21)

Back in verses 3-4, Moses instructed the elders to bring an ox and a ram for the sacrifice of peace offering. Here they were offered. The ceremony for these two offerings were detailed in chapter 3. Here is a snapshot of the sacrifice of peace offering.

- The animal, if it was a calf or ox, it was offered at the door to the Tent of Meeting. If it was a sheep

or ram, it was offered on the northside of the Brazen Altar.
- The laying of the hands occurred to transfer the sin.
- The animal was slain, skinned, and cut up.
- The blood was sprinkled around the Brazen Altar (not rubbed on the four horns).
- The fat portions of the animal were placed on the Brazen Altar.
- The fat of the breast was put on the Brazen Altar. The actual breast was waved before the LORD as a wave offering and then boiled to be eaten by the priest.
- The rest of the animal was given to the priests to eat.
- The hide was given to the priest.

With those guidelines from chapter 3, let us see what Moses said here in chapter 9. Verse 21. *"Then he slaughtered the ox and the ram, the sacrifice of peace offerings which was for the people; and Aaron's sons handed the blood to him and he sprinkled it around on the altar. As for the portions of fat from the ox and from the ram, the fat tail, and the fat covering, and the kidneys and the lobe of the liver, they now placed the portions of fat on the breasts; and he offered them up in smoke on the altar. But the breasts and the right thigh Aaron presented as a wave offering before the LORD, just as Moses had commanded."* (9:18-21).

All six offerings made by the elders were completed in perfect accord with the commands of the LORD found in the first six chapters of Leviticus. Nothing was amiss. Nothing was misplaced. The LORD was pleased.

C. The Appearance of the LORD to All the People (9:22-24)
1. The Blessing by Aaron (9:22-23a)

On that eighth day, after the offering for Aaron and his sons and the offerings of the elders for the Nation of Israel, Aaron stepped forward to present a blessing to the people. Verse 22. *"Then Aaron lifted up his hands toward the people and blessed them, and he stepped down after making the sin offering and the burnt offering and the peace offerings. Moses and Aaron went into the tent of meeting."* (9:22-23a).

Picture, if you will, this scene in your mind. Moses oversaw performing the ceremonies of these offerings on that day. The newly ordained priests were helping Moses. When the offerings were completed, Aaron, who, for the next thirty-nine years would preside over all the offerings, stepped toward the people, and spoke a blessing. It could have been Moses, but it was not. It was Aaron. Aaron was ordained and it was time for him to take the lead in presenting the offering to the LORD as the high priest. It was time for Moses to step aside from that position that he held only for the ordination of the first priests of the Nation of Israel. From that time on, the priests would ordain the priests. Aaron gave the blessing and he entered the Tent of Meeting with his brother, Moses. We must wonder what was said inside that tent that day. We do not know. But, they did not stay in the tent very long. The LORD had a plan and it involved showing Himself to His nation.

2. The Glory of the LORD from the Tent of Meeting (9:23b-24)
a) The Appearance of Moses and Aaron (9:23b)

After being in the Tent of Meeting for an unknown amount of time, Moses and Aaron came out before the people to bless them. Verse 23b. *"When they came out and blessed the people, the glory of the LORD appeared to all the people."* (9:23b).

Notice that the verse says, *"the glory of the LORD appeared to all the people."* What does that mean? The "glory" of the LORD means the radiance or glow from the LORD. Note this, when you see the glory of the LORD one day in your future, you will understand why the *glory of the LORD* means His radiance no matter where it was said in the Scripture and no matter the context.

Moving on, the Tabernacle stood inside the Tent of Meeting. Once both were in place it would seem to all the onlookers that they were the same structure, but they were not. The Tent of Meeting was erected by the people first. In that Tent of Meeting, the LORD met with Moses to give him the instructions presented in this book called Leviticus. Then, on the day of the ordination ceremony, the Tabernacle was erected inside the Tent of Meeting first, followed by the anointing of the Tabernacle and the first day of the priest's ordination. On that day, the LORD showed Himself above the Ark of the Covenant between the two cherubs on the Mercy Seat which acted as the top of the Ark of the Covenant. Hovering there between the two cherubs was the Shekinah Glory of the LORD. Perhaps our best description of it would be a radiating cloud that hovered between the two carved cherubs. It was so bright that it gave light to the entire Tabernacle even from behind the Veil. No doubt, when the door to the Tabernacle was opened by Moses and Aaron as they came out, the glow of the glory of the LORD shined forth and was clearly visible to all the people even in the daylight hours. But then, the LORD did something miraculous that only He could do.

b) The Fire of the LORD (9:24)

After exiting the Tent of Meeting and blessing the people, with the glory of the LORD radiating from the tent behind them, the spectacular occurred. Verse 24. *"Then fire came out from before the LORD and consumed the burnt offering and the portions of fat on the altar; and when all the people saw it, they shouted and fell on their faces."* (9:24).

Picture that. Fire came out of the door of the tent, passed around Moses and Aaron and consumed in an instant all the offerings on the Brazen Altar. It did not take hours. It only took a flash in the eyes of the people. No wonder they screamed and fell on their faces. You would too if you had been there. The presence of the living God is a fearful thing.

With that, the offerings of the Brazen Altar for the ordination of the Tabernacle and the priests were over and the Altar had been licked clean by the tongues of the fire of the glory of the LORD. It would not be the last time the people would see this glory of the LORD come from the tent in fire.

All the instructions and laws concerning the offerings to the LORD were given. The priestly system was in place. Moses had trained them himself. But before we go on, may we have one last law review concerning the offerings, just for good measure. It will be our last time.

The Place of the Offerings

The LORD allowed animals and agriculture to be brought as offerings to the Tent of Meeting and the Brazen Altar. Regardless of the kind of offering, the kind of animal or agriculture was always presented at the same place.

- If the offering was from the HERD, a male or female bull or cow oxen, without defect, was presented at the door to the Tent of Meeting.

- If the offering was from the FLOCK, a male or female sheep or goat, without defect, was presented at the north side of the Brazen Altar.
- If the offering was from the FLOCK, turtle dove or young pigeon without defect, was presented at the west side of the Brazen Altar.
- If the offering was grain, oil, and incense, without defect, was presented at the west side of the Brazen Altar.
- In all cases, that which was placed on the Brazen Altar was completely consumed with fire as a soothing aroma to the LORD.

None of the above was ever changed. It was always the same place for the same kind of animal or agriculture.

The Presentation of the Offerings

In all cases, regardless of the kind of animal being offered, once the animal was at its proper place (as seen in **"The Place of the Offerings"** above), the one bringing the animal would place his hands on the animal to symbolize the transfer from the person to the animal the reason the animal was being brought as an offering. Then the animal was slain and the blood was sprinkled according to a special instruction that will be listed in each offering below. This initial part of the presentation never changes. It is always the same.

The Procedures of the Offerings

Picking up with each offering based on the "Place" and Presentation" already settled we find these details in each kind of offering.

Chapter 9

THE BURNT OFFERING (Chapter 1)

Instructions for the **MALE** oxen, sheep, or goat:

- The priest sprinkles the blood around the Brazen Altar and then stokes the fire.
- The person bringing the offering skins the animal and cuts it into pieces.
- The entrails and the legs are washed in the basin of water to clean them.
- The priest places all the animal on the Brazen Altar except the hide and the offering burns in a raging fire until it is totally consumed.
- The hide belongs to the priest.

Instructions for the birds:

- The priest would wring the head off the bird.
- The blood would be sprinkled around the Brazen Altar.
- The wings would be torn, not cut off the bird.
- The feathers and the contents of the crop under the neck would be placed in the coals and ashes on the east side of the Brazen Altar.
- The animal is placed on the Brazen Altar to be totally consumed in fire.

THE GRAIN OFFERING (Chapter 2)

- The fine flour or grain, oil and incense are brought to the west side of the Brazen Altar and handed to the priest.
    - The ingredients can be raw, baked, griddle cooked, pan cooked or roasted.
    - No leaven or honey was allowed.

- The priest took a hand full of the offering and burned it completely on the Brazen Altar.
- Salt was added to season.
- The remaining grain offering belonged to the priests.

THE SACRIFICE OF PEACE OFFERING
(Chapter 3)

Instructions for the **MALE or FEMALE** oxen, sheep, or goat:

- The priest sprinkles the blood around the Brazen Altar and then stokes the fire.
- The person bringing the offering skins the animal and cuts it into pieces.
- The fat portions of the animal are given to the priest who places them on the Brazen Altar.
- The rest of the animal flesh and its hide belongs to the priest.

THE SIN OFFERING (Chapter 4)

Purpose of the in offering:

- The unintentional sin of a priest who brings guilt on the people.
- The unintentional sin of the whole nation that brings guilt on the people.
- The unintentional sin of a leader who brings guilt on himself.
- The unintentional sin of a common person who brings guilt on himself.

Chapter 9

Instructions for the **MALE** bull for the priest or whole nation:

- The priest takes the blood inside the Tent of Meeting and sprinkles the blood seven times in front of the Veil.
- The Priest rubs blood on the four horns on the four corners of the Altar of Incense in front of the Veil.
- The priest pours the rest of the blood at the base of the Brazen Altar were the coals and ashes are and then stokes the fire.
- The person bringing the offering removes the fat portions.
- The fat portions of the animal are given to the priest who places them on the Brazen Altar where they are totally consumed in the fire.
- The rest of the animal, including the hide is taken outside the camp to a clean place burned.

Instructions for the **FEMALE** goat or lamb for the leader or common people:

- The priest rubs blood on the four horns of the Brazen Altar.
- The priest pours the rest of the blood at the base of the Brazen Altar were the coals and ashes are and then stokes the fire.
- The person bringing the offering removes the fat portions.
- The fat portions of the animal are given to the priest who places them on the Brazen Altar where they are totally consumed in the fire.

- The rest of the animal, including the hide is taken outside the camp to a clean place burned.

THE GUILT OFFERING (Chapter 5)
Purpose of the in offering:

- The intentional sin of failing to come forth as a witness against sin.
- The intentional sin of touching unclean things.
- The intentional sin of swearing thoughtlessly through the lips.

Instructions for the FEMALE lamb or goat as a sin offering:

- The person bringing the offering must CONFESS his sin.
- The priest sprinkles the blood around the Brazen Altar.
- The priest pours the rest of the blood at the base of the Brazen Altar were the coals and ashes are and then stokes the fire.
- The person bringing the offering removes the fat portions.
- The fat portions of the animal are given to the priest who places them on the Brazen Altar where they are totally consumed in the fire.
- The rest of the animal, including the hide was given to the priest.

Or the instructions for the first turtle dove or young pigeon as a sin offering:

Chapter 9

- The person bringing the offering must CONFESS his sin.
- The head of the first bird is broken back but not severed.
- The blood of the bird is poured at the side of the Brazen Altar.
- The wings would be torn, not cut off the bird.
- The feathers and the contents of the crop under the neck would be placed in the coals and ashes on the east side of the Brazen Altar.
- The animal is placed on the Brazen Altar to be totally consumed in fire.

Or the instructions for a grain offering:

- The person bringing the offering must CONFESS his sin.
- The person brings one-tenth of an ephah of grain in an offering dry or with oil, raw, baked or pan griddled.
- The priest offers a hand full of the offering on the Brazen Altar.
- The rest of the grain offering belongs to the priest.
-

Instructions for the second turtle dove or young pigeon as a guilt offering.

- The person bringing the offering must CONFESS his sin.
- The priest would wring the head off the bird.
- The blood would be sprinkled around the Brazen Altar.
- The wings would be torn, not cut off the bird.

- The feathers and the contents of the crop under the neck would be placed in the coals and ashes on the east side of the Brazen Altar.
- The animal is placed on the Brazen Altar to be totally consumed in fire.

Purpose of the guilt offering:

- The intentional sin of unfaithful act against Holy things.
- The intentional sin of acts unaware.

Instructions for the ram of the guilt offering.

- The person bringing the offering must <u>CONFESS</u> his sin.
- The priest values of the ram according to the sanctuary silver shekel.
- The giver gives twenty-five percent of the value of the ram in shekels to the priest.
- The priest sprinkles the blood around the Brazen Altar.
- The priest pours the rest of the blood at the base of the Brazen Altar were the coals and ashes are and then stokes the fire.
- The person bringing the offering removes the fat portions.
- The fat portions of the animal are given to the priest who places them on the Brazen Altar where they are totally consumed in the fire.
- The rest of the animal, including the hide was given to the priest.

Chapter 9

THE ORDINATION OFFERING FOR THE PRIESTS

DAY ONE – A bull calf, two rams and a basket of unleavened bread

Instructions for the calf of the sin offering for Aaron and his sons:

- Aaron and his sons were anointed with oil then dressed in their holy garments.
- The calf was offered.
- The laying of the hands occurred to transfer the sin.
- The calf was slain, skinned, and cut up.
- The blood was sprinkled around the Brazen Altar and rubbed on its four horns.
- The rest of the blood was poured out at the base of the Altar.
- The fat was offered.
- All the rest of the animal, including the hide, was burned to ashes outside the camp.

Instructions for the first ram of the burnt offering for Aaron and his sons:

- The ram was offered on the northside of the Brazen Altar.
- The laying of the hands occurred to transfer the sin.
- The ram was slain, skinned, and cut up.
- The blood was sprinkled around the Brazen Altar (not rubbed on the four horns).
- The legs and entrails were washed and placed on the Brazen Altar.

- All the rest of the animal was burned to ashes on the Brazen Altar except the hide.
- The hide was given to the priest.

Instructions for the second ram and grain of the burnt offering for Aaron and his sons:

- The ram was offered at the door of the Northside of the Brazen Altar.
- The laying of the hands occurred to transfer the sin.
- The ram was slain, skinned, and cut up.
- The blood was placed on the right ear lobe, right thumb and right big toe of the priests being ordained and the rest of the blood was sprinkled around the Brazen Altar (not rubbed on the four horns).
- The fat, including the fat tail because this was a sheep, and the right thigh were presented.
- The grain offering of the ordination, which was introduced in chapter 6 verses 19-23, was presented. One cake, one cake with oil and one wafer was placed on both the fat and thigh. Aaron and his sons offered the fat and thighs as wave offerings. Moses then took them back and placed them on the Brazen Altar.
- The breast was presented as a wave offering.
- All the rest of the animal was burned to ashes on the Brazen Altar except the hide.
- The garments of Aaron and his sons were sprinkled with blood and anointing oil.
- The breast was boiled.

Chapter 9

- All the rest of the meat, cakes and wafers were burned.
- Then, Aaron and his sons entered the Tent of Meeting and stayed inside for seven days.

DAY EIGHT – A bull calf and ram for Aaron and his son's sin and burnt offerings.

- The bull calf was offered as a sin offering.
- The ram was offered as a burnt offering.
    - With the calf sin offering the fat was offered on the Brazen Altar and all the rest was burned outside the camp.
    - With the ram burnt offering the hide was given to the priest and all the rest was burnt on the Brazen Altar until it turned to ash.
    -

DAY EIGHT – A sin, burnt, sacrifice of peace and grain offering for the people.

Male goat – Sin offering

- The goat was offered at its proper place at the Tent of Meeting. In this case, because it is a goat, it is offered at the northside of the Brazen Altar.
- The laying of the hands to transfer the sin.
- The goat was slain, skinned, and cut up.
- The blood was sprinkled around the Brazen Altar and rubbed on the four horns.
- The fat was offered.
- All the rest of the animal, including the hide, was burned to ashes outside the camp.

Calf and lamb – Burnt offering

- The calf was offered at the door to the Tent of Meeting. The lamb was offered on the northside of the Brazen Altar.
- The laying of the hands occurred to transfer the sin.
- The calf and lamb were slain, skinned, and cut up.
- The blood was sprinkled around the Brazen Altar (not rubbed on the four horns).
- The legs and entrails and legs were washed.
- All the rest of the animal was burned to ashes on the Brazen Altar except the hide.
- The hide was given to the priest.

Ox and ram – Peace offering

- The ox calf was offered at the door to the Tent of Meeting. The ram was offered on the northside of the Brazen Altar.
- The laying of the hands occurred to transfer the sin.
- The ox and ram were slain, skinned, and cut up.
- The blood was sprinkled around the Brazen Altar (not rubbed on the four horns).
- The fat portions of the animal were placed on the Brazen Altar.
- The fat of the breast was put on the Brazen Altar. The breast (without its fat) was waved before the LORD as a wave offering and then boiled to be eaten by the priest.
- The rest of the animal was given to the priests to eat.

Chapter 9   137

- The hide was given to the priest.

Grain offering

- The ingredients of a tenth of an ephah of fine flour (about a pint), oil and incense were mixed. It could be raw, baked, pan fried on a griddle, cooked in a pot, or roasted. No leaven or honey could be used.
- The offering was handed to the priest on the westside of the Brazen Altar.
- Moses took a handful of the gain offering and placed it on the Brazen Altar as a memorial portion.
- The rest of the grain offering was given to the priest to eat.

When the ordination service was over and for the first time, Israel had a high priest and four regular priests. The high priest was Aaron; the four regular priests were Aaron's sons, Nadab, Abihu, Eleazar and Ithamar (Numbers 3:2). But on that eighth day, as the priests were finishing up the details of the offerings, two of Aaron's sons were about to die.

Chapter 10

V. The Rebellion of Two of Aaron's Sons (10:1-20)
  A. Nadab and Abihu Used Strange Fire and the LORD Killed Them (10:1-2)

The record of the rebellion and death of two of Aaron's sons is found here in chapter 10 of Leviticus, but Numbers 3:3-4 also mentions this rebellion. Nadab and Abihu used strange fire on the Altar of Incense and the LORD killed them. For this story, we must take it at face value. The Word of God does not interpret or explain it anywhere else but in Leviticus and Numbers. Verse 1. *"Now Nadab and Abihu, the sons of Aaron, took their respective firepans, and after putting fire in them, placed incense on it and offered strange fire before the LORD, which He had not commanded them. And fire came out from the presence of the LORD and consumed them, and they died before the LORD.* (10:1-2).

Inside the Tent of Meeting, in the Holy Place, the Altar of Incense sat in front of the Veil that separated the Holy Place from the Holy of Holies where the Ark of the Covenant rested and the LORD tabernacled (dwelt) there. The acacia wood Altar of Incense table was covered in gold. Incense was to burn on that table continuously. The LORD had instituted a certain blend of spices for the incense that was burned on that table. According to Exodus 30:7-8, the priests were to replace the coals and the incense at regular times through the day to keep the incense burning. What were the ingredients of that mixture of incense designed by the LORD?

Chapter 10

Here is the instruction for making the incense for the Altar in the Holy Place.

"Then the LORD said to Moses, "Take for yourself spices, stacte and onycha and galbanum, spices with pure frankincense; there shall be an equal part of each. With it you shall make incense, a perfume, the work of a perfumer, salted, pure, and holy. You shall beat some of it very fine, and put part of it before the testimony in the tent of meeting where I will meet with you; it shall be most holy to you. The incense which you shall make, you shall not make in the same proportions for yourselves; it shall be holy to you for the LORD. Whoever shall make any like it, to use as perfume, shall be cut off from his people." (Exodus 30":34-38).

The "testimony" mentioned here is the Ark of the Covenant or the Ark of the Testimony as some versions translate it. Notice in the warning at the end of this instruction. This mixture was never to be used outside the Holy Place by anyone or that person would be cut off.

But the issue in this passage with Nadab and Abihu was not the incense, it was the fire in the firepan. Some Bible versions translate these firepans as censors. For those of the Catholic faith, you have seen metal vessels with holes in them hung on long chains billowing smoke as the priest swings them around. That is not exactly the shape of the firepans described here but the function is similar. During the construction of all the Tabernacle complex, utensils to be used in holy ceremonies including firepans were hammered out of copper or bronze. These pans were like your nine-inch frying pan that you have in your home. A lid with holes was made for the pan. Coals from the Brazen Altar were put in the pan, incense was put on top of the coals and the lid was put on the pan. The smoke of the incense would seep through the holes and fill the room. The pan had a handle like a frying pan that was used to carry it to and from the Altar of Incense.

The issue was not the incense being used. It was not the pan being used. The issue was the fire being used. Where did Nadab and Abihu acquire the coals of fire they used in their firepans that they took into the Holy Place and put on the Altar of Incense?

Some commentators state that the fire on the Brazen Altar was started by the LORD and it was the responsibility of the priest to keep that fire going eternally. Their Scripture for that proof is found in chapter 9 verse 24 which states, *"Then fire came out from before the LORD and consumed the burnt offering and the portions of fat on the altar; and when all the people saw it, they shouted and fell on their faces."* What they fail to mention by using this passage is that this fire from the LORD occurred on the eighth day of the ordination of the priests. Eight days earlier, sacrifices were made on the first day of the ordination of the priests. Where did the fire on that first day come from? Did it go out between the eight days? Probably not. The fire on the Brazen Altar was probably set by Moses as he was the one directing the eight-day ceremony. The fire that came from the LORD had nothing to do with the original fire on the Altar. However, on that first day of the ordination, Moses consecrated the Altar, lit the fire and it burned constantly all week and on into the future – never extinguished.

So where did the fire come from that was "strange fire" according to the LORD. It came from some fire source that did not originate with the consecrated fire set by Moses originally. The boiling pots for the breasts and the thighs were not heated on the Brazen Altar but on other fires in the courtyard. The leftover meat from the offerings that belonged to the priests were cooked on different fires too. These fires were not required to be perpetual and were most likely struck as needed inside the courtyard during the daylight hours to cook the meat and grain for the meals of the priests. The source of these fires was most likely not the fire of the Brazen Altar because it was holy fire.

Because of the place where this incident is found in the context of Leviticus and Numbers, it had to occur on the eighth day of the ordination. These two boys were not priests for only a week and they made a terrible mistake. It was time for the Altar of Incense to be restocked with two new pans of incense. They each took their firepans and stepped to the nearest fire and filled the pans will hot coals. Incense was added. The top was placed on the pan. The two boys walked into the Holy Place and put them on the Altar of Incense. I doubt they knew what hit them. Verse 2 again. *"And fire came out from the presence of the LORD and consumed them, and they died before the LORD."* (10:2).

B. Aaron Kept Silent (10:3)

There they died in that sacred place, the Holy Place, the place with the Altar of Incense, the Table of Show Bread, and the Menorah. There stood Moses and Aaron with the two priests burned dead on the ground. Moses and Aaron had to be shocked by the supernatural event they just saw. What were they going to do? Verse 3. *"Then Moses said to Aaron, "It is what the LORD spoke, saying, 'By those who come near Me I will be treated as holy, And before all the people I will be honored.'" So Aaron, therefore, kept silent."* (10:3).

Keep your mouth shut brother, Moses said.

C. Nadab and Abihu Carried Away (10:4-5)

As the leader, Moses would handle things. Verse 4. *"Moses called also to Mishael and Elzaphan, the sons of Aaron's uncle Uzziel, and said to them, 'Come forward, carry your relatives away from the front of the sanctuary to the outside of the camp.' So they came forward and carried them still in their tunics to the outside of the camp, as Moses had said."* (10:4-5).

Mishael and Elzaphan were the second cousins of Nadab and Abihu and Moses called them into duty. (Uzziel was the youngest son of Kohath, the grandson of Levi. Uzziel was the father of three sons.[17]) Time was not wasted as Nadab and Abihu were swept up and carried out of the camp. Mind you, the camp was not small. To get the bodies out of the camp the men had to leave the courtyard of the Tabernacle, pass through the living area of the Levites surrounding the courtyard. Then they had to carry the bodies through one of the other tribal areas to get out of the whole camp. It was a difficult task.

   D. Instructions to Aaron and His Remaining Sons (10:6-20)
     1. Do Not Mourn (10:6-7)

And then we find Moses warning Aaron and his two remaining sons to not mourn the loss of Nadab and Abihu. If they did, the LORD would kill them. Verse 6. *"Then Moses said to Aaron and to his sons Eleazar and Ithamar, 'Do not uncover your heads nor tear your clothes, so that you will not die and that He will not become wrathful against all the congregation. But your kinsmen, the whole house of Israel, shall bewail the burning which the LORD has brought about. You shall not even go out from the doorway of the tent of meeting, or you will die; for the LORD'S anointing oil is upon you.' So they did according to the word of Moses."* (10:6-7).

In those ancient times, people mourned not only with bewailing tears and grief but they would also uncover their heads, tear their clothing and, although not mentioned here, throw dust or ashes into the air and let it fall back of them. Aaron, Eleazar and Ithamar were wearing their priestly turbans and garments which had been anointed and consecrated for the work of the Tabernacle complex for all

---

[17] Exodus 6:18, 22; Numbers 3:19; 1st Chronicles 6:1-3, 18; 23:12,20; 24:24

generations to come. It would have been a sacrilege to cast their turbans to the ground and tear the sacred garments. The LORD would surely kill them for that kind of response. The rest of the Nation of Israel could uncover their heads, tear their clothing, and bewail the loss, but Aaron and his two sons could not. They had a job to do. They still had the original anointing oil on their heads from when Moses ordained them. Their job was taking care of the business of the Tabernacle. Other relatives could bury the dead. They were to care for the living, sinful as they may be.

2. Do Not Drink (10:8-11)

Then, from behind the Veil, and from the Mercy Seat of the Ark of the Covenant, the LORD spoke to Aaron saying to him, "Do not drink." Verse 8. *"The LORD then spoke to Aaron, saying, 'Do not drink wine or strong drink, neither you nor your sons with you, when you come into the tent of meeting, so that you will not die—it is a perpetual statute throughout your generations—and so as to make a distinction between the holy and the profane, and between the unclean and the clean, and so as to teach the sons of Israel all the statutes which the LORD has spoken to them through Moses.'"* (10:8-11).

The Nation of Israel was a drinking nation. Wine was the common everyday drink of the common person - man, woman, boy and girl, with every meal.

Now when I was a little boy attending church, when the word "wine" came up in a passage, the Dr. Sam Tullock would always say something like, "wine in those days was like our grape juice today. It was not like our wine that the wino's drink on the streets." Baptist were drinkers and dancers before prohibition and I have proof of that from my family history in Mississippi in the 1840's. A Baptist church was started in Mantee, Mississippi by my family members. Back in those days, families would eat breakfast at home on Sunday mornings, pack a basket lunch and walk or ride in a buggy to church. They would be sober for church but as soon as the last Amen was said, everyone would join in a fellowship meal on the grounds with their sandwiches and favorite beverages. Wine, beer, and strong drink was always on hand in the baskets. As the meal time came to an end, the fiddle would come out and the dancing would start with the kids playing in the mix. About three o'clock a baptism or two might occur down at the creek or lake and everyone would head home for supper and bed time. During prohibition, Baptist formally took a no drinking stance, although, to be honest, I must say, I doubt that held true in their homes. Today, if just all the Baptist in Houston, Texas really did not drink, the world-wide brewery in our town would have to shut down for a lack of business. Since the end of prohibition, Baptist have held the stance of no drinking, at least from the lips of the preachers in the pulpits and the excuse has been, "the wine in the Bible was like our grape juice." It never made sense to me. But now it does. They were right. Most of them did not know why. Here is why.

In the Bible, there is a difference between wine and strong drink as Moses asserts in this passage. Wine that is purchased today would be considered strong drink in the Bible. The Hebrew word is *shecar* and it applies to any beverage that has fermented to the state of having an intoxicating quality. And, intoxicating wine was not as easy to make as just crushing the grapes and waiting for them to ferment. Today, the making of all intoxicating wines requires the fruit, sugar, and yeast (leaven). But it also requires the right temperature of between 62 – 65 degrees Fahrenheit. If the three ingredients are properly mixed and the temperature is within that specific range, the grape juice can ferment in fourteen days and be aged and ready by the end of the month. That is, if all things go perfectly. However, if the temperature is lower or higher than the temperature range stated, the process would take much longer. It just so happens that the average temperature in Israel in the winter is 57 degrees Fahrenheit and in the summer 79 degrees. So, intoxicating fermentation of wine in Israel would be hit or miss depending on the temperature. But then we come back to the ingredients and yeast was not used. The grapes were harvested in mid-September. Ah, the temperature would be cooling closer to the proper temperature at that time of year. So, the time clock started with the wine pressing which could take several days and then the wait for the natural fermenting process to take place as the sugars in the grapes began to break down and natural yeast would be introduced from the air. Not such a sure way to guarantee that all pressed grape juices would turn into intoxicating beverages on demand. But grape juice was in demand by all Jews for every meal. And that is the point. And that is why the LORD told Aaron and his sons not to drink wine or strong drink when it was time for them to enter the duty as priests in the Tabernacle complex. The normal wines of the ancient days could have sat long enough to become strong drink and that would have impaired their ability to do their jobs. The LORD was serious. Arriving to work as priest intoxicated brought an immediate death penalty from the LORD. It was the eternal statute for all priests.

But we also see the extra duties of the priests stated in a snapshot in this passage. "... *and so as to make a distinction between the holy and the profane, and between the unclean and the clean, and so as to teach the sons of Israel all the statutes which the LORD has spoken to them through Moses.*"

Making a distinction between the "holy and profane" would be easy for the Israelites to understand. The Holy would be all that the LORD had commanded them; the profane would be anything in opposition to the commands of the LORD. But then the LORD added the distinction between the "unclean and clean."

Coming to this point in the story, we have seen the words "clean" and "unclean" several times, but with no instructions. For instance, in 4:12 we are told the remains of the animal were to be burned outside the camp in a "clean" place. But what does that mean? In 5:2-3, unclean things were not to be touched, such as carcasses and beasts. But what makes a carcasses or beast unclean? In 7:19, nothing unclean was to be eaten. But what makes something unclean to eat? The clean and the unclean were not described or taught in the book of Exodus and it has not been taught thus far in the book of Leviticus. The book of Genesis was most likely complete by this time by Moses, but there was no description of what was clean or unclean in it. Deuteronomy is thirty-nine years away. What was clean and what was unclean that the priest was to teach as a perpetual statute had not been revealed by the LORD. The LORD just made the statement for the first time and we will have to wait for Chapter 11 for those details to be revealed by Him.

Be that as it may, the two sons were dead and the LORD took the opportunity to inform the priests that they had a job to do and they could not take the chance of being intoxicated when they were on the job.

3. Eat the Grain Offering (10:12-13)

But that day, the day of the death of the two sons of Aaron, Moses noticed a problem, the grain offering had not been eaten as required. Verse 10. *"Then Moses spoke to Aaron, and to his surviving sons, Eleazar and Ithamar, "Take the grain offering that is left over from the LORD'S offerings by fire and eat it unleavened beside the altar, for it is most holy. You shall eat it, moreover, in a holy place, because it is your due and your sons' due out of the LORD'S offerings by fire; for thus I have been commanded."* (10:12-13).

On the eighth day, Aaron, and his sons, after being in the Tent of Meeting for seven days, had exited the tent to presided for the first time over the final ceremony of the ordination. The elders had brought the grain offering and a handful of it was put on the Brazen Altar to be consumed by fire just as the instructions demanded. But the rest was to be eaten by the priests. It had not been eaten. Moses' sharp eye must have noticed the grain was uneaten and promptly instructed Aaron and his sons to complete their duty in that part of the offering ceremony. It was required.

4. Eat the Wave Offering (10:14-15)

Verse 14 is surely part of the instruction to eat the grain offering that was just addressed by Moses. We have separated it here in our study for two reasons. First, the leftovers of the grain offering were to be eaten by the priests in a holy place. But, second, starting in verse 14 we see an extended instruction for the wave offerings and it was also to be eaten in a clean place. Verse 14. *"The breast of the wave offering, however, and the thigh of the offering you may eat in a clean place, you and your sons and your daughters with you; for they have been given as your due and your sons' due out of the sacrifices of the peace offerings of the sons of Israel. The thigh offered by lifting up and the breast offered by waving they shall bring along with the offerings by fire of the portions of fat, to present as a wave offering before the LORD; so it shall be a thing perpetually due you and your sons with you, just as the LORD has commanded."* (10:14-15).

Did you notice, the breast and thigh offerings could be eaten by the sons and daughters too. That is new. In other words, the wave offerings were for the whole priestly families to eat, male and female. But they were to be eaten in a "clean place" not specifically a "holy place." Anywhere inside the curtain fence of the Tabernacle complex was considered a "holy place." It is never called a "clean place." That means the "clean place" must be outside the curtained area of the Tabernacle complex, in their tribal areas, in the camp. The living quarters of the priests surrounded the Tabernacle complex. Here is a layout of the camp and it was always the same no matter where they were when they camped. For Moses, Aaron and his sons, their living quarters were east of the door to the Tabernacle complex.

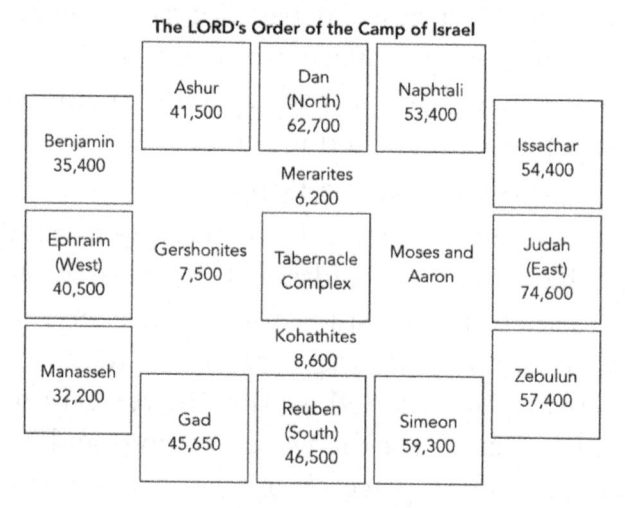

The LORD's Order of the Camp of Israel

	Ashur 41,500	Dan (North) 62,700	Naphtali 53,400	
Benjamin 35,400		Merarites 6,200		Issachar 54,400
Ephraim (West) 40,500	Gershonites 7,500	Tabernacle Complex	Moses and Aaron	Judah (East) 74,600
Manasseh 32,200		Kohathites 8,600		Zebulun 57,400
	Gad 45,650	Reuben (South) 46,500	Simeon 59,300	

5. Uneaten Goat Offering (10:16-18)

Moses had handled the offerings on the first day of the ordination. Those offerings were completed correctly according to the instruction of the LORD. But the offerings of the eighth day were completed by Aaron and his sons. Two of the sons had not followed the law of the fire in the firepans and died. Moses had also discovered the failure of the grain and wave offerings to be eaten as required. With two wrongs, Moses noticed another major infraction. Verse 16. *"But Moses searched carefully for the goat of the sin offering, and behold, it had been burned up! So he was angry with Aaron's surviving sons Eleazar and Ithamar, saying, 'Why did you not eat the sin offering at the holy place? For it is most holy, and He gave it to you to bear away the guilt of the congregation, to make atonement for them before the LORD. Behold, since its blood had not been brought inside, into the sanctuary, you should certainly have eaten it in the sanctuary, just as I commanded.'"* (10:16-18).

Moses accused Aaron and his sons of not following the commands of the LORD concerning the goat offering. It was a sin offering and Moses found the burning goat and hide outside the camp in a clean place. He thundered back to Aaron and his sons and questioned them harshly. *"Why did you not eat the sin offering at the holy place? For it is most holy, and He gave it to you to bear away the guilt of the congregation, to make atonement for them before the LORD."*

The reason we took the time to review the offerings was for this very sentence in this verse. Moses, in his panic, misjudged the goat offering on this eighth day. It was a sin offering, it was not the same as a sin offering associated with a guilt offering as Moses stated.

In a sin offering, the basics of the ceremony is the following.

- The priest takes the blood inside the Tent of Meeting and sprinkles the blood seven times in front of the Veil.
- The priest rubs blood on the four horns of the four corners of the Altar of Incense in front of the Veil.
- The priest pours the rest of the blood at the base of the Brazen Altar were the coals and ashes are and then stokes the fire.
- The person bringing the offering removes the fat portions.

- The fat portions of the animal are given to the priest who places them on the Brazen Altar where they are totally consumed in the fire.
- The rest of the animal, including the hide is taken outside the camp to a clean place burned.

But with a guilt offering, the sin offering portion was different as follows.

- The person bringing the offering must <u>CONFESS</u> his sin.
- The priest sprinkles the blood around the Brazen Altar.
- The priest pours the rest of the blood at the base of the Brazen Altar were the coals and ashes are and then stokes the fire.
- The person bringing the offering removes the fat portions.
- The fat portions of the animal are given to the priest who places them on the Brazen Altar where they are totally consumed in the fire.
- The rest of the animal, including the hide was given to the priest.

Moses had spoken incorrectly, the goat offering of the eighth day was not a guilt offering as Moses asserted. That is why Moses wanted to know why it was burned instead of eaten. It was a simple sin offering given by the elders for the people, not a sin offering associated with a guilt. It had been handled correctly. It was supposed to be burned outside the camp.

6. Aaron's Question (10:19)

The encounter with Moses's error caused Aaron to speak up. Verse 19. *"But Aaron spoke to Moses, 'Behold, this very day they presented their sin offering and their burnt offering before the LORD. When things like these happened to me, if I had eaten a sin offering today, would it have been good in the sight of the LORD?'"* (10:19).

Correctly Aaron said to Moses that the elders presented a sin offering and a burnt offering. Aaron did not say they presented a guilt offering which has its own order of service. If Aaron had eaten the sin offering associated with guilt, he would have sinned. So, with it being a sin offering instead of a guilt offering, Aaron asked Moses, *"if I had eaten a sin offering today, would it have been good in the sight of the LORD?"*

7. Moses' Thought (10:20)

Moses' thoughts had to have quickly reviewed in his mind the difference between a sin offering and a guilt offering. Aaron was right. The goat offering for sin had been handled correctly. Moses was wrong. And when Aaron corrected Moses, we find his answer in verse 20. *"When Moses heard that, it seemed good in his sight."* (10:20).

Aaron had done what was good in the Moses' sight, but also in the sight of the LORD. Aaron has kept the commands of the LORD.

The eighth day was about to be over. It had been a full day with may ups and downs. But it was no less over. It was time to hear an instruction from the LORD to determine what was clean and what was unclean. It was time to learn the details of that to teach it to all the people for all the generations to come. That we will discover in chapter 11.

Chapter 11

Here, we come to the first listing of clean and unclean foods in Leviticus chapter 11. This listing severely restricted the original list of animals and vegetation that man could eat following departure from Noah's Ark one-thousand and ninety years before the instruction in Leviticus. We find that story in Genesis 9.

> **Genesis 9:3** Every moving thing that is alive shall be food for you; I give all to you, as *I gave* the green plant. ⁴ Only you shall not eat flesh with its life, *that is,* its blood. ⁵ Surely I will require your lifeblood; from every beast I will require it. And from *every* man, from every man's brother I will require the life of man. ⁶ "Whoever sheds man's blood, By man his blood shall be shed, For in the image of God He made man.

Every animal that moved on the earth and every green plant on the planet was food for Noah and his family, including everyone that would live on earth until the time of the giving of Leviticus to the Nation of Israel. No animal or plant was unclean to anyone on earth for that one-thousand and ninety years. Now, as we come to Leviticus, the LORD will restrict only the Nation of Israel to eat animals that He deemed clean. The rest of the world could still eat all the animals and plants as with Noah's instruction.

VI. The Law of the Clean and Unclean Foods (11:1-46)
  A. Clean and Unclean Foods from the Land (11:1-2)

For the Nation of Israel, the LORD had a new food plan, and through Moses, He provided the law of the clean and unclean foods. He will begin with the clean and unclean foods from the land. As an introduction, we hear the LORD speaking to Moses in chapter 11 verse 1. *"The LORD spoke again to Moses and to Aaron, saying to them, "Speak to the sons of Israel, saying, 'These are the creatures which you may eat from all the animals that are on the earth."* (11:1-2).

When the LORD says, *"the animals that are on the earth,"* a better translation would be *all the animals on the land*. This is because, in this section, the LORD begins with land animals, then He moves to water animals and then to flying animals. Then He will summarize some special instructions that deal with all three kinds of animals.

1. Clean with Divided/Split Hoof and Chews the Cud (11:3)

In the law, clean animals have a divided or split hoof and chew the cud. Verse 3. *"Whatever divides a hoof, thus making split hoofs, and chews the cud, among the animals, that you may eat."* (11:3).

- First, after the animal swallows its food, it goes into a pouch called the *rumen*. From there, the animal can bring the food, now called a *cud*, back up into its mouth and chew it again. Some animals chew their cud several times before it finally goes into the stomach for full digestion.
- Second, the animal must have a completely cloven hoof. This means a hoof that splits into two toes.

This may seem like a general statement that fits either animal with a divided hoof or chews the cud, but that is not what the LORD intends. The two go together and must be together. Examples of clean animals that fit these two criteria are the oxen, sheep, goat, deer, gazelle, roebuck, ibex, and antelope. These animals are by far not an exhaustive list.

2. Unclean with any Deviation (11:4-8)

a) The Unclean Camel (11:4)

But the LORD tells the Nation of Israel that if the animal has one of the two but not the other, the animal is unclean, and he gives examples. Verse 4. *"Nevertheless, you are not to eat of these, among those which chew the cud, or among those which divide the hoof: the camel, for though it chews cud, it does not divide the hoof, it is unclean to you."* (11:4).

The camel is an unclean animal because it does not have the two criteria. It chews its cud, but it does not have a split hoof. With the unclean camel, its family includes the vicuna, alpaca, guanaco, llama, dromedary, and bactrian camel.

b) The Unclean Shaphan (Rock Badger) (11:5)

The second example is the same as the camel, and it is the unclean shaphan or rock badger. Verse 5. *"Likewise, the shaphan, for though it chews cud, it does not divide the hoof, it is unclean to you; ..."* (11:5).

The rock badger chews its cud, but it does not have a split hoof. The rock badger is found only in parts of Africa and extreme southwestern Asia. It is not related to the badgers we know today. Even if it was, the badgers we know are unclean. Instead, its closest living relatives are the elephants and manatees, which are also unclean animals.

c) The Unclean Rabbit (11:6)

The rabbit or hare is unclean as food for the Jews. Verse 6. *"...the rabbit also, for though it chews cud, it does not divide the hoof, it is unclean to you;"* (11:6). The reason it is unclean is the same as the camel and the rock badger. It chews its cud but does not have a split hoof.

What if the difference between a rabbit and a hare? The rabbit is much smaller in size, and it also has much shorter ears than a hare. The rabbit is born blind and furless and needs its mother to help until it is weaned. The hare is born

Chapter 11   155

with its eyes open and fully furred. Within hours after birth, it can begin to fend for itself.

d) The Unclean Pig (11:7)

Then the LORD gives an example of an animal with a split hoof that does not chew its cud. Verse 7. *"...and the pig, for though it divides the hoof, thus making a split hoof, it does not chew cud, it is unclean to you."* (11:7).

Some might ask the question, what is the difference between a pig and a hog. A pig is an animal that is a member of the Genus Sus family. A hog is a domestic subspecies of any one of the different family members of the Genus Sus. Pigs are found in the wild. Hogs are domestic, although some hogs have run free and become feral in various places in the world. Hogs are domestic pigs. Hogs and pigs, of any species, are unclean.

e) The Handling of the Unclean Animals (11:8)

But what about the handling of unclean animals? Could a Jew become unclean by handling such animals? Verse 8. *"You shall not eat of their flesh nor touch their carcasses; they are unclean to you."* (11:8).

The prohibition at this point in the instruction concerning these animals does not make them unclean to the Jew except that they cannot be eaten and their dead bodies cannot be touched. If one of these animals dies, a Jew could not dispose of the animal. That is not the point in this verse. Instead, the point in verse 8 is that the dead animal, which must be dead to be eaten, cannot be eaten because it is unclean.

B. Clean and Unclean from the Sea (11:9-12)
1. Clean Fins and Scales (11:9)

From the examples of the clean and unclean animals of the land, the LORD turns to the clean and unclean animals of the sea. For food, the sea animals were clean if they had fins and scales. Verse 9. *"These you may eat, whatever is in the water: all that have fins and scales, those in the water, in the seas or in the rivers, you may eat."* (11:9).

A scale is a rigid plate that grows on the animal's skin. In fish, the dermal scales are formed from mesoderm. They function to resist strong water currents and act as protective armor. The way they are formed allows the fish to move with great ease.

Many water animals have fins, but not all have scales. The fins are used to propel and guide the animal through the water. In this case, both fins and scales are required for the fish to be clean and edible. The two go together; both must be in place for the animal to be clean.

2. Unclean without Fins and Scales (11:10-12)

Like the land animals, the LORD explains that water animals that do not have both fins and scales are unclean. Verse 10. *"But whatever is in the seas and in the rivers that does not have fins and scales among all the teeming life of the water, and among all the living creatures that are in the water, they are detestable things to you, and they shall be abhorrent to you; you may not eat of their flesh, and their carcasses you shall detest. Whatever in the water does not have fins and scales is abhorrent to you."* (11:10-12).

As a fisherman, and the Jews will be fishermen in the Promised Land, it is impossible to fish without catching water creatures without fins or scales. They are not to be eaten. Even if they die, they are not to be eaten. They are unclean. Shellfish (shrimp, crayfish, crab, lobster, clams, scallops, oysters, and mussels), corals, and eels are examples of water creatures that do not have fins or scales and are unclean for Jews to eat. In general, all these animals survive on the waste of other animals. Because they eat the unclean excrement, the animal is unclean. It does not mean that the Jew cannot touch them; it just means they cannot be eaten.

C. Unclean Fowl (11:13-19)

The LORD then turns to the animals that fly, the unclean fowl he addresses first. Verse 13. *"These, moreover, you shall detest among the birds; they are abhorrent, not to be eaten: the eagle and the vulture and the buzzard, and the kite and the falcon in its kind, every raven in its kind, and the ostrich and the owl and the sea gull and the hawk in its kind, and the little owl and the cormorant and the great owl, and the white owl and the pelican and the carrion vulture, and the stork, the heron in its kinds, and the hoopoe, and the bat."* (11:13-19).

It is quite easy to see why these fowl are unclean; they all survive on dead decaying carcasses. They are scavengers. They eat that the unclean: therefore, they are considered unclean for the Jews to eat.

D. Clean and Unclean Insects (11:20-25)
1. Unclean walk on all fours (11:20)

Moving on to the clean and unclean insects, the LORD moves immediately to insects that walk on all fours. Verse 20. *"All the winged insects that walk on all fours are detestable to you."* (11:20).

Here we hit a slight problem. Wycliff translates this verse as follows. *"All thing of fowls that goeth on four feet, shall be abominable to you...."* Tyndale translates this verse as follows. *"And all foules that crepe ad goo apo all iiij. shalbe an abhominacion vnto you."* Both use the word "fowls", and that carried through to the King James Bible, which says, *"All fowls that creep, going upon all four, shall be an abomination unto you."* But all the modern translations use the word *insects*, including the New King James, which says, *"All flying insects that creep on all fours shall be an abomination to you."* So which is it?

The Hebrew word used is *oph*, and it means *flying creatures*. That does not help us because it can mean "fowl" or "insect." But what fowl have four legs? None. To add to the problem, fowl, in Wycliffe and Tyndale's days, means a feathered, warm-blooded vertebrate, and it comes from the Old English *fugel,* which comes from the Germanic word for bird. We are still no closer to the answer.

The only flying animal that walks on all fours that are not an insect is a bat. But it is not a fowl. It is not a feathered animal. Yet, it is a flying creature and fits the Hebrew word. But fowl do not have "all fours;" therefore, the translation cannot mean fowl and must mean insects, but here we run into another conundrum. All flying insects, such as bees, wasps, hornets, and more, have at least six legs but use only four for walking.

2. Clean with Jointed Legs and Jump – Locust, Crickets, Grasshoppers (11:21-22)

Not all flying insects are unclean. The LORD addresses the clean insects in verse 21. *"Yet these you may eat among all the winged insects which walk on all fours: those which have above their feet jointed legs with which to jump on the earth. These of them you may eat: the locust in its kinds, and the devastating locust in its kinds, and the cricket in its kinds, and the grasshopper in its kinds."* (11:21-22).

We find that flying insects that walk on all fours and can jump are clean and edible for the Jews. The LORD names them as *"locust in its kinds, ... crickets in its kinds; and grasshopper in its kinds."* Several varieties of locusts, crickets, and grasshoppers exist, and all are clean and edible.

3. Unclean if Touched until Evening (11:23-25)

But the LORD returns to the four-footed insects that, if touched, can cause you to be unclean until evening. Verse 23. *"But all other winged insects which are four-footed are detestable to you. By these, moreover, you will be made unclean: whoever touches their carcasses becomes unclean until evening, and whoever picks up any of their carcasses shall wash his clothes and be unclean until evening."* (11:23-25).

The LORD knew that it was impossible to live life without encountering these unclean insects. There are more kinds of insects on the earth than any other type of animals combined. How can you be unclean by these insects? By swatting them away? No. By flicking them off your clothing? No. By killing them with your hand? Yes. By killing them on your garments? Yes. How long will you be unclean? Until the end of the evening, which today is our *afternoon*. As soon as the new day starts at six o'clock pm, the Jew will once again be clean.

E. Unclean Summary Concerning Divided but Not Split Hoof (11:26)

The LORD returns to summarize His law concerning the animals with the divided but not split hoof and those which do not chew the cud. Verse 26. *"Concerning all the animals which divide the hoof but do not make a split hoof, or which do not chew cud, they are unclean to you: whoever touches them becomes unclean."* (11:26).

Here the LORD adds to the first prohibition of handing the unclean animals from the land. Now the LORD declares that animals such as the camel, rock badger, rabbit, and pig would make a Jew unclean even if he touched the animal.

F. Unclean Animals that Walk on Paws (11:27-28)

Also, the LORD prohibited the Jews from touching unclean animals that walk on paws. Verse 27. *"Also whatever walks on its paws, among all the creatures that walk on all fours, are unclean to you; whoever touches their carcasses becomes unclean until evening, and the one who picks up their carcasses shall wash his clothes and be unclean until evening; they are unclean to you."* (11:27-28).

Animals that walk on paws are not only unclean for eating purposes, but they are unclean to touch when they have died. What animals walk on paws? Felids – all cats, tigers, lions, leporids, bobcats, etc. Canids – all dogs, foxes, hounds, wolves, etc. Rabbits – all rabbits, hares pikas, etc. Bears and Raccoons. Rodents – mice, hamsters, rats, squirrels, prairie dogs, nutria, chipmunk, beaver, muskrat, porcupines, guinea pigs, gerbils, etc. Weasels – badgers, otters, ferrets, martens, minks, wolverines, etc. Not only are these animals unclean for Jews to eat if a Jew touches the dead body of one of these animals, but he is unclean until the end of the afternoon (evening).

- G. Unclean Animals that Swarm (11:29-31)
  1. What They Are (11:29-31)

The LORD then addresses the unclean animals that swarm and what they are. The first two have already been addressed because they fall into the category of animals with paws. Here, they are addressed again because they fall into animals that swarm in great numbers. *"Now these are to you the unclean among the swarming things which swarm on the earth: the mole, and the mouse, and the great lizard in its kinds, and the gecko, and the crocodile, and the lizard, and the sand reptile, and the chameleon. These are to you the unclean among all the swarming things; whoever touches them when they are dead becomes unclean until evening."* (11:29-31).

When we think of the word "swarm," most of us think about being attacked by thousands of wasps coming at us like the cloud of an angry flying army. We think of the danger coming our way. But that is not the meaning of the word "swarm" in this text. Here, when the English word was placed in the text, it meant *to gather together or to form a crowd*. When we think about it that way, when we use that definition for "swarm," it would include animals such as the mole (weasel), mouse, lizards, gecko, crocodiles, represent animals that are seen most often gathered in crowds of like kind. They are unclean to eat for the Jew as well as unclean to touch.

2. What they Touch that is Unclean (11:32-35)
a) Articles that Must Be Washed (11:32)

But more than that, the mole (weasel), mouse, lizards, gecko, crocodiles represent animals that cause regular articles of human life to be unclean too. Verse 32. *"Also anything on which one of them may fall when they are dead becomes unclean, including any wooden article, or clothing, or a skin, or a sack—any article of which use is made—it shall be put in the water and be unclean until evening, then it becomes clean."* (11:32).

Anything that these animals touch must be washed clean. These animals tend to constantly eliminate their body waste and therefore leave that waste on all items on which they crawl.

b) Clay Pots Must Be Broken (11:33)

We have already addressed the problem of porous earthenware or clay pots. When these animals are found in clay pots, the pots must be broken. Verse 33. *"As for any earthenware vessel into which one of them may fall, whatever is in it becomes unclean, and you shall break the vessel. Any of the food which may be eaten, on which water comes, shall become unclean, and any liquid which may be drunk in every vessel shall become unclean."* (11:33).

Why break the clay pots? The constant evacuation of the animal waste will soak into the clay pots' pores and cannot be washed well enough to be clean. Therefore, the pot must be broken and thrown away.

Also, any food that comes from the clay pots infected by these animals must be thrown away. Even the water is unclean. If wine, or any other liquid, kept in a clay pot, is found infected by these animals, that drink is unclean.

c) Ovens and Stoves Must be Smashed (11:35)

Even if these animals, moles (weasels), mice, lizards, geckos, crawl over an oven or a stove, the stove or oven must be smashed and discarded. Verse. 35. *"Everything, moreover, on which part of their carcass may fall becomes unclean; an oven or a stove shall be smashed; they are unclean and shall continue as unclean to you."* (11:35).

Why? Because they are unclean. Most stoves and ovens in that day were made of clay and were porous, and even with the presence of a fire, they cannot guarantee the purification from the waste of the animals.

3. What they Touch that is Clean (11:36-38)

a) Spring or Cistern (11:36)

But not all things that these animals touched were unclean. Springs and cisterns were still considered clean. Verse 36. *"Nevertheless a spring or a cistern collecting water shall be clean, though the one who touches their carcass shall be unclean."* (11:36).

Springs and cisterns contain water that is continuously moving. Moles, mice, lizards, and geckos are going to encounter springs and cisterns. If a mouse is found dead in the spring or cistern, the water is clean, but the person who retrieves the mouse is unclean.

b) Seeds to be Sown (11:37-38)

(1) Planted it is Clean (11:37)

Seeds sprout much better if they are soaked before they are planted. If the seeds are soaked in water that has been tainted by a dead mole, mouse, lizards, or gecko, the seeds are still clean to plant. Verse 37. *"If a part of their carcass falls on any seed for sowing which is to be sown, it is clean."* (11:37).

Chapter 11

(2) Watered with Clean Water (11:38)

However, once planted, the seeds were not to be tainted by a dead mole, mouse, lizards, or gecko. Verse 38. *"Though if water is put on the seed and a part of their carcass falls on it, it is unclean to you."* (11:38).

Here is what this means. A dead animal can be taken from the cistern or spring water, and the water is still clean to soak the seeds. But if, after the seeds have been soaked, a dead animal is found on the seeds, the seeds are unclean and should not be planted. Once soaked, the seeds can absorb diseases from the dead animal making the seeds susceptible to death. Therefore, they are unclean.

H. Unclean Dead Animals (11:39-40)
1. The One Who Touches it is Unclean Until Evening (11:39)

Now the LORD addresses the way clean animals can become unclean. Verse 39. *"Also if one of the animals dies which you have for food, the one who touches its carcass becomes unclean until evening."* (11:39).

The oxen, sheep, goat, turtle doves, or pigeons that die on their own or not killed and drained adequately of their blood are considered unclean, and once touched, the person is unclean until the end of the afternoon (evening).

2. The One Who Eats or Picks It Up is Unclean Until Evening (11:40)

The dead body of any edible animals which dies on their own or killed in some way other than by a person intentionally slaying the animal and processing it correctly at the time, causes that animal to be unclean to eat or even pick up. Verse 40. *"He too, who eats some of its carcass shall wash his clothes and be unclean until evening, and the one who picks up its carcass shall wash his clothes and be unclean until evening."* (11:40).

The dead animals even cause the clothes of the person picking them up to be unclean.

I. **Summary of Detestable Swarming Things (11:41-44)**

Finally, the LORD summarized the law for clean and unclean edible foods. Verse 41. *"Now every swarming thing that swarms on the earth is detestable, not to be eaten. Whatever crawls on its belly, and whatever walks on all fours, whatever has many feet, in respect to every swarming thing that swarms on the earth, you shall not eat them, for they are detestable. Do not render yourselves detestable through any of the swarming things that swarm, and you shall not make yourselves unclean with them so that you become unclean. For I am the LORD your God. Consecrate yourselves, therefore, and be holy, for I am holy. And you shall not make yourselves unclean with any of the swarming things that swarm on the earth."* (11:41-44).

J. **Clean and Unclean Declaration (11:45-46)**

Lastly, the LORD gives the reason for His clean and unclean declaration. Verse 45. *"For I am the LORD who brought you up from the land of Egypt to be your God; thus you shall be holy, for I am holy. This is the law regarding the animal and the bird, and every living thing that moves in the waters and everything that swarms on the earth, to make a distinction between the unclean and the clean, and between the edible creature and the creature which is not to be eaten."* (11:45-46).

Chapter 12

VII. The Law Concerning Childbirth (12:1-8)
   A. The Law for the Mother of a Male Child (12:1-4)
      1. Her Uncleanness (12:1-2)

From the Law concerning unclean foods, the LORD turned to the uncleanness concerning childbirth, and He begins with the uncleanness of the mother of a male child. We begin with her uncleanness in chapter 12, verse 1. *"Then the LORD spoke to Moses, saying, 'Speak to the sons of Israel, saying: When a woman gives birth and bears a male child, then she shall be unclean for seven days, as in the days of her menstruation she shall be unclean.'"* (12:1-2).

The LORD created females to have a time for cleaning their female organs used in reproduction. It takes seven days for this cleaning to take place. During that week, the females are considered unclean and therefore are not to have sexual relations with their husbands. A law concerning this issue for Israel had not been previously given. Yet, this instruction comes as the first indication that the female is considered unclean when the female body is cleaning itself. This will be addressed again in chapter 15.

But these seven days of uncleanness does not have anything to do with the time of her regular body cleaning; this is a regulation for childbirth of a male child. In this passage, we find that the LORD requires a mother of a male child to be considered unclean for the first seven days after the child's birth, in the same way, she is unclean during the time that her body's self-cleaning. It is in the same way, but it is not the same reason. During that uncleanness, there are several things she cannot do besides the prohibition of interacting physically with her husband. These include restrictions on where she can go, what she can do, and how she can do things. Being unclean, she cannot cook the clean foods. As soon as she touches them to prepare them for a meal, the food becomes unclean. Neither can she participate in holy things that are clean because her presence will make them unclean.

Be that as it may, the uncleanness to this degree is only for the first seven days. Why? Because on the eighth day of the male child's life, an important event in the child's life occurs.

2. Her Child's Circumcision (12:3)

On the eighth day of every male child's life in the line of Abraham and down through all the ages, the male is to be circumcised. Verse 3. *"On the eighth day, the flesh of his foreskin shall be circumcised."* (12:3).

The mother is permitted to be present at this holy ceremony because her strict seven days of uncleanness is over.

3. Her Days of Purification (12:4)

But even though her uncleanness is over, the law requires thirty-three more purification days when she delivers a male child. Verse 4. *"Then she shall remain in the blood of her purification for thirty-three days; she shall not touch any consecrated thing, nor enter the sanctuary until the days of her purification are completed."* (12:4).

For the following thirty-three days, the mother cannot go into the Tabernacle complex for any reason. In the context of Leviticus, it is the Tabernacle complex that is consecrated within the camp of the Israelites. When the text says, *"nor enter the sanctuary,"* the word *sanctuary* means *holy*.

As such, the holy would be the place of the offerings around the front of the Tent of Meeting, the holy basin of water, and the Brazen Altar. This law applied especially to the priests' wives who would be allowed to enter the Tabernacle complex's curtained area and eat the meals with their priestly families in the holy places. That would be forbidden during the seven days of her body's cleaning and the added thirty-three days of purification. In verse 6, we will learn that upon the end of her purification, she would be required to present an offering at the Tent of Meeting; therefore, proclaiming her purified and able to enter the holy area within the curtains of the Tabernacle complex at the appropriate times.

B. The Law for the Mother of a Female Child (12:5ab)
1. Her Uncleanness (12:5a)

But the law of the mother for the birth of a female child is different. Verse 5a. *"But if she bears a female child, then she shall be unclean for two weeks, as in her menstruation;"* (12:5a).

With the birth of a female child, uncleanness is extended from seven days to fourteen days. It is the same kind of uncleanness as during the time of her body's self-cleaning every month, but for a different reason. This time is for the birth of a female child.

2. Her Days of Purification (12:5b)

Also, the days of a mother's purification are extended from thirty-three days for a male child's birth to sixty-six days with a female child. Verse 5b. *"...and she shall remain in the blood of her purification for sixty-six days."* (12:5b).

Commentators of old try to explain the reasons for the difference in the unclean and purification law between a male child's birth versus a female child, but none makes sense. However, no doubt, commentators have made much about it, stating the difference in the status in culture between a male and a female birth and after-effects on the mother's body, but these tales cannot be proven.

C. The Law for the Offering of the Mother (12:6-8)
1. The Required Burnt and Sin Offerings (12:6-7)

To complete the law of the mother for the birth of a child, the LORD required a burnt and a sin offering. Verse 6. *"When the days of her purification are completed, for a son or for a daughter, she shall bring to the priest at the doorway of the tent of meeting a one-year-old lamb for a burnt offering and a young pigeon or a turtledove for a sin offering. Then he shall offer it before the LORD and make atonement for her, and she shall be cleansed from the flow of her blood. This is the law for her who bears a child, whether a male or a female."* (12:6-7).

Upon the end of her purification, thirty-three days for the birth of a male child and sixty-six days for the delivery of a female child, the mother delivers a lamb and a pigeon or turtle dove to the door of the tent of meeting. She is now clean and can enter the holy, sacred, consecrated Tabernacle complex. The offering is the same for a male or female child. The lamb will be the burnt offering, presented at the north side of the Brazen Altar. The mother will place her hand on the head of the lamb and kill it. The priest will catch the blood and sprinkle it around the altar and pour the rest at its base. He will then stoke the fire. The mother will skin and cut up the lamb. The legs and entrails will be washed, and the priest will place all the animals except for the hide on the altar, where it will burn all the rest of the day and all night for a burnt offering. The priest will be given the hide. The turtle dove or pigeon will be given to the priest at the west side of the Brazen Altar, where he will wring the head off, tear off the wings, sprinkle the blood around the altar, place the feathers and the crop in the coals on the east side of the altar and then put the bird parts on the Brazen Altar to be burned for a sin offering.

This passage will become especially important in the time of the birth of Jesus. He was born in Bethlehem. The family stayed there until the eighth day when He was circumcised. On the night of the eighth day, the angel told Joseph to take his family to Egypt to escape Herod's wrath. Joseph, Mary, and Jesus left in the middle of the night. In the days following, the babies in Bethlehem are killed, Herod kills his son and the son's mother. Herod dies on April 4th, 4 BC. An angel tells Joseph that he can return to Israel because Herod is dead. Thirty-three days after the circumcision of Jesus, Joseph, Mary, and Jesus arrived at the Temple in Jerusalem with her purification offering. It would have taken the family at least three days to travel from Egypt to Jerusalem. What is the conclusion? The birth of Jesus had to occur in March of 4 BC for all the days to fall in line with this law of the purification offering at the Temple in Jerusalem.

2. The Permitted Burnt and Sin Offerings (12:8)

But not every family could afford a lamb to give as a purification offering. Just as with most of the required offerings, the LORD permits an alternative burnt and sin offering. Verse 28. *"But if she cannot afford a lamb, then she shall take two turtledoves, or two young pigeons, the one for a burnt offering and the other for a sin offering; and the priest shall make atonement for her, and she will be clean."* (12:8).

Because we know the offerings presented in chapters 1 through 7, with this alternative offering, the head of the first bird was not snapped off the bird's body, it was broken backward, and the front of the neck was nipped to release the blood. The head of the second bird was wrung from the body. All the rest of the ceremony for the birds of the burnt and sin offerings were the same as always.

Chapter 13

In chapter 13, we will delve into the Law concerning unclean leprosy.

The straightforward law concerning leprosy needs only a few notes of commentary with each point. I think it would be helpful if I summarize the standard order of a leprosy diagnosis before we begin.

- First, the priest is the authority to diagnosed leprosy as clean or unclean in every situation.
- Second, the priest looks for a swelling, a scab, or a bright spot called the "mark."
- Third, with a mark present, the priest quarantines the person or item for seven days.
- Forth, the priest inspects the mark for spreading or changed, the quarantine continues for seven days.
- Fifth, the presence of white hair in the mark is an immediate sign of leprosy.
- Sixth, once the mark has turned entirely white, the priest declares the person clean.
- Seventh, once clean, the quarantine continues for seven days.
- Eighth, on the eighth day, the clean person presents his offerings at the Tent of Meeting.

With these points in mind, we can now discover them again as we read and study the law of leprosy. Chapters 13 and 14 contain the whole law of leprosy.

Chapter 13

VIII. The Law Concerning Leprosy (13:1-59)
  A. The Suspicion of Leprosy on a Man (13:1-8)
    1. Three Conditions – Swelling, Scab, Bright Spot (13:1-2)

The LORD gave the law concerning leprosy to both Moses and Aaron. When there was a suspicion of leprosy on a man, Aaron was to look for three conditions – swelling, scab, or a bright spot. The LORD spoke in chapter 13 verse 1. *"Then the LORD spoke to Moses and to Aaron, saying, 'When a man has on the skin of his body a swelling or a scab or a bright spot, and it becomes an infection of leprosy on the skin of his body, then he shall be brought to Aaron the priest or to one of his sons the priests.'"* (13:1-2).

The text says, *"When a man...."* We need to move this side point out of the way immediately. The Hebrew word for "man" is *adam*. You should recognize it because it was the formal name of the first man the LORD created. But it is the word that properly means *all humans – male and female together*. Therefore, most of the new versions render this verse as "When a person ...." We agree. The LORD is directing this instruction to the priests for both males and females.

Swelling skin, scabs, and bright spots were sure to come upon everyone living in tents out by a mountain as the Nation of Israel was doing at the time. The mere process of gathering wood for the fires lends to cuts and wounds. But the issue at hand deals with infected wounds. We have all had an infected wound. The skin around the wound becomes reddish; fever appears and, with that, the area becomes stiff and swollen, which is exactly what the LORD is addressing with Moses and Aaron.

a) Hair Turned White in Infection and Deep Infection – Declare Unclean (13:3)

When an infection appears in a wound, the person must go to the priest for a diagnosis. Verse 3 says, *"The priest shall look at the mark on the skin of the body, and if the hair in the infection has turned white and the infection appears to be deeper than the skin of his body, it is an infection of leprosy; when the priest has looked at him, he shall pronounce him unclean."* (13:3).

The "mark" on the skin is the infected area around the wound that has swollen, turned reddish, hard, and is hotter to the touch than the normal skin. We understand that. But the first sign of leprosy is the presence of a hair that has turned white, along with the infection appearing to be much deeper in the flesh than just a skin-deep scab. The white hair and the swelling are an immediate declaration that the person is unclean with leprosy.

b) Bright Spot with No Turned White Hair – Isolation Seven Days (13:4)

But not so fast. Men are hairy, and the hair in the wound may not have turned white, but the mark on the skin has turned whiter than the normal skin around it. What should the priest do? Verse 4. *"But if the bright spot is white on the skin of his body, and it does not appear to be deeper than the skin, and the hair on it has not turned white, then the priest shall isolate him who has the infection for seven days."* (13:4).

The diagnosis of the priest is, "I don't know if you are clean or unclean. Let us isolate you for seven days and take another look then." So, the priest isolates the person from all family and friends, most likely outside the camp for seven days.

c) Infection Not Changed - Isolate for Seven Days (13:5)

At the end of the seven days, the priest inspects the isolated person again. Verse 5. *"The priest shall look at him on*

Chapter 13 173

the seventh day, and if in his eyes the infection has not changed and the infection has not spread on the skin, then the priest shall isolate him for seven more days." (13:5).

With no change in the wound visible, the careful priest isolates the person for seven more days.

d) Scab Faded or Not Spread – Declare Clean (13:6)

At the end of the seventh day, making a total of fourteen days of isolation from family and friends, the priest inspects the person again. Verse 6. *"The priest shall look at him again on the seventh day, and if the infection has faded and the mark has not spread on the skin, then the priest shall pronounce him clean; it is only a scab. And he shall wash his clothes and be clean."* (13:6).

After fourteen days, if the mark fades with no spreading, the priest declares the person clean. The leper washes his clothes, the same clothes he has worn for fourteen days.

e) Scab Spread – Declare Unclean (13:7-8)

But on that fourteenth day, if the scab enlarges itself, there is a medical problem. Verse 7. *"But if the scab spreads farther on the skin after he has shown himself to the priest for his cleansing, he shall appear again to the priest. The priest shall look, and if the scab has spread on the skin, then the priest shall pronounce him unclean; it is leprosy."* (13:7-8).

When the priest sees the wound increased in size, he declares the person unclean with leprosy. Not spoken here, but the LORD will say later, the person with leprosy must isolate from family and friends outside the camp until the leprosy runs its course.

B. The Chronic Leprosy on a Man (13:9-23)
1. White Swelling, Hair Turned White, Quick Raw Flesh – Declare Unclean (13:9-11)

But not all leprosy runs its course in the same way. Some people experience chronic leprosy with raw open flesh. What should happen then? Verse 9. *"When the infection of leprosy is on a man, then he shall be brought to the priest. The priest shall then look, and if there is a white swelling in the skin, and it has turned the hair white, and there is quick raw flesh in the swelling, it is a chronic leprosy on the skin of his body, and the priest shall pronounce him unclean; he shall not isolate him, for he is unclean."* (13:9-11).

With this instruction, we can immediately conclude several kinds of leprosy exist with varying seriousness and length of ailment. Here we see the swelling in place, and the hair in the wound turned white as expected with leprosy, but the LORD adds the factor of *"quick raw flesh."* The word "quick" means *to have life*. The Hebrew word is *haya,* and it means *to live*. This means that the infected raw flesh reproduces itself with more infected raw flesh instead of healthy flesh. The priest must declare him unclean and isolate him for seven days. Not said here, but can be assumed by the way the LORD handled the previous leprosy instructions, the priest inspects at the end of the seven days. If the infection remains, he isolates another seven days, and the process continues until the leprosy runs its course.

2. White Leprosy Covers All of Body – Declare Clean (13:12-13)

The presence of white dead skin and flesh means the death of leprosy because it has run its course. We see that next in verse 12. *"If the leprosy breaks out farther on the skin, and the leprosy covers all the skin of him who has the infection from his head even to his feet, as far as the priest can see, then the priest shall look, and behold, if the leprosy has covered all his body, he shall pronounce clean him who has the infection; it has all turned white and he is clean."* (13:12-13).

With the chronic leper, the disease finally covers all the skin and flesh of the man. When it runs its course, the leprous skin and flesh turn completely white. When the person is completely white from head to toe, the priest proclaims him clean. As we will see, the leper remains isolated another seven days, and then on the eighth day, he presents his offering at the Tent of Meeting, but that information comes later in the text.

3. Presence of Raw Flesh – Declare Unclean (13:14-15)

When the priest inspects the leper at the end of the seven days, and raw flesh appears or is still present, the priest declares an immediate uncleanness. Verse 14. *"But whenever raw flesh appears on him, he shall be unclean. The priest shall look at the raw flesh, and he shall pronounce him unclean; the raw flesh is unclean, it is leprosy."* (13:14-15).

4. Raw Flesh Turned White Leper – Declare Clean (13:16-17)

But if, upon inspection, the raw flesh turned white, what is the priest to do? Verse 16. *"Or if the raw flesh turns again and is changed to white, then he shall come to the priest, and the priest shall look at him, and behold, if the infection has turned to white, then the priest shall pronounce clean him who has the infection; he is clean."* (13:16-17).

When all the raw flesh turns white, the appearance means the leprosy has run its course. The priest declares the person unclean. No doubt he must remain in isolation seven more days for a final inspection as with the others.

5. Boil Turns to Deep White Swelling or Reddish White Spot – Declare Unclean (13:18-20)

Perhaps we come to a third strain of leprosy that begins with a boil. Verse 18. *"When the body has a boil on its skin, and it is healed, and in the place of the boil there is a white swelling or a reddish-white, bright spot, then it shall be shown to the priest; and the priest shall look, and behold, if it appears to be lower than the skin, and the hair on it has turned white, then the priest shall pronounce him unclean; it is the infection of leprosy, it has broken out in the boil."* (13:18-20).

The Hebrew word for "boil" is *bashal,* and it means *seethe.* An archaic English word, *seethe* needs defining in today's language. It is a hard tumor-like wound that bubbles up in size and oozes out liquid as if it is "boiling from within."

In the case of the "boil," the priest relies on two signs. First, does it look like the boil goes deep past the skin into the flesh? Second, does it contain the presence of a hair turned white in the wound? In either case, the priest must declare the man unclean. Out to isolation, he must go.

6. **Boil, No White Hairs, and Skin Deep – Isolate Seven Days (13:21)**

But what if the priest looks for the two signs that we just mentioned, and they are not there? What does the priest do? Verse 21. *"But if the priest looks at it, and behold, there are no white hairs in it, and it is not lower than the skin and is faded, then the priest shall isolate him for seven days; … "* (13:21).

As we should expect by now, the priest does not know if leprosy remains in the wound, so the person isolates for seven days.

7. **Boil, White Swelling or Reddish Spot Spreads – Declare Unclean (13:22)**

But, if upon inspection, the priest finds the boil spreading, what does he to do? *"… and if it spreads farther on the skin, then the priest shall pronounce him unclean; it is an infection."* (13:22)

With a spreading boil, the priest declares the man unclean. He remains in isolation.

8. **Scar from Boil – Declare Clean (13:23)**

If upon inspection on the seventh day, the priest finds a bright spot or a scar in place of the boil, verse 23 says, *"But if the bright spot remains in its place and does not spread, it is only the scar of the boil; and the priest shall pronounce him clean."* (13:23).

In this case, the priest declares the man clean.

C. The Burn Turned to Leprosy on a Man (13:24-)
1. Burn Turns to Deep Bright Spot, Reddish-white, or White – Declare Unclean (13:24-25)

Alas, the LORD introduces another source of leprosy, one from a burn. Verse 24. *"Or if the body sustains in its skin a burn by fire, and the raw flesh of the burn becomes a bright spot, reddish-white, or white, then the priest shall look at it. And if the hair in the bright spot has turned white and it appears to be deeper than the skin, it is leprosy; it has broken out in the burn. Therefore, the priest shall pronounce him unclean; it is an infection of leprosy."* (13:24-25).

The source of this wound comes from a fire burn. No doubt fire burns were common in the camp, but in this case, the burn becomes infected beyond the expected. The priest looks for two things— the deepness of the infection and the presence of a white hair. With one or both present, the priest declares the leper unclean. Isolation begins.

2. No White Hair No Deep Spot – Isolate Seven Days (13:26)

But with neither of the two signs present, the priest still protects the other people. Verse 26. *"But if the priest looks at it, and indeed, there is no white hair in the bright spot and it is no deeper than the skin, but is dim, then the priest shall isolate him for seven days..."* (13:26).

Nothing new here. If the priest does not know for sure, isolation continues.

3. Bright Spot Spreads Deeper – Declare Unclean (13:27)

Seven days later, upon inspection, if the wound becomes worse, we know the prescription by now. Verse 27. *"... and the priest shall look at him on the seventh day. If it spreads farther in the skin, then the priest shall pronounce him unclean; it is an infection of leprosy."* (13:27).

The spread of the wound immediately prescribes the declaration of an unclean leper. Isolation continues.

4. Bright Spot Stays the Same – Declare Clean (13:28)

But if, on that seventh day, healing appears, the prescription changes. Verse 28. *"But if the bright spot remains in its place and has not spread in the skin, but is dim, it is the swelling from the burn; and the priest shall pronounce him clean, for it is only the scar of the burn."* (13:28).

The declaration becomes clean, but the person must stay in isolation seven more days before coming to the camp as in the previous cases.

D. The Infection of Leprosy in the Hair of Man and Women (13:29-37)

Now the LORD introduces when leprosy found in the hair on the head or beard. Verse 29. *"Now if a man or woman has an infection on the head or on the beard, ..."* (13:29).

Concerning leprosy, all the way to this point in the law, the LORD uses the Hebrew word *adam;* we have already discussed that it means *humans or persons*. Here the LORD gives specific instructions to a *"man or woman."* What is the difference? The Hebrew word for man here is *wə·'îš*, and it means *male*. The Hebrew word for a woman here is *'iš-šāh*, and it means *female*. So, the LORD carefully contrasts the male and the female because the male typically wears a beard in Jewish life.

1. Deep in Skin with Thin Yellowish Hair – Declare Unclean (13:30)

Whether male or female, when an infection appears, the person must go to the priest. Verse 30. *"... then the priest shall look at the infection, and if it appears to be deeper than the skin and there is thin yellowish hair in it, then the priest shall pronounce him unclean; it is a scale, it is leprosy of the head or of the beard."* (13:30).

The priest inspects the infection with the only two signs he knows how to use upon the first visit. He looks for the

Chapter 13

depth of the infection and the color of the hair in the infection. Here we see a difference in the color of the hair. On the body, he looks for a white hair. On the head or beard, he looks for yellowish hair. If the two are present, the person is unclean. To isolation the person goes.

2. Skin Deep with No Black Hair – Isolate Seven Days (13:31)

The presence of white or yellow hair causes an immediate unclean declaration. But if the wound does not have hair in it, it makes the diagnosis difficult. But what the absence of hair? Verse 31. *"But if the priest looks at the infection of the scale, and indeed, it appears to be no deeper than the skin and there is no black hair in it, then the priest shall isolate the person with the scaly infection for seven days."* (13:31).

The people of the Nation of Israel were black-headed. As age came along, many of them would become gray-headed. In this inspection, the wound seems to be on the surface, but the black hair is missing. A bald spot appeared. Just to be safe, the priest orders isolation for seven days.

3. Not Spread, Shave – Isolate Seven Days (13:32-33)

After seven days, the priest inspects the person again. Verse 32. *"On the seventh day the priest shall look at the infection, and if the scale has not spread and no yellowish hair has grown in it, and the appearance of the scale is no deeper than the skin, then he shall shave himself, but he shall not shave the scale; and the priest shall isolate the person with the scale seven more days."* (13:32-33).

With no changes in the wound, the person shaves all the hair but not the wound area. The person stays in isolation for another week.

4. No Change – Declare Clean (13:34)

With another week behind, the priest inspects again. Verse 34. *"Then on the seventh day the priest shall look at the scale, and if the scale has not spread in the skin and it appears to be no deeper than the skin, the priest shall pronounce him clean; and he shall wash his clothes and be clean."* (13:34).

If the wound does not change over the fourteen days, the priest declares the person clean. He washes his clothing. No doubt, the person stays in isolation for seven more days because it is part of the routine before bringing an offering to the Tent of Meeting.

5. Change – Declare Unclean (13:35-36)

But if the wound spreads after shaving all the hair, a prescription changes. Verse 35. *"But if the scale spreads farther in the skin after his cleansing, then the priest shall look at him, and if the scale has spread in the skin, the priest need not seek for the yellowish hair; he is unclean."* (13:35-36).

If the wound grows, it does not matter if yellow hair appears, the mere size of the growing wound requires the declaration of uncleanness and isolation away from the camp.

6. Spot Remains with Black Hair Growing – Declare Clean (13:37)

But if the wound contains black hair, the news was good. Verse 37. *"If in his sight the scale has remained, however, and black hair has grown in it, the scale has healed, he is clean; and the priest shall pronounce him clean."* (13:37).

Black hair is the normal color for Israelites. With black hair growing in the old wound, the person is clean.

E. The Infection of Leprosy in the Skin of Man and Women (13:38-39)

1. Bright Spots Faint White Eczema – Declare Clean (13:38-39)

Not all spots on the skin which dry to scales are leprosy. Nevertheless, when a spot occurs, the priest must be notified to give a diagnosis. Verse 38. *"When a man or a woman has bright spots on the skin of the body, even white bright spots, then the priest shall look, and if the bright spots on the skin of their bodies are a faint white, it is eczema that has broken out on the skin; he is clean."* (13:38-39).

Faint white skin with a little scale is not leprosy; it is eczema. The Hebrew word that we translate as *eczema* is *bohaq*. It means a *white spot*. The English word "eczema" means *something thrown out by heat, or to boil over, break out, or bubble*. The ancient physicians called it "eczema" because it began as a *fiery pustule on the skin*. It is associated with yeast, and as it grows on the skin, its fiery nature causes great itching. Nevertheless, it is not leprosy, and the person is clean. No isolation.

F. The Infection of Leprosy on a Bald Man (13:40-46)
1. Just the Loss of the Hair – Declared Clean (13:40)

Eczema is not leprosy, and neither is the natural baldness of a man. Verse 40. *"Now if a man loses the hair of his head, he is bald; he is clean."* (13:40).

The Hebrew word for *man* is the word that means a *male*, as we formally explained. The natural process of baldness is not leprosy; the man is clean.

2. Bald on Front and Sides – Declared Clean (13:41)

Israelites and men in all nations can lose hair on the front and sides of their heads. Verse 41. *"If his head becomes bald at the front and sides, he is bald on the forehead; he is clean."* (13:41).

With the normal bald patterns of men – he is still clean.

3. Bald Head or Forehead with Reddish-white Infection – Declared Unclean (13:42-46)

But if with the loss of hair comes the mark of the tale-tell sign of the reddish-white infection, the priest must make a diagnosis. Verse 42. *"But if on the bald head or the bald forehead, there occurs a reddish-white infection, it is leprosy breaking out on his bald head or on his bald forehead. Then the priest shall look at him; and if the swelling of the infection is reddish-white on his bald head or on his bald forehead, like the appearance of leprosy in the skin of the body, he is a leprous man, he is unclean. The priest shall surely pronounce him unclean; his infection is on his head."* (13:42-44).

We have already seen this diagnosis before. In all other situations, the priest looks for the deepness of the infection and the hair color. Even in the case of the loss of hair with a spreading infection, it would likely be leprosy. When a man begins to become bald with a leprous sore mark, the priest must to declare him unclean. Off to isolation, he must go to live. We will learn that soon.

a) Tear Cloths, Cover Hair and Mustache – Cry Unclean (13:45)

Once diagnosed as a leper, the leper must follow a process. Verse 45. *"As for the leper who has the infection, his clothes shall be torn, and the hair of his head shall be uncovered, and he shall cover his mustache and cry, 'Unclean! Unclean!'."* (13:45).

First, torn clothing must be discarded. Second, the rest of the hair on his head, mustache, or beard is shaved. Third, when coming near anyone, the leper must declare the with words, "unclean."

b) Liver Alone Outside of Camp (13:46)

Where does the leper live once diagnosed? Verse 46. *"He shall remain unclean all the days during which he has the infection; he is unclean. He shall live alone; his dwelling shall be outside the camp."* (13:46).

The leper's isolation was not just for seven days, it was for all the days he was infected, and his isolation was to be outside the camp away from all family and friends.

G. The Infection of Leprosy on Garments (13:47-59)

Now we come to the most difficult part of this section to understand. We clearly understand that leprosy is an infection that attacks humans. So far, the LORD has dealt with what might be six different kinds or varieties of leprosy in humans. But now, the LORD speaks of a kind of leprosy that attacks garments and walls. We begin this leprosy in verse 47. *"When a garment has a mark of leprosy in it, whether it is a wool garment or a linen garment, whether in warp or woof, of linen or of wool, whether in leather or in any article made of leather, if the mark is greenish or reddish in the garment or in the leather, or in the warp or in the woof, or in any article of leather, it is a leprous mark and shall be shown to the priest. Then the priest shall look at the mark and shall quarantine the article with the mark for seven days."* (13:47-50).

We all recognize the terms *"wool ... linen ... leather."* But what does the LORD mean by *"warp or woof"*? Threads in a material running lengthwise are called *warp*. Threads running crosswise are called *woof*. These threads create a texture on the wool and linen fabrics. The priest inspects the material to discover green or yellowish growing marks anywhere, front, back, between the layers, or in the undergarment structure. If an organic mark is present, the garment is quarantined for seven days. We are not told where the quarantined garment is kept, but surely outside the camp for the safety of all.

a) If Leprous Mark Has Spread – Burn Garment (13:51-52)

As with humans, the priest inspects the garments at the end of seven days. Because we know how the LORD has dealt with all the human wounds, we can assume correctly how He deals with the garments, but with an added twist. *"He shall then look at the mark on the seventh day; if the mark has spread in the garment, whether in the warp or in the woof, or in the leather, whatever the purpose for which the leather is used, the mark is a leprous malignancy, it is unclean. So he shall burn the garment, whether the warp or the woof, in wool or in linen, or any article of leather in which the mark occurs, for it is a leprous malignancy; it shall be burned in the fire."* (13:51-52).

At the end of seven days of isolation for the garment, if the diseased mark grows, the garment does not remain in isolation; it is burned.

b) If Leprous Mark Has Not Spread – Quarantine Seven Days (13:53-54)

At the end of seven days of isolation for the garment, if the diseased mark had not spread in any part of the garment, the priest would do the same thing that he had done with humans. Verse 53. *"But if the priest shall look, and indeed the mark has not spread in the garment, either in the warp or in the woof, or in any article of leather, then the priest shall order them to wash the thing in which the mark occurs and he shall quarantine it for seven more days."* (13:53-54).

With no disease growth in seven days, the garments are washed and remain in isolation for seven more days.

c) Wash Garment and If Mark Remains – Burn It (13:55)

At the end of the second week, one week after the garment is washed, the priest inspects the garment again. Verse 55. *"After the article with the mark has been washed, the priest shall again look, and if the mark has not changed its appearance, even though the mark has not spread, it is unclean; you shall burn it in the fire, whether an eating away has produced bareness on the top or on the front of it."* (13:55).

If the mark is not washed away and remains at the end of the week, the garment is unclean and must be burned. The last phrase of the verse says, *"... whether an eating away has produced bareness on the top or on the front of it."*

No doubt, we would not call this leprosy today; we would call it fungus. We understand that word, and we know that when a fungus is growing on a garment and not treated, it will destroy the threads of the material or eat holes in leather. Today we have cleaners for such funguses, but in the ancient days, they did not. When a fungus will not die and fade away after being washed, it cannot die. Therefore, the only option given by the LORD is to burn the article. It did not matter where the fungus mark was, in full view or hidden underneath.

d) Wash Garment and the Mark Faded – Tear It Out and Burn It (13:56)

If the priest finds upon inspection that, after the washing seven days before, the mark is faded, the LORD has a different plan. *"Then if the priest looks, and if the mark has faded after it has been washed, then he shall tear it out of the garment or out of the leather, whether from the warp or from the woof; ...."* (13:56).

When the priest sees the mark faded after the washing and quarantined for seven days, the faded area must be torn out, and new material sewn in to repair the garment. The part that is torn out is burned.

e) Mark Returns – Burn It (13:57)

If the priest finds upon inspection that, after the washing seven days before, the mark is still present, we have a new instruction. Verse 57. *"...and if it appears again in the garment, whether in the warp or in the woof, or in any article of leather, it is an outbreak; the article with the mark shall be burned in the fire."* (13:57).

f) Wash Garment and Mark Departed Wash Again– Declare Clean (13:58-59)

If the priest finds upon inspection that, after the washing seven days before, that the mark is gone, then verse 58 says, *"The garment, whether the warp or the woof, or any article of leather from which the mark has departed when you washed it, it shall then be washed a second time and will be clean. This is the law for the mark of leprosy in a garment of wool or linen, whether in the warp or in the woof, or in any article of leather, for pronouncing it clean or unclean."* (13:58-59).

With chapter 14 of Leviticus, we discover the law for the offerings of a leper after being declared clean, as well as the issue of leprosy growing on the walls of one's home.

Alas, we transgress a problem that we must quickly settle. What kind of leprosy attacks linen, wool, and leather? The answer resides in the word we call "leprosy." With all our experience in the Word of God so far, we find many instances where our definitions lead us wrong. So, too, it is the reason that we see here, for what we think about leprosy today, is not the meaning in the pages of Leviticus.

Our definition of the word "leprosy" restricts us to a poor, poor man with rotting oozing sores and open raw decaying flesh right down to the bone. The Hebrew word for "leprosy" is *cara'ath*. Obviously, we did not receive our word from ancient Hebrew. Instead, the Middle English word *leper*, which simply meant *disease*, came from the Latin *lepra,* which encompasses all kinds of illness. Modern English, in the late 1500s, began to separate diseases into classes with different names. At that time, our definition and understanding of leprosy disease began to emerge to define a person with the kind of leprosy we expect and apply to this text in chapters 13 and 14. But we are misguided in a crisis of obsolete definitions.

The Hebrew word *cara'ath* was defined in earlier times in the English language as a *smiting or a stroke*. But these, too, are obsolete definitions for the Hebrew word. Today, we can change the words *smiting or stroke* because they imply a battery with some object to the word *infliction*. As such, we understand that a person can be infected with some disease and, so, too, the garment can be inflicted with an illness. Whether on the human or the garment, the effect is the same; the disease destroys the fabric of a humans' skin just as it does the garment's fabric. The humans' covering is the skin; therefore, we must determine the LORD is speaking of a skin disease for which, we know, there are many besides what we define as leprosy today. Leprosy did the trick when Wycliffe and Tyndale put the word in their translations because, at that time, it meant any kind of skin disease. Today, because we restrict the definition of the word leprosy, most new versions replace the word with the words *skin disease*.

Chapter 14

Chapter 13 left us with just the disease diagnosis; chapter 14 directs us to the law concerning the disease. Because our text uses the words *leper and leprosy*, we, too, will continue to do the same.

IX. The Law Concerning the Cleansing of Leprosy (14:1-57)
   A. Inspection by the Priest Outside the Camp (14:1-3a)

Now we come to the law concerning the cleansing of leprosy. Week after week, a priest makes his way to inspect the lepers outside the camp. Skin diseases do not heal quickly, and the contagiousness of such diseases is not readily known. As such, great care and caution are needed. But, the condition runs its course at some point, and the day of the cleansing offering will be at hand. We see that in chapter 14, verse 1. *"Then the LORD spoke to Moses, saying, 'This shall be the law of the leper in the day of his cleansing. Now he shall be brought to the priest, and the priest shall go out to the outside of the camp.'"* (14:1-3a).

The leper makes his home outside the camp. From this verse, we ascertain that the priest did not go all the way to the leper's dwelling; rather, the priest departed the camp, and once outside the boundary, the leper came to the priest.

   1. Ceremony for the Healed Leper (14:3b)

The ceremony for the healed leper began with an inspection of the infection. Verse 3b. *"Thus the priest shall look, and if the infection of leprosy has been healed in the leper..."* (14:3b).

Chapter 14

a) Ingredients (14:4)

Once the priest declares the infection healed, the priest proclaims the cleanness and orders the healed man to gather the ceremony's ingredients. Verse 4. *"... then the priest shall give orders to take two live **clean** birds and cedar wood and a scarlet string and hyssop for the one who is to be cleansed."* (14:4).

Two birds, cedarwood, a scarlet string, and hyssop, are the ingredients for the leper's offering on the day of his cleansing ceremony. The birds can be turtle doves or young pigeons. The amount of the cedar wood, we do not know. The length of the red thread we do not know. The amount of hyssop we do not know. What is hyssop? Hyssop is found in the plants we call grasses. We first see it used in Exodus's book when the hyssop is used to apply the blood on the doorpost of each Jewish home. The Hebrew word for hyssop means a *bunch*. It is merely a bunch of long grass bound together in a bundle and used as a paintbrush.

b) First Bird Slain (14:5)

Two birds are brought to the priest, and the first is slain. Verse 5. *"The priest shall also give orders to slay the one bird in an earthenware vessel over running water."* (14:5).

The leper takes one bird down to the spring of running water and kills it over a clay pot with the running water. The pot catches the blood of the bird and the water. No doubt, the leper then returns to the priest with the pot of bird blood mixed with water.

c) Second Bird Dipped (14:6)

While still alive, the second bird is dipped in the blood and water mixture with the other ingredients. Verse 6. *"As for the live bird, he shall take it together with the cedarwood and the scarlet string and the hyssop, and shall dip them and the live bird in the blood of the bird that was slain over the running water."* (14:6).

The ingredients dipped in the pot's soupy bloody water, the bird, the cedar, the thread, and the bundle of hyssop.

d) Leper Sprinkled Seven Times (14:7a)

The priest then takes over with the ceremony. Verse 7a. *"He shall then sprinkle seven times the one who is to be cleansed from the leprosy and shall pronounce him clean, ..."* (14:7a).

Seven times the priest sprinkles the leper with the bloody water and declares him clean.

e) Second Bird Freed (14:7b)

And as for the second bird, he flies free. Verse 7b. *"... and shall let the live bird go free over the open field."* (14:7b).

Forthwith we must notice something. This ceremony is not done at the Tent of Meeting nor around the Brazen Altar. It is performed outside the camp where the priest met the leper. For when the ceremony is over, the live bird is set free in the open field. No open field exists within the camp.

2. Leper Waits Seven Days Outside Camp (14:8-9)

To prove our point that the ceremony occurs outside the camp with the leper, the leper remained outside the camp for seven days to complete the other steps in his ritual cleansing. Verse 8. *"The one to be cleansed shall then wash his clothes and shave off all his hair and bathe in water and be clean. Now afterward, he may enter the camp, but he shall stay outside his tent for seven days. It will be on the seventh day that he shall shave off all his hair: he shall shave his head and his beard and his eyebrows, even all his hair. He shall then wash his clothes and bathe his body in water and be clean."* (14:8-9).

For seven days after the bird ceremony, the leper waits outside the camp. Then, on the seventh day, the leper shaves all his hair. He washes his clothing and bathes himself. Clean as a whistle he would be.

3. Offering on the Eighth Day (14:10-11)

Next, we find the cleansed leper entering the Tent of Meeting on the eighth day with his offering. Verse 10. *"Now on the eighth day he is to take two male lambs without defect, and a yearling ewe lamb without defect, and three-tenths of an ephah of fine flour mixed with oil for a grain offering, and one log of oil; and the priest who pronounces him clean shall present the man to be cleansed and the aforesaid before the LORD at the doorway of the tent of meeting."* (14:10-11).

This cleansed leper does not enter the Tabernacle complex alone. He is ushered in by the priest who declared him clean eight days before. In toe, the cleansed leper brings two spotless male lambs, a ewe lamb, a pint of the most refined seed flour mixed with olive oil, and a "log of oil." How much was a "log of oil?" It is the smallest of the liquid measurements used by the Jews. It amounts to the volume of about six hen eggs or just short of a pint of liquid.

a) First Male Lamb Guilt Offering (14:12a)

The first male lamb is for a guilt offering. Verse 12a. *"Then the priest shall take the one male lamb and bring it for a guilt offering, ..."* (14:12a).

By now, we know the ceremony of the guilt offering - no need for an order of service here. We see the lamb slain at the proper place; blood sprinkled around the Altar. Entrails washed and the fat placed on the Altar. All the rest of the meat belongs to the priest to be eaten.

b) Oil for Wave Offering (14:12b)

But we find a wave offering included with the log of oil. Verse 12b. *"...with the log of oil, and present them as a wave offering before the LORD."* (14:12b).

The order of the ceremony is not presented here. With the mention for the log of oil, we already know it is to be waved before the LORD in the smoke of the Altar last, but not placed on the Altar.

(1) Slay the Lamb (14:13)

Be that as it may, the order of worship in this offering has a twist that is more important and needed in the details concerning the slaying of the lamb and its blood that the priest catches. Verse 13. *"Next he shall slaughter the male lamb in the place where they slaughter the sin offering and the burnt offering, at the place of the sanctuary—for the guilt offering, like the sin offering, belongs to the priest; it is most holy."* (14:13).

The guilt offering is not the sin offering, but it is like the sin offering in its holiness. The sin offering does not belong to the priest. Every part of a sin offering must be burned outside the camp, including the hide. The only part of a sin offering that is not burned outside the camp is the fat portions burned on the Brazen Altar. It is a most holy offering.

The guilt offering is just as holy as the sin offering, except that the parts of the offering that are not placed on the Brazen Altar are given to the priest for food.

(2) Blood on Right Ear Lobe, Thumb and Toe (14:14)

The blood that the priest catches is sprinkled around the Brazen Altar, but here we see another twist in the instruction. Verse 14. *"The priest shall then take some of the blood of the guilt offering, and the priest shall put it on the lobe of the right ear of the one to be cleansed, and on the thumb of his right hand and on the big toe of his right foot."* (14:14).

In this deviation from the ordinary person with the regular guilt offering, the leper's right earlobe, thumb, and big toe are anointed. The only other time we see this kind of anointing is for the ordination of the priests. Before we address the reason, let us address the log of oil.

Chapter 14

(3) Priest Pours Oil in Left Palm and Sprinkles Seven Times (14:15-16)

After anointing the right ear, thumb, and toe of the leper, the priest pours the log of oil in his left hand. Verse 15. *"The priest shall also take some of the log of oil, and pour it into his left palm; the priest shall then dip his right-hand finger into the oil that is in his left palm, and with his finger sprinkle some of the oil seven times before the LORD."* (14:15-16).

The last words that say, *"with his finger sprinkle some of the oil seven times before the LORD,"* tells us that the priest enters the Tabernacle and sprinkles the oil seven times in front of the Veil that is in front of the Ark of the Covenant. The LORD's presence hovers in the Shekinah Glory over the Mercy Seat on top of the Ark of the Covenant. It is the place that defines the phrase "before the LORD." The same is done with the priests at their ordination.

(4) Oil on Right Ear Lobe, Thumb, Toe and Head (14:17-18)

But oil remains in the left palm of the priest's hand. Out from the Holy Place, the priest returns to the leper standing in front of the Tent of Meeting door. Verse 17 tells us of the next part of the ceremony. *"Of the remaining oil which is in his palm, the priest shall put some on the right ear lobe of the one to be cleansed, and on the thumb of his right hand, and on the big toe of his right foot, on the blood of the guilt offering; while the rest of the oil that is in the priest's palm, he shall put on the head of the one to be cleansed. So the priest shall make atonement on his behalf before the LORD."* (14:17-18).

Of the remaining oil, the priest places it, too, on the right ear, thumb, and toe of the leper, and the rest he put on the head of the leper. The blood and the oil sprinkled before the LORD in the Holy Place of the Tabernacle are for the leper's atonement. As we have already discovered, the word *atonement* means the "reconciliation between God and a person or group of people."[18] The leper is reconciled before the LORD in the ceremony, and he is also reconciled to his family, his tribe, and his nation. How will that be done? Through a sin offering.

4. Second Male Lamb for Sin Offering (14:19a)

The atonement of the leper is made with the second lamb for a sin offering. Verse 19a. *"The priest shall next offer the sin offering and make atonement for the one to be cleansed from his uncleanness."* (14:19a).

That is all the instruction for this second male lamb given by the LORD. It is a sin offering with no changes from the original instructions. The lamb slain, the blood rubbed on the Brazen Altar's four horns, the fat offered on the Brazen Altar, and all the rest is burned outside the camp.

5. One Ewe Lamb for Burnt Offering and the Grain Offering (14:19b-20)

Following the sin offering is the burnt offering with a ewe lamb. The grain offering is included at this point. Verse 19b. *"Then afterward, he shall slaughter the burnt offering. The priest shall offer up the burnt offering and the grain offering on the altar. Thus the priest shall make atonement for him, and he will be clean."* (14:19b-20).

The two lambs were male, but an ewe is a female lamb. She was a burnt offering. No instructions are needed here. We know the recipe. She was slain, the blood sprinkled around the Brazen Altar. Every part of her was placed on the Brazen Altar except her hide. It was given to the priest.

---

[18] Brockway, D. (2016). Atonement. In J. D. Barry, D. Bomar, D. R. Brown, R. Klippenstein, D. Mangum, C. Sinclair Wolcott, ... W. Widder (Eds.), *The Lexham Bible Dictionary*. Bellingham, WA: Lexham Press.

Chapter 14

The grain offering was the regular offering of about a pint of flour made from fine (perfect) seeds mixed with oil and incense – raw, fried griddled, pan-cooked, baked, roasted but with no honey or leaven. A handful was placed on the Brazen Altar, and the rest was given to the priest. Nothing new here.

6. Offering Substitute for the Poor (14:21-32)
a) Approved Items for the Substitute Offering (14:21-23)

The LORD, our God, is a gracious LORD Who provides for the needs of those in a relationship with Him. He understands when a person does not have the means to give an offering comparable to the masses. But the offering of the poor is just as important to the LORD as the offering of others. When a person goes through worldly diseases such as leprosy, He allows for a substitute offering for the poor. Verse 21. *"But if he is poor and his means are insufficient, then he is to take one male lamb for a guilt offering as a wave offering to make atonement for him, and one-tenth of an ephah of fine flour mixed with oil for a grain offering, and a log of oil, and two turtledoves or two young pigeons which are within his means, the one shall be a sin offering and the other a burnt offering. Then the eighth day he shall bring them for his cleansing to the priest, at the doorway of the tent of meeting, before the LORD."* (14:21-23).

The original offering for the leper's cleansing requires two male lambs and a female lamb with the grain offering and the log of oil. With this substitute offering, the LORD allows the change to be one male lamb, the grain offering, the log of oil, and two turtle doves or two young pigeons.

b) The Lamb and Oil Substitution (14:24-29)

The lamb, the oil, and the grain of this substitute guilt offering are handled in the same way as the three were handled in the original instructions. Verse 24. *"The priest shall take the lamb of the guilt offering and the log of oil, and the priest shall offer them for a wave offering before the* LORD. *"Next he shall slaughter the lamb of the guilt offering; and the priest is to take some of the blood of the guilt offering and put it on the lobe of the right ear of the one to be cleansed and on the thumb of his right hand and on the big toe of his right foot. The priest shall also pour some of the oil into his left palm; and with his right-hand finger the priest shall sprinkle some of the oil that is in his left palm seven times before the* LORD. *The priest shall then put some of the oil that is in his palm on the lobe of the right ear of the one to be cleansed, and on the thumb of his right hand and on the big toe of his right foot, on the place of the blood of the guilt offering. Moreover, the rest of the oil that is in the priest's palm he shall put on the head of the one to be cleansed, to make atonement on his behalf before the* LORD.*"* (14:24-29).

   c)   **The Two Dove and Grain Substitution (14:30-32)**

The LORD knows the means of a person to give to Him as an offering. In the Nation of Israel's camp, everyone can give at least one male lamb, a log of oil, a grain offering, and two doves. He says so as much in His instruction for the dove offerings and the grain. Verse 30. *"He shall then offer one of the turtledoves or young pigeons, which are within his means. He shall offer what he can afford, the one for a sin offering and the other for a burnt offering, together with the grain offering. So the priest shall make atonement before the* LORD *on behalf of the one to be cleansed. This is the law for him in whom there is an infection of leprosy, whose means are limited for his cleansing."* (14:30-32).

The LORD said about the doves, *"…which are within his means. He shall offer what he can afford…."* No leper is without excuse. One dove is for a sin offering. One is for the burnt offering. And the grain offering is offered with the two. Nothing new here. A sin-offering as part of a guilt offering with a bird is the same as always. A burnt offering as part of a guilt offering of a bird is the same as always. The grain offering as part of the guilt offering is the same as always.

We covered those in detail in chapter 5, verses 7-11. No need to cover those details here.

7. The Leprosy in the Promised Land (14:33-53)
a) In the House – Quarantine Seven Days (14:33-38)

Just as the LORD threw a curve with the leprosy of garments, the LORD now addresses leprosy of a house. Just as garments do not possess flesh and blood to feed the leprosy, there is no flesh and blood in a mud-brick wall to feed the walls of a house. But the Israelites are not living in brick houses at the time of the giving of this law; they lived in tents. But the LORD is not giving this law for the time the Israelites are in the wilderness; it is for the time they are living in the Promised Land. Verse 33. *"The LORD further spoke to Moses and to Aaron, saying: 'When you enter the land of Canaan, which I give you for a possession, and I put a mark of leprosy on a house in the land of your possession, then the one who owns the house shall come and tell the priest, saying, 'Something like a mark of leprosy has become visible to me in the house.' The priest shall then command that they empty the house before the priest goes in to look at the mark, so that everything in the house need not become unclean; and afterward the priest shall go in to look at the house. So he shall look at the mark, and if the mark on the walls of the house has greenish or reddish depressions and appears deeper than the surface, then the priest shall come out of the house, to the doorway, and quarantine the house for seven days."* (14:33-38).

The LORD begins with, *"When you enter the land of Canaan, which I give you for a possession...."* This instruction is not for the time in the wilderness; it is for their lives in the land of Canaan. The LORD, perfect in knowledge, looks ahead and prepares His nation for what they will encounter in the Promised Land.

Then the LORD says, *"...and I put a mark of leprosy on a house in the land of your possession...."* The mark of the diseases will be the LORD's doing. How can that be? He knows the ills of the house and its construction. He knows what has taken place in that house in years past. He knows, and He protects His own by placing a mark of disease on the house.

From there, the story is the same as with a disease on a human or a garment. It is time to employ the priest for his opinion. But the priest will not just run over and look. The house must be empty of all its furniture, fixtures, and people before he arrives. When the priest arrives, he looks for two signs, the same signs he looks for on the garment — greenish or reddish color and how deep it seems to be. Well, obviously, the house cannot be exiled out of the city for isolation, so the priest declares that the house must be shut up and quarantined for seven days. The priest's formula is always the same; if it has the signs, it is seven days.

Shutting a house for seven days is the best and the worst thing that can be done for any type of fungus to grow. It is the best thing because if it grows, the dark, damp, closed house will cause the fungus to grow exponentially. It is the worst thing because if you want to kill a fungus, the bright sun's UV lights with fresh air will kill the fungus. The LORD knew about UV lights long before we did. He invented them on the first day of creation. But the point of the LORD instruction here is to grow the disease, not to cure it.

b) Mark of Leprosy Spread House Renovated – Declared Unclean (14:39-42)

On the seventh day, if the disease spreads, a renovation is required. Verse 39. *"The priest shall return on the seventh day and make an inspection. If the mark has indeed spread in the house walls, then the priest shall order them to tear out the stones with the mark in them and throw them away at an unclean place outside the city. He shall have the house scraped all around inside, and they shall*

Chapter 14

dump the plaster that they scrape off at an unclean place outside the city. Then they shall take other stones and replace those stones, and he shall take other plaster and replaster the house." (14:39-42).

No doubt this is a costly renovation for the unclean house. Ancient plasters have been found in Israel and examined. It consists of lime, sand, water, and most often, hair to bind it together. There it is. The hair of a man or beast used in the plaster is the protein source for the fungus' growth. Now fungus is everywhere. It is in the air, our foods, in the soil, and the water. Not all fungi are detrimental. The things they need to grow are fungi-specific. However, all fungi need protein and nitrogen to grow. If the temperature is right and food is there, the fungus can double its mass every five hours.

The flooding waters of Tropical Storm Allison inundated the Houston area in 2001. The Corman family were members of my church, and their house was flooded. When the waters receded, the mother called to tell me she had fuzzy mold growing on her baseboards. I had teams tearing out sheetrock all over Southeast Houston, and I did not have a team to go to her house that day, so I went to look. Down near the floor was a green mold line ranging from a half-inch to an inch wide. I promised her a team would be out the next day. When the team arrived after lunch the following day, the green mold had grown up the walls, three-foot-high all around the house inside walls. The simple, minor problem had grown into a major health problem in just twenty-four hours. Just think about what the Canaan Land family was facing after the home had been shut up for seven days. For the Corman's, the old gypsum sheetrock was removed. The paper on the sheetrock was an ample and sufficient source of protein for the fungus mold. The rooms were dried and treated. New sheetrock was hung. All was well until Hurricane Ike came, and the whole problem reoccurred again.

c) Second Breakout in House Tear Down House (14:43-47)

That brings us to the next instruction of the LORD. After the renovation occurs, if the fungus breaks out again, the LORD has a new instruction. Tear down the house. Verse 43. *"If, however, the mark breaks out again in the house after he has torn out the stones and scraped the house, and after it has been replastered, then the priest shall come in and make an inspection. If he sees that the mark has indeed spread in the house, it is a malignant mark in the house; it is unclean. He shall therefore tear down the house, its stones, and its timbers, and all the plaster of the house, and he shall take them outside the city to an unclean place. Moreover, whoever goes into the house during the time that he has quarantined it, becomes unclean until evening. Likewise, whoever lies down in the house shall wash his clothes, and whoever eats in the house shall wash his clothes."*

There are to be no second chances with diseases within the houses in the Promised Land. Tear down the house and dump it outside the city in an unclean place. Every bit of it. But do you also see the problem it is causing the workers laboring to tear down and dispose of it outside the city? They are becoming unclean each day they work on the house. Each day they must bathe in a culture where baths are not taken so often.

8. House with Mark Not Spread after the Renovation – Declare Clean (14:48)

But suppose that the mark has not spread on the seventh day, the priest will declare the house clean. *"If, on the other hand, the priest comes in and makes an inspection and the mark has not indeed spread in the house after the house has been replastered, then the priest shall pronounce the house clean because the mark has not reappeared."* (14:48).

Chapter 14

Because the house has been replastered, we know that the priest required the renovation. Because it seems in this instruction that inspection occurs once a week, every seventh day, and it is reasonable to assume that after the renovation is completed, the house waits for an inspection from the priest before it can be inhabited again - just like the guideline for the leper in quarantine. With no mark on the repair site, the house is declared clean. It is time for a ceremony.

a) Ceremony Two Birds, Cedar Wood, Scarlet String, and Hyssop (14:49-53)

Back in verses 3 through 7 of this 14th chapter, we saw the clean leper's ceremony that occurred outside the camp. It involved two birds, cedarwood, scarlet string, and hyssop. Here we have a clean house, and it needs a ceremony too. Let us see how close the two ceremonies are alike. Verse 49. *"To cleanse the house then, he shall take two birds and cedarwood and a scarlet string and hyssop, and he shall slaughter the one bird in an earthenware vessel over running water. Then he shall take the cedarwood and the hyssop and the scarlet string, with the live bird, and dip them in the blood of the slain bird as well as in the running water, and sprinkle the house seven times. He shall thus cleanse the house with the blood of the bird and with the running water, along with the live bird and with the cedarwood and with the hyssop and with the scarlet string. However, he shall let the live bird go free outside the city into the open field. So he shall make atonement for the house, and it will be clean."* (14:49-53).

The ceremony is the same for the healed leper as it is for the house. Two birds are offered. One slain over a pot with running water. The cedarwood, scarlet string, hyssop, and the second live bird, are dipped in the bloody water. The bloody water is sprinkled seven times in the house, and the live bird is released outside the city in the field. The house is ceremonially clean.

Much has been made about the living bird, cedar, red string, and hyssop. Whether the red string is used to tie them all together for the dipping, we do not know. Some commentators delve into the cedar's antiseptic nature and the symbol of the red, but that is all speculation, and we will not delve into it, for nothing is said about it in the Word of God. We will just leave it as it is, items used in the ceremony of a house's cleanings in the Promised Land.

B. The Law of Leprosy Conclusion (14:54-57)

And in conclusion, the LORD states a summary of the law and its purpose. Verse 54. *"This is the law for any mark of leprosy—even for a scale, and for the leprous garment or house, and for a swelling, and for a scab, and for a bright spot— to teach when they are unclean and when they are clean. This is the law of leprosy."* (14:54-57).

Whatever the leprous disease is on a human's body, the fabric of a garment, or the walls of a house, all leprous diseases of any kind must be handled by the priest in the orderly prescription of this law for any mark of leprosy.

I must admit, I have read chapter 15 of Leviticus more times than I can remember, but I have not taught a single lesson on the contents of this chapter. I have read every commentary available to me of the famous commentators as well as the lesser-known scholars. Not one of them has discussed the content in these chapters satisfactory to my understanding. Therefore, I have forgone any attempt to explain the contents of the chapter altogether. Yet, I am here, and it would be a disgrace to skim over the intended message to disregard its sensitive and personal topic. I have thought long and hard about this text considering what the scholars have said before me and determined in my heart and mind that the others have restricted their attention too quickly to the private parts of a man or woman and missed the real intent of the passage. I contend that this law concerning a man or woman with a discharge deals with general places where these diseased discharges can occur. Then the LORD discusses the specific natural functions of the body that are not diseases. With that, let us delve into this sensitive yet significant instruction that can be applied in 1464 BC and might well be truthful today.

Chapter 15

X. The Law Concerning a Man or Woman with a Discharge (15:1-33)
   A. For the Man in General (15:1-15)
      1. The Person of the Man with a Discharge (15:1-4)

As we open our Bibles to Leviticus 15, we find ourselves facing the LORD's law concerning a man or woman with a discharge from the body. First, the LORD will issue His instruction for the man in general. Verse 1. *"The LORD also spoke to Moses and to Aaron, saying, 'Speak to the sons of Israel, and say to them, 'When any man has a discharge from his body, his discharge is unclean. This, moreover, shall be his uncleanness in his discharge: it is his uncleanness whether his body allows its discharge to flow or whether his body obstructs its discharge. Every bed on which the person with the discharge lies becomes unclean, and everything on which he sits becomes unclean.'"* (15:1-4).

While most commentators have immediately directed their attention to the most private parts of the man's body, I contend that that is not the specific intent in this passage. Before I delve into that, let us deal with the subject of this instruction. The text says, *"When any man...."* If the word for man is the Hebrew *adam,* this passage would address men and women. But the word "man" here is the Hebrew word *'is.* It means *male.* Factually, the Hebrew text uses the word twice in the phrase. "When any *'is 'is ....*" It reads, "When any male male ..." There must not be any confusion about this opening passage in chapter 15 dealing with males. It means men – males.

Now I want to ask the question. "How many natural places on a man's body can a discharge come from in times of sickness?" Count them on your head first. Did you count seven on your head? Two eyes, two ears, two nostrils, and one mouth. Are there not seven natural, normal, God-designed places on the head where in times of sickness, nasty discharges can ooze? Now, when you evaluate the rest of man, down below the neck, you will find two more natural, normal, God-designed places where nasty discharges can ooze in times of sickness. For now, in this passage, let us leave it at that. A male has nine bodily places where diseases can ooze discharges on his body.

Now in case you might think that I am wrong in expanding the intent of this passage to the head instead of focusing solely on the below, I ask this question. "Where else in the Bible does the LORD discuss the discharges of diseases of the ears, eyes, nose, and mouth?" If not here, then where? It is my contention that the LORD begins this passage with the available openings wherewith diseases can naturally ooze as signs of sickness, be it at the head or below. One reason for this opinion is found in the words "...*whether his body allows its discharge to flow or whether his body obstructs its discharge....*" As soon as our nose begins to flow or our nose stops up, it is an immediate sign that we are sick. The Bible, in the context of Leviticus, would call it *unclean*. We are unclean with an illness of the nose. The same occurs with the eyes, the ears, the mouth, and from the openings down below. The LORD has already dealt with the diseases of the general flesh that break open in the unnatural places, and He called it leprosy – which means *disease*. In this text, the LORD moves to discuss the disorders of the natural places that are open orifices.

The passage we read ends with, *"Every bed on which the person with the discharge lies becomes unclean, and everything on which he sits becomes unclean."* Is that not true that the signs of flue begin with a runny nose, itchy eyes, draining ears, and flehm coughed up from the mouth? We must go ahead and add that which often accompanies the cold is diarrhea and thick dark urine. It is God's natural design of the body's functions to tell us when we are sick. But in our sickness, is it not true that everything we touch while in a disease of this kind contaminates everything we touch, lay on, sit on, eat on, lean on, sneeze on, and cough on? We contaminate everything - unclean as the Bible would say. And everything that we make sick can make others sick.

2. The Nurse of the Man with a Discharge (15:5-7)

Then we hear the LORD address the "anyone" who comes near such a sick man. In our minds, we can imagine this as the doctor or nurse of the man with a discharge. Verse 5. *"Anyone, moreover, who touches his bed shall wash his clothes and bathe in water and be unclean until evening; and whoever sits on the thing on which the man with the discharge has been sitting, shall wash his clothes and bathe in water and be unclean until evening. Also whoever touches the person with the discharge shall wash his clothes and bathe in water and be unclean until evening."* (15:5-7).

In general, sick people with issues that come from the orifices of the body need the assistance of some kind of nurse to tend to their needs of food, water, medicines, and clean linens. Whomever that person is, with any sickness whatsoever puts themselves in the dead center of the bullseye for contracting the disease too. Simply by being around the sick, one makes them unclean also. Thus, everything they touch that has been touched by the sick may transfer the sickness to the nurse. What is the answer? It is the universal cleaning agent given by the LORD – water.

Wash, wash, wash, wash, we see over and over in this passage. Wash everything touched by the sick man. What is the prescription to keep yourself from catching the illness? You are to bathe and wash your clothing if you have touched anything touched by the sick man.

a) The Spit of the Sick (15:8a)

But colds and diseases often come with a cough and a sneeze. With the cough or a sneeze comes spit. When spit comes, so does the contagious disease. Verse 8b. *"Or if the man with the discharge spits on one who is clean, he too shall wash his clothes and bathe in water and be unclean until evening."* (15:8a).

In 2020 AD, the world we live in shut down by necessity because of a disease called Covid 19. As we know it, the infection spreads by airborne contagious particles coming from the infected mucus glands of the infected person. What does the LORD prescribe for the healthy person if he or she has been in the vicinity of a sick person with a cough or sneeze? It is the same prescription given by our doctors now three thousand years later, wash and bathe. Notice that even with the wash and the bath, the nurse or attendant must *"... be unclean until evening."* We know that as quarantine. It is for the protection of others. The LORD set this barrier to give the body time to show symptoms if the infection transferred during contracted with the sick person.

b) The Seat of the Sick (15:8b-10)

People help sick people. At times, the need to transfer the sick for medical help occurs. In that transfer process, sickness spreads. Even the seat of the sick can infect others. Verse 8b. *"Every saddle on which the person with the discharge rides becomes unclean. Whoever then touches any of the things which were under him shall be unclean until evening, and he who carries them shall wash his clothes and bathe in water and be unclean until evening."* (15:8b-10).

As before, the only preventable solution for a healthy person comes with a wash and a bath. Then, as before, a quarantine time gives the helper time to show symptoms of infection.

c) The Spread of the Sick (15:11)

The helpers' problem is not touching the sick; the helper can control the amount of handling of the sick. The problem occurs with the ill person touches the helper. This problem brings us to the spread of the sick by the sick. Verse 11. *"Likewise, whomever the one with the discharge touches without having rinsed his hands in water shall wash his clothes and bathe in water and be unclean until evening."* (15:11).

Once again, we come to the universal answer to control the spread of sicknesses. Rinse the hands, wash the clothing, take a bath, and quarantine until evening. In all cases, *"until evening"* would naturally mean until the next day. In those days, when nightfall came, the ordinary, trustworthy people returned to their homes and remained there until the break of light in the morning when they went back to work.

d) The Saucer of the Sick (15:12)

But sick people need to eat too. Clay and wooden vessels held the prepared foods and drink. The ill person touched these vessels as they partook. Then, the LORD gave the instruction for the saucer of the sick. Verse 12. *"However, an earthenware vessel which the person with the discharge touches shall be broken, and every wooden vessel shall be rinsed in water."* (15:12).

Clay, earthenware, vessels were porous and could not be adequately cleaned. Repeatedly, in the past chapters, when items were cooked in clay pots, the destruction of the pots was mandatory. But that is not the case with wooden or brass utensils that can be cleaned appropriately. The point of the LORD's message here indicates that humans need to know that the items touched by a sick person, especially those used for food and drink, can transmit disease.

Before we move on to the atonement of the man once he is clean, we must address all mentioned too this point concerning the man and, by reason, apply it to the woman also. The LORD will not make these same points concerning diseases that occur in these same nine natural orifices with a woman, but the woman is just as prone to have these diseases as a man. Can these warnings be applied to the woman too? I think so. Here is the reason. Throughout the Bible, when a man and woman unite in marriage, the two become one. Factually, in all the common law that came to America through England, the biblical standard concerning marriage stands as the statute that when the two become one, the one is the man. In the history of most nations, a married woman could not own anything of value in the marriage in her name until the death of her husband. Of course, there are exceptions in every nation, especially among royalty, but that is not common among the regular people. The same is true in the Nation of Israel during the days of the Exodus. In forty years from the giving of this message, the details of how to divide the Promised Land to each family's patriarch occurred. However, five sisters who had no male counterparts to own the new land complained (Numbers 27:1-7). The decision rendered by the LORD and Moses gave them land in their dead father's name. With that, the sisters could live on their own land. I believe that the general instruction concerning the flow and blockage of the natural male openings that arise at the first signs of disease can, and should, apply to the man's wife and, by extension, to all women. Why? The nine natural openings on a male have the same counterparts on the female; therefore, there would be no need to repeat the instruction concerning these openings' diseases. More will come for this reasoning when we reach a woman's disorders in this chapter's following passages.

3. The Atonement of the Man with a Discharge (15:13-15)

The human body is amazing, and with time and care, healing often comes, and a diseased man can be declared clean. With what we already know about the holy ceremony upon the healing of any disease, we can almost predict what Moses is about to say. Verse 13. *"Now when the man with the discharge becomes cleansed from his discharge, then he shall count off for himself seven days for his cleansing; he shall then wash his clothes and bathe his body in running water and will become clean. Then on the eighth day he shall take for himself two turtledoves or two young pigeons, and come before the* LORD *to the doorway of the tent of meeting and give them to the priest; and the priest shall offer them, one for a sin offering and the other for a burnt offering. So the priest shall make atonement on his behalf before the* LORD *because of his discharge."* (15:13-15).

Once the discharge stopped, the seven-day waiting period presents no surprise. The washing and cleanings present no surprise. The eighth-day celebration presents no surprise. The two turtle doves or two young pigeons presents no surprise. The sin and burnt offerings present no surprise. The atonement by the priest presents no surprise. Nothing is a surprise in this atonement of the man with a discharge. It is all expected if, and only if, you have learned all that has come before in this book of laws. For the Jewish, it was mandatory.

B. For the Man in Specific (15:16-18)
1. Of the Man (15:16-17)

After addressing the needs for cleanliness during sicknesses that can spread through the natural openings in the man's body for which a religious ceremony always concluded the healing process, the LORD turns to address the regular and normal specific emission for the man that does not require a religious ceremony. It is a function that only a man can have and not a woman. Verse 16. *"Now if a man has a seminal emission, he shall bathe all his body in water and be unclean until evening. As for any garment or any leather on which there is seminal emission, it shall be washed with water and be unclean until evening."* (15:16-17).

The LORD does not address an illness in this passage; He addresses the regular operation of a male's bodily function. When this emission occurs from a man in everyday life, the remedy requires the washing of any item touched by the sick and the body's bathing. And as usual in all cases, the man needs to seclude himself that day after the cleaning. This cleansing does not require a holy ceremony down at the Tabernacle. It is normal. It is how the LORD created a man's body.

2. Of the Man with a Woman (15:18)

The LORD made the man's body to connect with a woman's body to bring babies into the world. The LORD made man for that purpose. As a man interacts with his wife in the marriage routine, the LORD gave instructions for both following the union. Verse 18. *"If a man lies with a woman so that there is a seminal emission, they shall both bathe in water and be unclean until evening."* (15:18).

The seminal emission from a man to a woman in the marriage relationship often results in a child's birth. Such is the LORD's plan for man and woman. However, after the union together, both need to wash and be separated from the world around them; no religious ceremony required.

C. For the Woman in General (15:19-30)
1. The Person of the Woman with a Discharge (15:19-20)

The LORD then addresses discharges of the woman in general. When we count the natural openings in a man's body, the number was nine. When we count the natural openings of the woman, there are ten. The nine found in the male have the same counterparts in the female. But the tenth in a woman does not have a counterpart in the male. It is that particular part of the woman's body that the LORD address. All the illnesses that we addressed with the male's nine parts can be associates with the counterparts found in the woman. Therefore, the LORD did not need to cover those possible illnesses in the female. Here, the LORD addresses the person of the woman with a natural normal discharge in her unique organ. Verse 19. *"When a woman has a discharge, if her discharge in her body is blood, she shall continue in her menstrual impurity for seven days; and whoever touches her shall be unclean until evening. Everything also on which she lies during her menstrual impurity shall be unclean, and everything on which she sits shall be unclean."* (15:19-20).

First, the LORD addresses the regular monthly time for the woman. The LORD made her organ function with a monthly cleansing naturally induced by her body. I wonder if you have ever thought about the cleaning process of anything? In the cleaning process, something must become dirty for something to become clean. The washcloth becomes dirty when we use it to clean our bodies. We find the same truth with the woman's body. The seven-day flow of the blood causes other things to become unclean in the body's process of becoming clean. Whatever the woman touches during her monthly time becomes unclean to everyone around her.

Chapter 15

2. The Man of the Woman with a Discharge (15:21-24)

A woman can care for the normal discharge from her body without help during her regular time of the month. For a single woman, her time of uncleanness should not affect anyone. But for a married woman, marital relationships occur, and her monthly uncleanness will affect her husband. Verse 21. *"Anyone who touches her bed shall wash his clothes and bathe in water and be unclean until evening. Whoever touches any thing on which she sits shall wash his clothes and bathe in water and be unclean until evening. Whether it be on the bed or on the thing on which she is sitting, when he touches it, he shall be unclean until evening. If a man actually lies with her so that her menstrual impurity is on him, he shall be unclean seven days, and every bed on which he lies shall be unclean."* (15:21-24).

The man, touching anything during the time of his wife's regular uncleanness, needs only to wash and bathe each day. If the man and woman have a marital union during her seven days of natural body cleaning, the man becomes unclean for seven days. Every pallet he sleeps on during those seven days also becomes unclean. However, the LORD does not mention a need for an atonement ceremony with the priest because of this interaction between a husband and wife in the course of their marriage relationships and the normal functions of the woman's body.

3. The Illness of the Woman with a Discharge (15:25-26)

The woman's standard monthly body cleaning does not cover all the issues that can discharge from her unique organ. Verse 25. *"Now if a woman has a discharge of her blood many days, not at the period of her menstrual impurity, or if she has a discharge beyond that period, all the days of her impure discharge she shall continue as though in her menstrual impurity; she is unclean. Any bed on which she lies all the days of her discharge shall be to her like her bed at menstruation; and every thing on which she sits shall be unclean, like her uncleanness at that time."* (15:25-26).

When a general sickness in the woman's unique organ occurs, the first order of business requires the same treatment of that discharge as in the manner of the monthly body's cleaning., but they are not the same. This disease makes her unclean for the entire time of the infection in the same way her monthly body's cleaning makes her unclean, but they are not the same. No doubt, with an illness such as this, a doctor, or nurse at the least, would attend to her needs.

4. The Nurse of the Woman with a Discharge (15:27)

Just as the nurse or doctor who attended the male with an infectious discharge became unclean, so, too, the same applies to the female. Verse 27. *"Likewise, whoever touches them shall be unclean and shall wash his clothes and bathe in water and be unclean until evening."* (15:27).

The LORD's prescription repeats what we found in the instruction for the man. In short, the law requires the washing of the clothing, the bathing of the body, and the segregation from clean persons.

5. The Atonement of the Woman with a Discharge (15:28-30)

Just as with the male, the atonement of the woman with a discharge agrees. It is the same. Verse 28. *"When she becomes clean from her discharge, she shall count off for herself seven days; and afterward she will be clean. Then on the eighth day she shall take for herself two turtledoves or two young pigeons and bring them in to the priest, to the doorway of the tent of meeting. The priest shall offer the one for a sin offering and the other for a burnt offering. So the priest shall make atonement on her behalf before the LORD because of her impure discharge."* (15:28-30).

This atonement offering for the woman with an infectious discharge of her unique organ is the same as that of the man. No difference at all. The two required turtle doves or the two young pigeons become the sin and burnt offerings on the eighth day following the woman's healing.

D. For the Ceremony in General (15:31)

Uncleanness from a discharge of a person's body and all associated with that person brings deathly consequences at the Tabernacle with the presentation of offerings. Verse 31. *"Thus you shall keep the sons of Israel separated from their uncleanness, so that they will not die in their uncleanness by their defiling My tabernacle that is among them."* (15:31).

Someone may hide illnesses from the public, but no one can conceal conditions from the LORD. Anyone who tries to approach the LORD with a regular offering without declaring to the priest a hidden disease will die. Outside the normal bodily functions of a man and woman, illnesses would defile the LORD's Tabernacle, and the penalty would result in immediate death before the LORD. A sickness of an abnormal discharge from the body required the oversight of the priest. The normal functions of marital life that made a person unclean did not require the priest. Both had their times of uncleanness; both had their times of cleanness. The LORD forbids any unclean person from approaching Him in His Tabernacle.

E. For the Man and Woman in General (15:32-33)

Ending this portion of the law, the LORD concludes with His statement of the statute for the man and woman in general. Verse 32. *"This is the law for the one with a discharge, and for the man who has a seminal emission so that he is unclean by it, and for the woman who is ill because of menstrual impurity, and for the one who has a discharge, whether a male or a female, or a man who lies with an unclean woman."* (15:32-33).

Notice that the stated law agrees with my interpretation of this chapter. First, the LORD addresses the discharge of a man in general. He does not specify where the disease discharges from on the man. He is not specific, and neither should we be. The created male has nine places that can discharge fluids associates with an illness. Illnesses can also block the normal healthy discharge from those nine places on the body. Then, the LORD addresses the regular specific emission of the male body. It does not call it a discharge, which would assume an illness.

With the women, the LORD addressed the regular specific body's cleaning of her unique organ and then addresses general discharges that are not normal, but infectious. Finally, the LORD addresses the state of uncleanness the man and woman find themselves in when interacting with one another. All of this agrees perfectly with this commentary on this chapter. It is by far the most extensive explanation found among the commentaries for this chapter.

With the cleansing from the infectious diseases of the male and female, both required an atonement offering before coming in the presence of the LORD. That thought offers a natural transition to the atonement offerings. The next topic in the LORD's instruction deals with the once-a-year Day of Atonement for the sins of the people.

Most of the content of the Book of Leviticus was new to the Israelites camped at Mount Sinai. We spoke of that fact often while studying the LORD's required offering in chapters 1 through 7. It was new as well to the Jews concerning the laws of clean and unclean food, childbirth, leprosy, the discharges of man and woman, and it is new as we come to the all-important Day of Atonement. The first mention of this day in the Bible comes in this chapter.

Chapter 16

XI. The Law Concerning the Day of Atonement (16:1-34).
   A. The Time of the Giving of the Law for the Day of Atonement (16:1-28).
      1. The Prohibition of Entry into the Holy of Holies (16:1-2).

In this book's order, the LORD gave the essential instructions for Jewish life's required offerings, but extremely important for the priests' ordination. The LORD explained the offerings and then directed that the erection of the Tabernacle inside the Tent of Meeting. Upon completion, Moses consecrated it and proceeded with the ordination of the priests. All happened on the first day of the ordination ceremony. According to Exodus 40:17, the Tabernacle erection, consecration, and the ordination of the priest occurred on the first day or the first month of the second year after leaving Egypt – Nisan 1, 1465 BC. At the end of the first-day observance, the priests entered the Tabernacle for seven days. On the eighth day, Nisan 8, 1465 BC, the priests exited the Tabernacle for the ceremony of the day to complete the process. Later that day, two of Aaron's sons were killed by the LORD when they brought fire from the wrong source into the Tabernacle, defiling the sacred hall. The LORD notes this topic in His address to Moses as the LORD puts a prohibition of entry into the Holy of Holies by the priest. Chapter 16, verse 1. *"Now the LORD spoke to Moses after the death of the two sons of Aaron, when they had approached the presence of the LORD and died. The LORD said to Moses: 'Tell your brother Aaron that he shall not enter at any time into the holy place inside the veil, before the mercy seat which is on the ark, or he will die; for I will appear in the cloud over the mercy seat."* (16:1-2).

Evidently, Aaron's two sons' sin was more extensive than just taking strange fire in their firepans to the Altar of Incense in the Holy Place. The two may have entered the Holy of Holies behind the Tabernacle's veil at the same time. With verse 2, the LORD puts an end to anyone entering the Holy of Holies except the High Priest. The next time the High Priest can enter the Holy of Holies is six months away. In the following passage, we will discover that the High Priest could enter the Holy of Holies only one day per year, the Day of Atonement. Aaron was the High Priest at the time, but this instruction stands for all High Priests into Israel's future.

2. The Permission of Entry into the Holy of Holies (16:3-5).
   a) The Preparation for the Day of Atonement (16:3-5).

For three hundred and fifty-four days out of every year, the Lord prohibits everyone, including the High Priest, from entering the Holy of Holies. However, He grants permission to enter into the Holy of Holies to only the High Priest on one day of the year, provided the successful and proper preparation for the Day of Atonement. Verse 3. *"Aaron shall enter the holy place with this: with a bull for a sin offering and a ram for a burnt offering. He shall put on the holy linen tunic, and the linen undergarments shall be next to his body, and he shall be girded with the linen sash and attired with the linen turban* (these are holy garments). *Then he shall bathe his body in water and put them on. He shall take from the congregation of the sons of Israel two male goats for a sin offering and one ram for a burnt offering."* (16:3-5).

In preparation for the Day of Atonement, Aaron was to select two animals for his two offerings. He also took three animals from the nation as an offering for the people. The High Priest's requirement was always to be a bull for a sin offering and a ram for a burnt offering. The nation's required animal selection was still to be a bull for the sin offering and a ram for the burnt offering. The nation's choice of animals needed was always two male goats for the sin offering and a ram for a burnt offering. This prescription was never to change. Once the priest entered the holy Tabernacle complex, the LORD required that he bathe and put on his priestly garb.

b) The Instruction for the Day of Atonement (16:6-10).

When the priest arrived at the complex, the LORD had specific instructions for the Day of Atonement. Verse 6. *"Then Aaron shall offer the bull for the sin offering which is for himself, that he may make atonement for himself and for his household. He shall take the two goats and present them before the LORD at the doorway of the tent of meeting. Aaron shall cast lots for the two goats, one lot for the LORD and the other lot for the scapegoat. Then Aaron shall offer the goat on which the lot for the LORD fell, and make it a sin offering. But the goat on which the lot for the scapegoat fell shall be presented alive before the LORD, to make atonement upon it, to send it into the wilderness as the scapegoat."* (16:6-10).

In preparation for the day's ceremony, the LORD's instruction directed Aaron to offer the bull for the sin offering immediately and then cast lots between the two goats. One goat will become the people's sin offering; one is released alive, ladened with the nation's guilt, but completely atoned before the LORD.

3. The Program of Entry into the Holy of Holies (16:28).
a) The Offering for Aaron and His Family (16:14).
(1) The Bull of the Sin Offering (16:11).

With the timing and instructions for the Day of Atonement settled, the LORD provides the program or the High Priest's entry into the Holy of Holies. After bathing and dressing in the priesthood's holy garments, the offering for Aaron and his family comes first. As noted already, the first offering is the bull of the sin offering. Verse 11. *"Then Aaron shall offer the bull of the sin offering which is for himself and make atonement for himself and for his household, and he shall slaughter the bull of the sin offering which is for himself."* (16:11).

The details of this sin-offering were not recorded in this passage — no need to do so. The LORD covered those details in chapter 4. The slain animal's blood was sprinkled in front of the veil and rubbed on the Altar of Incense's horns. While inside the Tabernacle, with the bowl of blood in his hand, the priest had a task to do. But before completing the task with the blood, the next order of business was the smoke of the incense.

(2) The Smoke of the Incense (16:12-13).

The High Priest did not have to gather the supplies for this step of the ceremony. The utensils and incense were stored in the Holy Place. This step was the important smoke of the incense before the LORD. Verse 12. *"He shall take a firepan full of coals of fire from upon the altar before the LORD and two handfuls of finely ground sweet incense, and bring it inside the veil. He shall put the incense on the fire before the LORD, that the cloud of incense may cover the mercy seat that is on the ark of the testimony, otherwise he will die."* (16:12-13).

Every day, at regular intervals, the priests supplied a firepan with fresh coals and incense for the Altar of Incense in front of the veil. Aaron knew how to do this. However, on the Day of Atonement, the firepan with incense was prepared to take behind the veil into the Holy of Holies where the LORD resided in the cloud above the Mercy Seat on top of the Ark of the Covenant. Aaron could not have performed this step in the ceremony with firepans without remembering the deadly results with the firepans and his two sons that died. Their deaths would be ever in his mind.

Chapter 16

With this step, if Aaron missteps, the penalty of the LORD is the same fate as his sons. For the sons, their presentation was in front of the veil; for Aaron on the Day of Atonement, his presentation was behind the veil. The firepan with the incense was Aaron's ticket to give him safe passage to enter behind the veil.

(3) The Blood of the Bull (16:14).

Once behind the veil with the firepan and the bowl of bull's blood in hand, the program's next step required the blood's sprinkling precisely on the Mercy Seat. Verse 14. *Moreover, he shall take some of the blood of the bull and sprinkle it with his finger on the mercy seat on the east side; also in front of the mercy seat he shall sprinkle some of the blood with his finger seven times."* (16:14).

I have always assumed that the Mercy Seat front was one of the long sides of the rectangle case. As such, I have always thought that the front side faced the veil in front of it that separated the Holy of Holies from the Holy Place. But my assumptions could not be correct according to this verse. Here is the reasoning. If the front of the Mercy Seat faced the veil, it would be facing east. How could Aaron sprinkle blood on the east side of the Mercy Seat and the front of the Mercy seat if both were the same? Therefore, my conclusion from this passage, the front of the Mercy Seat faced either north or south, and the end of the Mercy seat faced the veil to the east.

Having completed the presentation with the incense and the bull's blood, Aaron was to turn and leave the Holy of Holies for the next step in the ceremony.

b) The Offering for the People (16:15).
(1) The Goat of the Sin Offering (16:15a).

At the north side of the Brazen Altar, the selected goat for the people's offering was slain as a sin offering outside the Tabernacle. Verses 15a. *"Then he shall slaughter the goat of the sin offering which is for the people..."* (16:15a). It is a sin offering, too, as described in chapter 4.

(2) The Blood of the Goat (16:15b).

The priest caught the goat offering's blood, took that blood behind the veil, and sprinkled it on the Mercy Seat just like he did with the bull's blood. Verse 15b. *"... and bring its blood inside the veil and do with its blood as he did with the blood of the bull, and sprinkle it on the mercy seat and in front of the mercy seat."* (16:15b).

We might make a note at this point. Aaron is to do everything with the bull and goat sin offerings. He cannot be in two places at once. To this point, he has caught the blood of the animals for the sprinkling, but he has not processed the fat portions as required to present to the LORD. That part of these offerings will come later in the ceremony.

c) The Atonement of the Holy Place (16:16).

When Aaron sprinkles the bull's blood and goat blood on the Mercy Seat, all the defilement found within the people of Israelite camp will be forgiven, and the Holy Place will be atoned. Verse 16. *"He shall make atonement for the holy place, because of the impurities of the sons of Israel and because of their transgressions in regard to all their sins; and thus he shall do for the tent of meeting which abides with them in the midst of their impurities."* (16:16).

Surrounded by sin, the Tent of Meeting, which held the Tabernacle, was atoned.

d) The Restriction of the Holy Place (16:17a)

But for the atonement to occur on that special day, the whole Tent of Meeting was restricted. Verse 17a. *"When he goes in to make atonement in the holy place, no one shall be in the tent of meeting until he comes out..."* (16:17a).

The only one allowed in the Tent of Meeting was the High Priest. The first celebration in the wilderness and the celebrations for the next thirty-nine years would be Aaron, alone with the LORD, behind the veil.

e) The Atonement for the People (16:17b).

We come to a solemn thought. By the faithfulness of one man, the High Priest, he, his family, and all the Nation of Israel found the favor of the LORD. We call it the atonement of the people. Verse 17b. *"... that he may make atonement for himself and for his household and for all the assembly of Israel."* (16:17b).

The ceremony was the job of the High Priest and no one else. But the ceremony was not over.

f) The Atonement for the Brazen Altar (16:18-19).

The Tent of Meeting was atoned, but what about the Brazen Altar. Verse 18. *"Then he shall go out to the altar that is before the LORD and make atonement for it, and shall take some of the blood of the bull and of the blood of the goat and put it on the horns of the altar on all sides. With his finger he shall sprinkle some of the blood on it seven times and cleanse it, and from the impurities of the sons of Israel consecrate it."* (16:18-19).

Not all of the blood of the bull and goat was used on the Mercy Seat. Leaving the Mercy Seat from behind the veil, the priest marched to the Brazen Altar and sprinkled the blood on it seven times too.

g) The Man with the Scapegoat Departs (16:20-22).

Then we come to the next point in the order of worship on the Day of Atonement. A man will take the goat selected to live out to the wilderness and let it go free. Verse 20. *"When he finishes atoning for the holy place and the tent of meeting and the altar, he shall offer the live goat. Then Aaron shall lay both of his hands on the head of the live goat, and confess over it all the iniquities of the sons of Israel and all their transgressions in regard to all their sins; and he shall lay them on the head of the goat and send it away into the wilderness by the hand of a man who stands in readiness. The goat shall bear on itself all their iniquities to a solitary land; and he shall release the goat in the wilderness."* (16:20-22).

Picture, if you will, the goat. Two goats were led into the place by Aaron. Lots were cast, and one goat was to die; one goat was to live. The goat to die was dead; his blood had been sprinkled in front of the veil, on the Mercy Seat, and the Brazen Altar. Aaron approached the living goat that had watched it all. I have often wondered what a goat thinks when he sees another goat die. I wonder what that live goat thought when Aaron took him by the head, just as he took the head of his dead fellow friend. But instead of a knife to the throat, he received a talking.

What he heard, none of it was his fault. He had not been to the local school of counseling a day in his life. He did not know all the coping skills needed to deal with such a mess of sin and shame in human life. He was a goat. He spoke goat. He did not speak human. I dare say he did not understand a word that old Aaron said. Yet, all the sin of all the Nation of Israel's people was placed on that goat on that day – a burden too heavy to be carried by any human alone. But a solitary goat was selected for the task of bearing that load far away from the camp, into the wilderness. Oh, he would not do it alone, to begin with; a man would help direct him to the wilderness. But in the wilderness, the man would let him go, alone, with no one to protect this lone goat. One solitary goat, released in a solitary grove, to give a solitary grace to a solitary group. A group of sinful Israelites was saved by the hand of the LORD from Egypt's land with an assurance of a Promised Land.

h) The Bathing of the High Priest (16:23).

Aaron, the High Priest, watches as the man leads the goat out of the Tabernacle complex. Just outside the front curtain to the fence surrounding the complex, Aaron cannot see the man and goat any longer. Through one of the tribal areas, the man leads the goat. The people watch. They look at the goat; the goat looks at the people. They know about the goat. The goat knows nothing about them. The goat knows nothing about the ceremony or the reason he is such a big part. But a significant role he is playing! The people watch as the goat passes by bearing all their sins. Aaron is not done. He is dirty. Verse 23. *"Then Aaron shall come into the tent of meeting and take off the linen garments which he put on when he went into the holy place, and shall leave them there. He shall bathe his body with water in a holy place and put on his clothes ..."* (16:23).

In the wilderness and the Promised Land, the priests' holy garments were kept in the Tabernacle's front room. It was there that Aaron would take them off and go outside to the Basin of water to bathe. Once clean, he returned to the Tabernacle's front room and put his holy garment on again.

i) The Ram of the Burnt Offering (16:24).

Dressed anew, Aaron exited the Tent of Meeting and took the two rams in his hands. Verse 24. *"...and come forth and offer his burnt offering and the burnt offering of the people and make atonement for himself and for the people."* (16:24).

In the beginning instructions for the Day of Atonement, we found that two rams were selected to prepare the ceremony. One was for Aaron and his family; the other was for the people of Israel's nation. Both rams were for burnt offerings. At this point in the ceremony, each was offered by Aaron. Aaron slew the rams on the north side of the Brazen Altar. He sprinkled their blood seven times at the altar. The remaining blood was poured at the base of the altar. The entrail and legs were washed. The entrails symbolized a cleansing of the old sinful life; the legs symbolized the new way of walking in life's newness. The cleaned parts were placed on the altar. The rest of the ram's bodies were placed on the altar, except the hides. The hides belonged to Aaron.

    j)   **The Fat of the Sin Offerings (16:25).**

Now comes the fat of the bull and goat offerings. Verse 25. *"Then he shall offer up in smoke the fat of the sin offering on the altar."* (16:25).

For a reminder, the blood of the bull and goat was caught by Aaron and used to sprinkle in the Mercy Seat, the veil, and the Brazen Altar. The meat had not been processed. It was time for that in the ceremony. Aaron extracted the kidneys, loins, and liver considered the "fat" and placed them on the Brazen Altar. The rest of this bull and goat's bodies were held shortly for another part in the ceremony.

    k)   **The Man with the Scapegoat Returns (16:26).**

Outside the camp, the man had released the scapegoat and returned. But before coming into the camp, that man had to bathe. Verse 26. *"The one who released the goat as the scapegoat shall wash his clothes and bathe his body with water; then afterward he shall come into the camp."* (16:26).

Only after bathing could the man enter the boundaries of the tribal areas of the camp again.

    l)   **The Bull and Goat of the Sin Offering Burned (16:27-28).**

Aaron was waiting for the man who released the scapegoat to return. He and another job for the man. It involved the bodies of the bull and goat sin offerings being burned. Verse. 27. *"But the bull of the sin offering and the goat of the sin offering, whose blood was brought in to make atonement in the holy place, shall be taken outside the camp, and they shall burn their hides, their flesh, and their refuse in the fire. Then the one who burns them shall wash his clothes and bathe his body with water, then afterward he shall come into the camp."* (16:27-28).

The only thing left to do for the Day of Atonement was too burned the entire bodies, including the hides, but excluding the fat, outside the camp. The man who led the scapegoat to the wilderness bathed and returned to the camp was tasked with burning the bodies. Once again, the man was required to wash before returning to the camp.

B. The Day of the Day of Atonement (16:29).

We mentioned the date of the day of the Day of Atonement at the beginning of this section. The only reason we could do that is that I read and studied ahead before I started this commentary. Finally, we come to the LORD's text, and we hear Him speak. Verse 29, *"This shall be a permanent statute for you: in the seventh month, on the tenth day of the month..."* (16:29).

The date is set. It cannot be changed. It is the 10th day of the 7th month of every year. Years late in Jewish, like the seventh month, will be given the name Tishri. The 10th of Tishri is always the Day of Atonement.

1. A Statute for Cessation (16:30-31).

The law of the Day of Atonement imposed a statute for cessation on that day. Verse 30. *"...you shall humble your souls and not do any work, whether the native, or the alien who sojourns among you; for it is on this day that atonement shall be made for you to cleanse you; you will be clean from all your sins before the LORD. It is to be a sabbath of solemn rest for you, that you may humble your souls; it is a permanent statute."* (16:30-31).

The cessation of all work was required of all Jews and anyone living with the Jews. It is a sabbath of solemn rest.

The Hebrew word for "sabbath" means the *day of rest* or *cease to do*. We often think that the word "sabbath" means *seventh*, but it does not. Be that as it may, it will come to be associated hand in glove with the seventh day at the Ten Commandments' giving. In Genesis 2:2, the Hebrew word *shebii* is used. It is the ordinal number for seven. In Exodus 20:8, the text says, "Remember the sabbath day ...." The Hebrew word for *sabbath* is *hassabbat*. It means a *day of rest*. But the Exodus passage ties the sabbath to the six-day of work. Therefore, for the Nation of Israel, the seventh day becomes the *day of rest* perpetually.

With the Day of Atonement, regardless of the day of the week that Tishri 10th occurs, that day must be celebrated as a *day of rest from all labors* for all persons within Jewish camps, villages, cities, and tribal areas.

2. A Statute for Succession (16:32-33).

Aaron was the first High Priest, but he was eighty-four years of age by this time in the story. He would not live forever – the LORD would not let him. Therefore, the LORD included in this law the statute for succession. Verse 32. *"So the priest who is anointed and ordained to serve as priest in his father's place shall make atonement: he shall thus put on the linen garments, the holy garments, and make atonement for the holy sanctuary, and he shall make atonement for the tent of meeting and for the altar. He shall also make atonement for the priests and for all the people of the assembly."* (16:32-33).

You might ask, why did the LORD not include the Temple that Israel would construct in Jerusalem in this statute? Surely the LORD knew about the Temple. After all, the LORD is all-knowing. Of course, the LORD knew about that place called Jerusalem and the Temple that Solomon would build. The city that would someday be called Jerusalem was still the Jebusite Citadel, and Israel would not take it until King David's seventh year. Then, Solomon would not start building the Temple for thirty-seven years after David takes the city. Solomon will start the Temple four-hundred and eighty years after the Exodus (1 Kings 6:1). All the Israelites needed to know at this time was concerning the Tabernacle that the camp had just completed building.

3. A Statute for Expiation (16:34).

The LORD's final statement in this law states the statute for expiation. Verse 34. *"Now you shall have this as a permanent statute, to make atonement for the sons of Israel for all their sins once every year. And just as the LORD had commanded Moses, so he did."* (16:34).

"And just as the LORD had commanded Moses, so he did." What did Moses do? This instruction returns to the beginning of the law in 16:2, which says, *"The LORD said to Moses: "Tell your brother Aaron that he shall not enter at any time into the holy place inside the veil...."* So Moses told Aaron this complete law six months before it was time to observe it. However, the law had to be communicated immediately to Aaron. His life and the lives of all his descendants would be on the line if Moses failed to warn them of the statute of expiation, that is, the penalty they would face if they did not obey the law and only enter the Holy of Holies on the Day of Atonement, Tishri the 10th. And, *"so he did."*

Chapter 17

XII. The Law Forbidding the Egyptian and Canaanite Ways (17:1-18:30).

Now we come to the law forbidding Egyptian and Canaanite ways among the Nation of Israel in the Promised Land. We have spoken often about the Jews being in Egypt for four hundred and thirty years, where all they knew was Egyptian life. We need to set the background to understand why the LORD's words become specific and graphic in chapters 17 through 20.

First, who are the Egyptians and Canaanites? They are cousins. When Noah's family and descendants were divided at the Tower of Babel, ninety-eight years after the flood and coming off the Ark, the sons born to Ham were Cush, Mizraim, Phut, and Canaan. When the LORD confounded the languages at the Tower of Babel and forced the families to move apart from each other to populate the world, Cush, Mizraim, Phut, and Canaan headed in the same direction from Babylon. Canaan stopped in the territory we call Canaan Land, which the LORD will take away from them and give to the Jews as the Promised Land. Mizraim stopped at the Nile River and settled in that territory. The Hebrew name

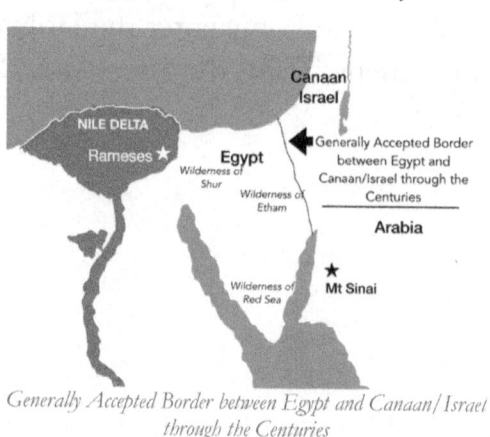

Generally Accepted Border between Egypt and Canaan/Israel through the Centuries

"Mizraim" has been translated into English as "Egypt." Phut continued west along the Mediterranean Sea coast and settled just past Mizraim/Egypt. The Hebrew name "Phut" has been translated into English as "Libya." Cush traveled south of Mizraim/Egypt and settled in the Mountains along the upper Nile. The Hebrew name "Cush" has been translated into English as "Ethiopia." Looking at a map, we see that the border of Mizraim/Egypt touches Canaan on the east, Phut on the west, and Cush on the south.

Second, the relationship between Mizraim and Canaan's descendants over thousands of years is particularly close. The borderline between the two nations lies where the Wadi Egypt enters the Mediterranean Sea. From there, the line runs straight to the northern tip of the Sea of Aqaba, the eastern gulf finger attached to the Red Sea. As cousin nations, with no real natural boundaries that would segregate the countries from each other, the people of Mizraim/Egypt and Canaan shared many cultural practices, including their gods, customs, morals, sexual relationships, and ways of life.

Third, because the Nation of Israel grew from infancy in Egypt, all they knew was Egyptian life and ways. Entering Egypt, Israel had no restrictions upon it. It had no theology, no religion, no laws of its own. It had no true national heritage. It was a family of seventy people. Leaving Egypt, it had the Egyptian theology, religion, laws, and ways ingrained in its heart and soul. Worse than that, most Egyptian ways were matched in the Canaanite ways, and the LORD wanted a complete break from all of that for Israel. In short, all that was evil in Egypt was also found in Canaan. Evil always concerns humans and the human ways of life. For that reason, the LORD instructed Israel to destroy all the Canaanites and their ways of life upon taking the

Promised Land. Why? The LORD gave Israel His specific laws, and He did not want any Israelite living in the Promised Land to fall back into or replicate their ways of life for four hundred and thirty years in Egypt.

Fourth, more needs to be said. The ways of Egypt and Canaan were the ways of the entire world. Every person in the world practiced some form of the same gods, morals, sexual relationships, and ways of life. The gods worshiped across the world had different names but were no less the same gods. The only thing different across the world was the specific local norms and customs. Israel was the LORD's new nation, and He wanted it to be different from the world as a whole. He wanted Israel to be a holy nation, set apart from the rest of the world, for His holy purpose. For that purpose, the LORD gave laws. But, in the next four chapters, the LORD is going to be specific with His directions. No detail is too small to be dismissed or overlooked. He knows the Canaanites' ways that He forbids the Israelites to replicate; He also knows the gullibility of Israelites and that they will repeat the Egyptian ways if He is not specific.

Finally, just to be sure we understand and remember, the laws in this book were for the Nation of Israel, not the rest of the world. Israel will be the only nation held accountable to the LORD for breaking these laws. However, any non-Jew who comes to live in the nation will be expected to abide by these laws. If an immigrant comes to live in the Nation of Israel and seeks to hold to his past ways of life, import them into Israel, the penalty for doing so is death. Foreign customs and ways of life mean nothing to the LORD and His new nation. He has a plan for Israel, and it is different from the ways of life found in the rest of the world.

A. The Forbidden Worship (17:1-9).
  1. The Sacrifice (17:1-7).
    a) Offered in the Wrong Place (17:1-4).

The LORD comes to the law forbidding Egyptian and Canaanite ways by addressing worship. What better place to begin? It is the worship the LORD will not tolerated. Specifically, it is the worship of a sacrifice in the wrong place. Chapter 17, verse 1. *"Then the LORD spoke to Moses, saying, Speak to Aaron and to his sons and to all the sons of Israel and say to them, 'This is what the LORD has commanded, saying, Any man from the house of Israel who slaughters an ox or a lamb or a goat in the camp, or who slaughters it outside the camp, and has not brought it to the doorway of the tent of meeting to present it as an offering to the LORD before the tabernacle of the LORD, bloodguiltiness is to be reckoned to that man. He has shed blood and that man shall be cut off from among his people.'"* (17:1-4).

The LORD's instruction to begin this section says, *"Speak to Aaron and to his sons and to all the sons of Israel and say to them...."* Often, we have seen the LORD say in Leviticus, *"Speak to Aaron,"* or *Speak to Aaron and to all his sons,"* but here the LORD adds *"... and all the sones of Israel...."* He took the long way around to say *this instruction is for everyone in the Nation of Israel.* Still, the LORD had to be specific with the Israelites because He knew they were the kind of people to split hairs and to get around the law in generations to come.

The topic is not instantly apparent in these first four verses, but it will be in the remaining context. The LORD is not talking about the routine slaughter of clean animals for food; the LORD is talking about the sacrificial process in worship. For the nation of Israel, all sacrifice worship, for a prescribed offering, is to be slain at the Tabernacle, or, as we will discover later in the Book of Deuteronomy, at the place in every tribal area where the LORD chooses for worship. The shedding of the animal's blood anywhere, instead of where the LORD approves, is a sacrifice in the wrong place, for the wrong purpose, and, as we will soon see, for the wrong god. The key to this passage is found in the words "... *in the camp ... outside the camp....*" In general, all sacrifices of all people and religions of the world before the time of the Exodus were slain at a designated altar for a specific god except one. The altar may be part of an elaborate temple complex or as simple as a stone altar built for their favorite god or goddess. These altars were permanent structures for the people to plead with a specific god for a particular need. But not so with one of the gods. For him, a sacrifice could be made in an open field outside of a populated area. It was never a specific and permanent place for that god. But that god was not the God. That god was a figment of man's imagination. He is a fake god. Israel is forbidden to make any sacrifices to any gods in any place that is the wrong place. Shedding the blood of an animal to a fake god in the wrong place means the slayer is to be cut off from the Nation of Israel. Why? Shedding the blood of an animal for food is to feed a body, and the LORD approves. Shedding the blood of an animal before the LORD is for worship. But shedding an animal's blood to a fake god is the same as the shedding of innocent blood, and the LORD calls that murder.

b) Offered for the Right Reason (17:5).

Israel is warned by the LORD not to make a sacrifice in the wrong place but to make a sacrifice for the right reason. Verse 5. *"The reason is so that the sons of Israel may bring their sacrifices which they were sacrificing in the open field, that they may bring them in to the LORD, at the doorway of the tent of meeting to the priest, and sacrifice them as sacrifices of peace offerings to the LORD."* (17:5).

Chapter 17

While in Egypt, one of the favorite gods to be worshipped is the god whose sacrifices are made in the open fields. It is the herdsmen and shepherds' favorite god because it is the god of fertility of herds and flocks. If you will remember, when Joseph brought his father and brothers to Egypt, he placed them in the land of Goshen as the herdsmen and shepherds of pharaoh's herds and flocks. In that capacity, they served all the pharaohs for four centuries until a pharaoh came along that did not know Joseph and did not care about all the hundreds of thousands of Hebrews in his kingdom. The Jews worshiped the Egyptian god of herds and flocks in Egypt. They were to worship him no longer in the fields. Instead, the LORD instructed the Jews to have no other gods before Him. Israel is to abandon all other gods and bring its sacrifices to the LORD in His Tabernacle. He is the right reason for a sacrifice in worship.

The LORD makes a switch in this verse that we should not overlook. By abandoning the offering to a false god in the wrong place in the open field and bringing it for the right reason before the LORD, the offering becomes *"... sacrifices of peace offerings to the LORD."* The LORD gave the instructions for this kind of offering in chapter 3. In that chapter, we learned that the *sacrifice of peace offering* is not for sin but gratitude. It is a thank you gift to the LORD for safety, wellbeing, or prosperity. The sacrifice to the false god in Egypt's open fields is a bribe to encourage the god to grant fertility to their herds and flocks. The LORD changes the reason for the gratitude in the sacrifice of peace offering to after the blessing has already come upon the herds and flocks with abundant offspring.

c) Offered in the Right Way (17:6).

A sacrifice in the right place provides the way for a sacrifice in the right way. Verse 6. *"The priest shall sprinkle the blood on the altar of the LORD at the doorway of the tent of meeting, and offer up the fat in smoke as a soothing aroma to the LORD."* (17:6).

With this passage, the LORD makes sure Israel's people understand the difference between offerings He will accept and those He will reject. The LORD puts the priestly system in place for a purpose, to make sure the offerings are handled and presented in the right and proper way according to His instruction. Sacrifices include blood; the blood must be handled correctly. At home, when slaying an animal for a meal, the blood is simply poured on the ground and covered with dirt. But with a sacrifice, that is different. Blood is holy with the sacrifice, and it belongs to the LORD. It is to be sprinkled on the altar where the fat portions of the animal are to be offered. Through the shedding of the blood, atonement comes.

d) Offered to the Wrong God (17:7)

Now we come to the problem of a sacrifice to the wrong god. The LORD puts the hammer down on the false god for the Israelites and names the god worshiped in the open field that He detests. Verse 7. *"They shall no longer sacrifice their sacrifices to the goat demons with which they play the harlot. This shall be a permanent statute to them throughout their generations."* (17:7).

Chapter 17

The goat demons. Other versions say "the goat idols." The goat. There we have it. Today, we have all studied in school the topic called *mythology*. We learned the names of pagan gods worshiped in the past and still today in many places on earth in mythology. These prevalent false gods were called by different names in different nations, but they were still the same gods. For instance, Zeus was also Jupiter. Poseidon was Neptune. Cronus was Saturn. Aphrodite was Venus. Ares was Mars. Hermes was Mercury. All these pagan gods had their glorious temples or altars built at great expense in multiple locations worldwide, except one that we have not named – the goat.

He Goat in Hebrew - Known in Greece as Pan

What mythological god was a goat? His name is Pan. Long before the Greeks gave him the name Pan, he was called *he goat*. The Hebrew word for *goat demons* is *sa'ir*. *Sa'ir* is a title more than a name. It means *he goat*. It is found as a title here in Leviticus 17:7 and in 2 Chronicles 11:15. All worship, throughout time of the He Goat, was far away from the populated cities and villages. His name is Pan. He did not have large temples built to worship him. Worship of this god occurred out in nature, in the open fields, or caves. Pan was the god who ruled over shepherds, herdsmen, hunters, and rustic music. Some of the most disgusting and obscene, godless sculptures and paintings of the Pan's He Goat's worship have been created by followers. Such art always represents what has happened in the past, and the worship of the He Goat was nothing less than godless. When the LORD says, *"with which they play the harlot,"* it would be easy to read into that the sexual deviance associated with the He Goat god displayed in the sculptures and paintings of Pan. But the LORD considered any worship of any false god as harlotry. Israel is to love the LORD God and Him only. He is a jealous God and will not allow those who love Him to interact in worship with false, fabricated gods. To Him, it is no different than a married man offering money to a woman to whom he is not married for sexual favors – harlotry.

When the LORD says, *"They shall no longer sacrifice their sacrifices to the goat demons with which they play the harlot,"* it means that the Israelites had already committed such sin in acts of worship to the He Goat. Where did they learn to worship the He Goat? The only place they could have learned to worship the goat was in Egypt, where they had been for four centuries. The problem would persist in Canaan if not stopped by the LORD. Canaanites worshiped the He Goat too. In fact, because the Nation of Israel will not fulfill the order to destroy all the Canaanites when it enters the Promised Land, the influence of Canaanite culture will be a thorn in the Israelite flesh through all time as it is still today. The Canaanite worship of Pan remains so strong after taking the Promised Land that a temple to Pan is built in Caesarea Philippi, which is said to be Pan's birthplace. Before being named Caesarea, the town was named Paneas, after the god, Pan. It sits on the ancient major trade route called *The Way of the Sea*. All trade headed east of Mount Hermon and down the Euphrates or Tigris Rivers to the gulf passed by Paneas. The surrounding area was called Panion. The LORD knew about the worship of this god and demands that Israelites never do it again.

We find one more interesting fact in this passage. Remember, the LORD says, *"They shall no longer sacrifice their sacrifices to the goat demons."* As we have said, the Hebrew word for *goat demons* is literally *He-Goats*. The LORD is not addressing one particular He-Goat god, but all the He-Goat gods. In mythology, *Pan* gave birth to twelve *he-goats* named *Kelaineus, Argennon, Aigikoros, Eugeneios, Omester, Daphoenus, Phobos, Philamnos, Xanthos, Glaukos, Argos, and Phorbas*. They are all *he-goat* gods that people in all nations worship by these and other names.

Additionally, two other *Pans* are *Agreus* and *Nomios*. Neither of these was related in mythology to the first *Pan* we mentioned with the twelve sons. Although all of these *He-Goats* were fictitious, they were created by the minds of man, worshiped as real, and the very thought of the worship of these gods detested the LORD. Therefore, the LORD rightly forbids the worship of them all in the one Hebrew word, *sa'ir* - He-Goats, goat demons. Once again, history books and ancient literature proves the truth found in God's Word about these *He-Goats*.

2. The Burnt (17:8-9).

The sacrifice of peace offering to any god other than the LORD God is important to the LORD, but the burnt offering is just as important. Verse 8. *"Then you shall say to them, 'Any man from the house of Israel, or from the aliens who sojourn among them, who offers a burnt offering or sacrifice, and does not bring it to the doorway of the tent of meeting to offer it to the LORD, that man also shall be cut off from his people."* (17:8-9).

The LORD summarizes this point in short order, and we can explain it quickly. Any sacrifice or offering is to be presented to the One LORD God at His chosen place. The Israelites and those living with the Israelites are never to sacrifice to any god but the LORD God. The penalty for being caught making a sacrifice or offering to any other god is to be *"... cut off from his people."* The death penalty is not the point here; excommunication from being a member of the Nation of Israel is the point.

- B. The Forbidden Blood (17:10-16).
  1. The Animal's Life Taken by Man (17:10-16).
     a) The Blood Which Atones the Soul (17:10-12).

From the forbidden worship, we come to the forbidden blood associated with the animal's life taken by a man that contains the blood which atones for the soul. In chapter 3, verse 17 says, *"It is a perpetual statute throughout your generations in all your dwellings: you shall not eat any fat or any blood."* Chapter 3 contains the instructions for the *Sacrifice of Peace Offering*. You might ask, "Why did the LORD wait until the third chapter to forbid the eating of blood. First, chapter 1 contains the instructions for the burnt offering. With that offering, the blood is sprinkled on the Brazen Altar, with the remaining blood poured at the base of the altar. The entire animal is burnt to ashes on the altar except for the hide. With nothing about the burnt offering eaten, there is no need for the instruction. Chapter 2 contains the instructions for the grain offerings. No blood is present; no blood is eaten. Chapter 3 moves to the instruction for the *Sacrifice of Peace Offering,* which requires placing the fat and entrails on the Brazen Altar but all the rest of the meat is given to the priests to eat. The instruction concerning the meat and its blood became an issue, and the LORD declared the statute forbidding the eating of the blood associated with the *Sacrifice of Peace Offering*. In the chapter 3, we asked if the statute was just for the animal offerings where the meat is eaten applies to all animals slain for daily food. I stated then that in chapter 17, we would learn that the statute applies to all slain animals for the offerings or at home for food. Here we come to that statute. Verse 10.

Chapter 17

"And any man from the house of Israel, or from the aliens who sojourn among them, who eats any blood, I will set My face against that person who eats blood and will cut him off from among his people. For the life of the flesh is in the blood, and I have given it to you on the altar to make atonement for your souls; for it is the blood by reason of the life that makes atonement. Therefore I said to the sons of Israel, 'No person among you may eat blood, nor may any alien who sojourns among you eat blood.'" (17:10-12).

We find a stark warning in this passage. The LORD says, *"I will set My face against that person who eats blood and will cut him off from among his people."* For the LORD to set His face against a person means that He is angry with that person. In this case, the LORD will cast the person out of the Nation of Israel.

We also find here that *"For the life of the flesh is in the blood, and I have given it to you on the altar to make atonement for your souls; for it is the blood by reason of the life that makes atonement."* In Exodus, the story of the Passover occurs. On the 14th of Abib, the lamb was slain and roasted. The blood was painted on the doorframes of every Jewish family. The death came at midnight to every firstborn whose home did not have the blood on the doorframes. The life blood died in every firstborn in Egypt without the blood on the home's doorframe. Do we know how many Egyptians, from man to beast, died that night because their blood died? Yes. The exact number of the living firstborn sons of Israel and their beast. The book of Numbers tells us the story about the deaths of the Egyptians that night.

[11] Again the LORD spoke to Moses, saying, [12] "Now, behold, I have taken the Levites from among the sons of Israel instead of every firstborn, the first issue of the womb among the sons of Israel. So the Levites shall be Mine. [13] For all the firstborn are Mine; on the day that I

struck down all the firstborn in the land of Egypt, I sanctified to Myself all the firstborn in Israel, from man to beast. They shall be Mine; I am the LORD." (Numbers 3:11-13).

The death of the blood of every firstborn man and beast in Egypt on the night of the Passover paid the atonement for every firstborn man and beast in the Nation of Israel. It is the death of the blood that atones, for life is in the blood. When the blood dies, the flesh dies. Therefore, he blood of all animals slain for an offering or food is forbidden.

b) The Blood Which Contains the Life (17:13-14).

The blood which atones the soul is also the blood that contains the life. Verse 13. *"So when any man from the sons of Israel, or from the aliens who sojourn among them, in hunting catches a beast or a bird which may be eaten, he shall pour out its blood and cover it with earth. For as for the life of all flesh, its blood is identified with its life. Therefore I said to the sons of Israel, 'You are not to eat the blood of any flesh, for the life of all flesh is its blood; whoever eats it shall be cut off."* (17:13-14).

When taking an animal for food, the blood must be drained on the ground and covered with dirt. Why? To the LORD, *"its blood is identified with its life."*

2. The Animal's Life Taken by Nature (17:15-16).

But what about when you find the animal's life taken by nature? Verse 15. *"When any person eats an animal which dies or is torn by beasts, whether he is a native or an alien, he shall wash his clothes and bathe in water, and remain unclean until evening; then he will become clean. But if he does not wash them or bathe his body, then he shall bear his guilt."* (17:15-16).

The LORD addressed the law for an animal found dead in Chapter 11. *"Also, if one of the animals dies which you have for food, the one who touches its carcass becomes unclean until evening. He too, who eats some of its carcass shall wash his clothes and be unclean until evening, and the one who picks up its carcass shall wash his clothes and be unclean until evening."* (11:39-40). Here in chapter 17, the LORD simply adds the penalty for not washing or bathing after touching an animal not slain by man. The LORD says, *"...then he shall bear his guilt."* In such cases, for his sin, at some time, the man will need to present a guilt offering to the LORD.

With that, we conclude Leviticus 17. From forbidden worship to forbidden blood, we will come to the forbidden relationships in chapter 18.

Chapter 18

C. The Forbidden Relationships (18:1-30).
1. When Israel Enters Canaan Land (18:1-5).

And now we come to the forbidden relationships when Israel enters Canaan Land. The people of Egypt and Canaan are close enough cousins that many of their customs and practices are the same. Chapter 18, verse 1. *"Then the LORD spoke to Moses, saying, 'Speak to the sons of Israel and say to them, 'I am the LORD your God. You shall not do what is done in the land of Egypt where you lived, nor are you to do what is done in the land of Canaan where I am bringing you; you shall not walk in their statutes. You are to perform My judgments and keep My statutes, to live in accord with them; I am the LORD your God. So you shall keep My statutes and My judgments, by which a man may live if he does them; I am the LORD.'"* (18:1-5).

First, the LORD confirms the closeness of the Egyptian and Canaanite cousins when He says, *"You shall not do what is done in the land of Egypt ... nor ... what is done in the land of Canaan...."* Egypt and Canaan live by the same standards and morals. Today, we would say the same absence of standards and morals, but our position is from a more complete knowledge of the desires of the LORD. For those of us who have been living under godly instruction all our lives, we find it quite hard to stomach the thoughts found in much of the rest of the book of Leviticus. We mostly see the incest regulations challenging to wade through in our yearly Bible reading. We must understand that until the Exodus days, the whole world lived by the same basic standards and morals that we find so offensive. As a child, I remember how horrible it was when I first heard that

Adam and Eve's sons married the daughters of Adam and Eve. But being the first family on earth from which all other families would derive, where could a son find a girl to marry except his sister. No other humans lived at the time. I remember Abram and Sarah's issue when they went to Egypt and lied concerning their family relationship. They told the officials Sarah was Abram's sister instead of his wife. It was a partial truth because Sarah was Abram's half-sister. The two had the same father but different mothers. We can go on through the Scripture and mention many, such as Isaac marrying his cousin Rebekah and Jacob marrying two sisters. But all those incestual relationships which allowed the world to be populated are coming to an end with the Nation of Israel immediately. No other nation of people in the world will abide by these new standards and morals until the coming of the LORD and the Church's establishment.

Second, the LORD says, *"So you shall keep My statutes and My judgments, by which a man may live if he does them; I am the LORD."* Instead of living life in the world's way, the LORD warns Israel's people to live life in His way according to His statutes and judgments. We must remember, *statutes* mean *legal regulations,* and *judgments* mean *the penalty for breaking a legal regulation.*

And with all of that, we enter the statute and judgment section of the book of Leviticus. It is the last section of the book, which spans chapters 18 through 27. In general, it is nothing but a list of the LORD's legal instruction for Israel to follow despite what the people of the entire world are doing around them.

a) Abominations with Blood Relatives (18:6).

The LORD begins the list of statues with a warning about repulsive abominations with blood relatives. Verse 6.

"None of you shall approach any blood relative of his to uncover nakedness; I am the LORD." (18:6).

What does the LORD mean when He says, *"uncover nakedness?"* Let us go back to Genesis 3:7 and the Adam and Eve story to understand these words' meaning. The two have eaten the forbidden fruit, and the following occurs. *"Then the eyes of both of them were opened, and they knew that they were naked; and they sewed fig leaves together and made themselves loin coverings."* (Genesis 3:7). Thus, Adam and Eve saw their nakedness and covered their naked loin parts. The Genesis verse uses the word *loin,* we call them sexual organs. The same meaning applies here in Leviticus.

Our translation uses the words *"blood relatives."* However, the Hebrew should be translated *flesh of your flesh.* In Genesis 2:24, the LORD says, *"For this reason a man shall leave his father and his mother, and be joined to his wife; and they shall become one flesh."* (Genesis 2:24). When a man marries a woman, and they join in a marital union in the process of intercourse, the flesh of the two become one flesh. Therefore, the husband and the wife are of one flesh, and all their parents, siblings, and offspring are of the same flesh. Basically, once a man marries a wife, the families of both become one flesh, and the families become off-limits to new sexual encounters. First, we see the statutes for the abominations with blood relatives.

(1) Your Father and Mother (18:7).

The LORD begins these instructions with the closest relationships possible, that of a child to a father and mother. Verse 7. *"You shall not uncover the nakedness of your father, that is, the nakedness of your mother. She is your mother; you are not to uncover her nakedness."* (18:7).

A child is truly constructed from the flesh and blood of its biological father and mother. Without the union of the two, the child could not be born. Biologically it holds parts of each within its physical being. In these new guidelines, a child is never to mate with a father or mother. We can look back in the book of Genesis and see where this occurred with Lot and his two daughters; however, when the daughters mated with their father, the LORD's law was not in place.

(2) Your Father and Step-Mother (18:8).

Now we come to the relationship with a father and a step-mother. Verse 8. *"You shall not uncover the nakedness of your father's wife; it is your father's nakedness."* (18:8).

Even though a child does not have a biological blood relationship with the step-mother, no sexual relationship can be had with her because she is in a sexual relationship with the biological father. As your father's wife, she is now one flesh with your father.

(3) Your Sister or Step-Sister (18:9).

The LORD addresses the sexual relationship with a sister or step-sister and forbids any acts between the two. Verse 9. *"The nakedness of your sister, either your father's daughter or your mother's daughter, whether born at home or born outside, their nakedness you shall not uncover."* (18:9).

Your sister is of the same biological makeup as you with your father and mother; therefore, your sister cannot be taken into a sexual relationship. Neither can a half-sister be a sexual partner because she has half of your biological makeup. Many years after giving this law, David's son, Amnon, sexually assaulted his half-sister, Tamar. Absalom brought justice for Amnon's transgression by killing him for the sin. But this law was not in place when Amnon and Tamar mated.

The step-sister is also addressed here. Even though she is not biologically related in flesh and blood, her mother is one flesh with your father making your step-sister off limits to you as a sexual partner.

(4) Your Granddaughter (18:10).

Next, we come to the sinful sexual relationship with a granddaughter. Verse 10. *"The nakedness of your son's daughter or your daughter's daughter, their nakedness you shall not uncover; for their nakedness is yours."* (18:10).

You have now grown to be the father or mother, and the same stipulation applies to you as did with your father and mother. You cannot enter a sexual relationship with a granddaughter.

(5) Your Half-Sister (18:11).

The half-sister comes next. Her flesh and blood will only match half of yours, but she is still forbidden. Verse 11. *"The nakedness of your father's wife's daughter, born to your father, she is your sister, you shall not uncover her nakedness."* (18:11).

Simply having your father's flesh and blood within your half-sister is enough to restrict her from a relationship with you.

(6) Your Aunts and Uncles (18:12-14).

Then the LORD addresses the aunts and uncles. Verse 12. *"You shall not uncover the nakedness of your father's sister; she is your father's blood relative. You shall not uncover the nakedness of your mother's sister, for she is your mother's blood relative. You shall not uncover the nakedness of your father's brother; you shall not approach his wife, she is your aunt."* (18:12-14).

The bloodlines of your aunts and uncles are the same as your fathers and mothers. Therefore, they cannot be included in any sexual relationships.

(7) Your Daughter-in-law (18:15).

The wife of your son is your daughter-in-law. She is off-limits. Verse 15. *"You shall not uncover the nakedness of your daughter-in-law; she is your son's wife, you shall not uncover her nakedness."* (18:15).

Even though she is not related by flesh and blood, she is one flesh with your biological son, which makes her out of bounds for a sexual relationship with you.

(8) Your Sister-in-law (18:16).

Your sister-in-law will be the wife of your brother or sister. Once again, she is not the flesh of your flesh and blood of your blood, but she is one flesh with your brother or sister. You cannot have a sexual relationship with her. Verse 16. *"You shall not uncover the nakedness of your brother's wife; it is your brother's nakedness."* (18:16).

Your flesh and blood are the same as your brother's flesh and blood. Flesh and blood sexual relationships are strictly forbidden in the Nation of Israel.

b) Abominations with Neighbors (18:17-23).

From the abomination with blood relatives, we come to the abominations with neighbors. The LORD begins with a woman and her daughter together.

(1) A Woman and Her Daughter Together (18:17a).

The LORD is no longer speaking of a wife or a mother; He has changed His words to *a woman* and her daughter. Verse 17a. *"You shall not uncover the nakedness of a woman and of her daughter..."* (18:17a).

First, a sin exists because a sexual relationship with a woman you are not married is strictly forbidden. Second, the statute exposes a different corruption, a sexual relationship with a woman and her daughter at the same time. Neither are blood relatives, neither are married to you. Both encounters are strictly forbidden.

(2) A Daughter-in-law and the Granddaughter (18:17b).

Because He has just addressed the problem of a man entering a sexual relationship with a woman and her daughter in an unmarried state, the LORD addresses a daughter-in-law and a granddaughter in an unholy state. Verse 17b. *"...nor shall you take her son's daughter or her daughter's daughter, to uncover her nakedness; they are blood relatives. It is lewdness."* (18:17b).

The LORD uses the word *"lewdness."* The word means a *lustful indulgence*. When the word was first used in the English translations, it meant a *habitual lustful indulgence* indicating that the man would continually lust for a sexual encounter with a woman, daughter, daughter, and granddaughter.

(3) A Marriage to Two Sisters (18:18).

Now we come to the prohibition of marrying two sisters. Verse 18. *"You shall not marry a woman in addition to her sister as a rival while she is alive, to uncover her nakedness."* (18:18).

The classic example of this problem is found in the story of Jacob marrying Rachel and Leah. The book of Genesis makes it clear that the two were rivals in every way. This restriction means that a man cannot be married to two sisters at the same time. If he is married to one sister and she dies, then he can marry the second sister. This verse does not condone multiple wives in a marriage. It supports a monogamous marriage between one man and one woman.

(4) A Menstruating Woman (18:19).

Every woman has a time each month when the sexual organs clean themselves. The LORD addresses this prohibition. Verse 19. *"Also you shall not approach a woman to uncover her nakedness during her menstrual impurity."* (18:19).

This is the second time the LORD has given this instruction. We found it in the instruction for the discharge from a woman's body in chapter 15. This statute, in this verse, applies to any woman to whom you are married or not.

(5) A Neighbor's Wife (18:20).

A neighbor's wife is also forbidden. Verse 20. *"You shall not have intercourse with your neighbor's wife, to be defiled with her."* (18:20).

Interestingly, the word *intercourse* is used in this verse. The Hebrew word is *shekobeth*, and it means to *lie carnally*. The word *intercourse* was first used in the 1500s to explain a conversation between different parties. It meant to communicate to and fro. It was not used to mean a sexual relationship until the late 1770s. For that reason, the older English translations and versions use the words *lie carnally*. They both mean the same thing. The word *carnal* means *a sensual immoral passion and appetite of the flesh*. A Jewish man is forbidden from having a sexual relationship with a woman he has not married.

(6) A Child Sacrifice to Molech (18:21).

Child sacrifice to Molech is strictly forbidden. Verse 21. *"You shall not give any of your offspring to offer them to Molech, nor shall you profane the name of your God; I am the LORD."* (18:21).

Molech is the name of the Canaanite fire deity over children. Molech is the ancient Ammonite name. Remember, Ammon was the son born to Lot after the destruction of Sodom and Gomorrah. It is interesting that Moabites, Ammon's brother, also worshipped this deity but called him Chemosh. These are the Moabite and Ammonite names for this single deity. We do not know the name used for this deity in the Canaanite or the Egyptian language. However, in Mesopotamia, he is called *Nergal*, in Syria,

Shamash, in Ebia, *Kamish*. They are all the names of the same deity. The Smith Bible Dictionary says the following about Molech.

> *Fire-gods appear to have been common to all the Canaanite, Syrian, and Arab tribes, who worshipped the destructive element under an outward symbol, with the most inhuman rites. According to Jewish tradition, the image of Molech was of brass, hollow within, and was situated without Jerusalem. "His face was (that) of a calf, and his hands stretched forth like a man who opens his hands to receive (something) of his neighbor. And they kindled it with fire, and the priests took the babe and put it into the hands of Molech, and the babe gave up the ghost."*[19]

(7) A Male with a Male (18:22).

A man having a sexual relationship with a man is forbidden. Verse 22. *"You shall not lie with a male as one lies with a female; it is an abomination."* (18:22). Here we come to the abomination of a man having a sexual relationship with another man. The LORD's statute forbids it. The word used to describe this today is homosexuality. The word *abomination* means *fifth*.

(8) A Human with an Animal (18:23).

A sexual relationship with an animal is forbidden. Verse 23. *"Also you shall not have intercourse with any animal to be defiled with it, nor shall any woman stand before an animal to mate with it; it is a perversion."* (18:23).

For the word *intercourse*, see the notes on verse 18:20. Today, to lie carnally with an animal is called bestiality. The word *perversion* means *the alteration of something from its original course*. It is strictly forbidden in Israel.

---

[19] Smith, W. (1986). In *Smith's Bible Dictionary*. Nashville: Thomas Nelson.

2. When Israel Sees Canaan Land (18:24-30).
a) The Punishment of the Canaanites (18:24-25).

The LORD ends this section of the forbidden relationships by explaining that when Israel sees Canaan Land, she will see the LORD's punishment of the Canaanites for their ways. Verses 24. *"Do not defile yourselves by any of these things; for by all these the nations which I am casting out before you have become defiled. For the land has become defiled, therefore I have brought its punishment upon it, so the land has spewed out its inhabitants."* (18:24-25).

The LORD saw the evil of the Canaanites and their rejection of Him long before He delivered these laws to the Nation of Israel. Six hundred and twenty years before giving this law, the LORD promised to give Abram's descendants Canaan's Land. At that time, all the Canaanite tribes had long past offended the LORD, and he planned to destroy the Canaanites. The Canaanites were guilty of all the forbidden relationships listed in this chapter.

b) The Pattern of the Canaanites (18:24-30).

From the punishment of the Canaanites, we come to the pattern of the Canaanites. The LORD warns Israel to abstain from copying the pattern of the ways of Canaan when they take possession of the land. Verse 24. *"But as for you, you are to keep My statutes and My judgments and shall not do any of these abominations, neither the native, nor the alien who sojourns among you (for the men of the land who have been before you have done all these abominations, and the land has become defiled); so that the land will not spew you out, should you defile it, as it has spewed out the nation which has been before you. For whoever does any of these abominations, those persons who do so shall be cut off from among their people. Thus you are to keep My charge, that you do not practice any of the abominable customs which have been practiced before you, so as not to defile yourselves with them; I am the LORD your God."* (18:24-30).

The LORD took the land away from the Canaanites. If Israel follows the Canaanite's practices, the LORD will take the land away from Israel too. Sadly, we know the end of the story. The Israelites did fall into the ways of the Canaanites, and the LORD took the land away from Israel when He sent them into exile eight hundred and eighty years after He gave them this law.

Chapter 19

Now we come to the law of the ways of life in the Promised Land.

XIII.   **The Law of the Ways of Life (19:1-37).**

The LORD turns His attention to delivering His law of the ways of life for the Nation of Israel when she enters the Promised Land.

  A. The Ways of the LORD's Holiness (19:1-18).
    1. You Shall (19:1-10).
      a) Be a Holy People (19:1-2).

First, we come to the ways of the LORD's Holiness in the Promised Land. These are the things He expects of the Jewish people. He begins with the holiness of the people. Chapter 19, verse 1. *"Then the LORD spoke to Moses, saying: "Speak to all the congregation of the sons of Israel and say to them, 'You shall be holy, for I the LORD your God am holy."* (19:1-2).

The Hebrew word for *holy* is *qadosh*. It means *sacred*. As we begin this section, we must remember that the whole world is living according to man's customs, laws, and practices. Just one year before the LORD delivers the text in this book, no Scripture existed on earth from the LORD. Every man did as he pleased in his own heart and mind. Because man acted according to his own desires, sin ran rampant across the world. With the Nation of Israel being the LORD's chosen people, He wanted them to hold to His standards of life, not the worlds. He wanted them to be holy as He is holy. The whole world will consider the ways of Israel odd. They are not odd; they are merely following the instructions of the Creator and how He intends for them to live. That is the reason He instructs them to be a holy people.

b) Be a Respectful People (19:3a).

The LORD also wants the Jews to be a respectful people. Verse 3a. *"Every one of you shall reverence his mother and his father..."* (19:3a). The LORD does not require His people to agree with the ways of their fathers and mothers. Instead, He demands His people to be respectful or reverent toward their fathers and mothers. In the Ten Commandments, the LORD says, *honor your father and mother.* *Honor* means to show respect or reverence. But with the Ten Commandments, the LORD desires for His people to bring honor to the parents regardless of their character, nature, or ways. How do you do that? By being an honorable, respectful person of integrity, even if it means your parents were the worst of the worst.

c) Be a Faithful People (19:3b).

The LORD desires you to be a faithful people to Him. Verse 3b. *"... and you shall keep My sabbaths; I am the LORD your God."* (19:3b). The day of rest is important to the LORD. He watches His creation; He cares for His creation. He created the sabbath day for rest and declared it to be so.

d) Be a Loyal People (19:4).

The LORD wants a loyal people. Verse 4. *"Do not turn to idols or make for yourselves molten gods; I am the LORD your God."* (19:4). No other gods exist. The LORD is the only God. He addresses this in the first commands of the Ten Commandments. It detests the LORD when His people worship man's fabrications rather than the LORD Himself as God.

e) Be a Thankful People (19:5-8).

The LORD wants a thankful people. Therefore, He reminded the people of how He provided a way to show thankfulness to Him in the *sacrifice of peace offering*. Verse 5. *"Now when you offer a sacrifice of peace offerings to the LORD, you shall offer it so that you may be accepted. It shall be eaten the same day you offer it, and the next day; but what remains until the third day shall be burned with fire. So if it is eaten at all on the third day, it is an offense; it will not be accepted. Everyone who eats it will bear his iniquity, for he has profaned the holy thing of the LORD; and that person shall be cut off from his people."* (19:5-8).

Nothing new here. The LORD simply reminds His people how to show thanks to Him for the provisions He provides for their daily needs.

f) Be a Giving People (19:9-10).

The LORD gives in order to provide for the needs of His people. He also requires that His people pass on from what He has given to others with needs. Verse 9. *"Now when you reap the harvest of your land, you shall not reap to the very corners of your field, nor shall you gather the gleanings of your harvest. Nor shall you glean your vineyard, nor shall you gather the fallen fruit of your vineyard; you shall leave them for the needy and for the stranger. I am the LORD your God."* (19:9-10).

To *glean* means to *scrape the edges*. The main part of the all the crops belong to the owner, whom the LORD blesses. But the LORD wants the owners to bless the poor by leaving the produce at the edges of the fields for the poor to collect. In this way, the poor, needy, and stranger did not have to leave the road to gather a meal. They could just step to the edge of the road without transgressing the whole property of a farmer.

2. You Shall Not (19:11-18).
   a) Be a Thief Among the People (19:11).

Now the LORD turns in this section to the things you shall not do among the Promised Land people. You shall not be a thief among the people. Verse 11. *"You shall not steal, nor deal falsely, nor lie to one another."* (19:11).

To steal, deal falsely, or lie is all theft in one way or another. It is the theft of property, of misleading, or of untruth. These three are uniquely joined together because they always seem to be present in people's evil actions. When a child tells a lie to a parent, the lie is attached to a false dealing with the parent face to face. It also included the theft of something. Think about these three the next time you watch a Hallmark movie. Although they are rated for all audiences, within the plot, someone deals falsely with another, steals something from that person, and lies about the theft. You may question property theft, but please keep in mind that there are many kinds of property – movable and immovable, tangible, and intangible, private and public, personal and real, corporeal and incorporeal.

   b) Be a Profaner Among the People (19:12).

Then comes the profaner among the people. Verse 12. *"You shall not swear falsely by My name, so as to profane the name of your God; I am the LORD."* (19:12).

To *swear* means to *take an oath*. In this verse, the LORD does not allow for someone to take an oath using His name with the intent of being dishonest, deceitful, or deceptive. It profanes the name of the LORD when He is included in such evil.

   c) Be an Oppressor Among the People (19:13).

Jews were not to be an oppressor among the people. Verse 13. *"You shall not oppress your neighbor, nor rob him. The wages of a hired man are not to remain with you all night until morning."* (19:13).

An oppressor exercises *undue severity in the use of power or authority*. Two kinds of oppressors are listed here – the oppressor of the neighbor, the oppressor of the employee. First is the oppressor who is unreasonable to neighbors, demanding this and that with something new every day. Or the oppressor who treats his neighbor's property as his own. taking what he wants without asking, never returning what does not belong to him. A robber he is. Second, we come to the employer who holds the wages of the employee. The Bible teaches to pay hired men at the end of each day.

d) Be a Stumbling Block Among the People (19:14).

The Jews were not to be a stumbling block among the people. Verse 14. *"You shall not curse a deaf man, nor place a stumbling block before the blind, but you shall revere your God; I am the LORD."* (19:14).

Moses begins by saying, *"You shall not curse a deaf man."* The Hebrew word for *curse* is *qalal,* and it does not carry the same meaning we use today for the word *curse. Qala* means *to treat lightly*. As such, in the context here, it means to cause trouble for a deaf person by making life difficult. That falls right in line with the second part of the sentence, *"nor place a stumbling block before the blind."* Both make the way difficult for the deaf and the blind. Then the LORD ends with *"you shall revere your God."* The word *revere* means *to have a reverence for the LORD*. He would not want the way of the deaf and blind to be hindered by anyone, and neither should His people.

e) Be a Partisan Among the People (19:15).

The Israelites must not be a partisan among the people. Verse 15. *"You shall do no injustice in judgment; you shall not be partial to the poor nor defer to the great, but you are to judge your neighbor fairly."* (19:15).

Most injustices in life come from partisanship. To be partial means to be one-sided, biased, inclined to favor one party in a cause or one side of a question more than the other. All people should be treated with fairness, the rich and the poor alike.

f) Be a Defamer Among the People (19:16).

As a Jew, no one should be a defamer among the people. Verse 16. *"You shall not go about as a slanderer among your people, and you are not to act against the life of your neighbor; I am the LORD."* (19:16).

Simply, in the Promised Land, the people are not to disgrace, dishonor, or impair others' reputation in the nation.

g) Be a Hater Among the People (19:17).

The Israelites are not to be a hater among the people. Verse 17. *"You shall not hate your fellow countryman in your heart; you may surely reprove your neighbor, but shall not incur sin because of him."* (19:17).

Hate is an interesting thing. Those who hate others let the hate consume their lives, hearts, and souls. It is a constant ill-will toward others. The problem and the sin are with the person who hates instead of the one being hated. In opposition, some people need to be reproved. Part of the word *reprove* is the word *prove*. When it was first used in the original English translation, it meant to *present the proof, or to prove* the truth. It is the same in this passage. Some people, especially those who have hate for someone, need to have the facts presented to them to prove the wrongness of their ways. The last part of the verse says, *"but shall not incur sin because of him."* Proving wrong does not mean you are doing wrong.

h) Be a Revenger Among the People (19:18).

Finally, the people of Israel are not to be a revenger among the people. Verse 18. *"You shall not take vengeance, nor bear any grudge against the sons of your people, but you shall love your neighbor as yourself; I am the LORD."* (19:18).

Vengeance involves a passionate, often unrestrained desire to punish. *Grudge* involves ongoing envy, jealousy, or contempt for another person. The people of the Nation of Israel should never participate in either. They are to *love* their neighbors as they want to be loved, in the same way, the normal person loves themselves.

B. The Ways of the LORD's Statutes (19:19-37).
1. Concerning the Different Kinds of Things (19:19).

From the ways of the LORD's Holiness, we come to the ways of the LORD's statutes. We begin with the statutes concerning the different kinds of things. Verse 19. *"You are to keep My statutes. You shall not breed together two kinds of your cattle; you shall not sow your field with two kinds of seed, nor wear a garment upon you of two kinds of material mixed together."* (19:19).

The breeding of two kinds of animals is strictly forbidden. We understand why. Left alone, the natural attraction of animals will be with like-kind. However, in other nations worldwide, breeding experiments had begun, and the LORD disapproved of such practices. As for the sowing of seed and mixing of materials as garments, we struggle. We find similar statements in Moses' summary in Deuteronomy.

> Deuteronomy 22:9 *"You shall not sow your vineyard with two kinds of seed, or all the produce of the seed which you have sown and the increase of the vineyard will become defiled.*

Deuteronomy 22:9 changes the planting of the seed from the word "field" in Leviticus to the word "vineyard." The end of verse 9 says concerning the mixing of the seeds, *"the increase of the vineyard will become defiled."* This verse explains the reason. The fruits of different seeds mature at different times. The harvest of two different crops from the same field becomes almost impossible. Damage to the crop which grows last will occur with the gathering of the first. Thus, the increase becomes defiled.

Concerning the mixed materials, we see a similar statement in Moses' summary in Deuteronomy.

> Deuteronomy 22:11 *"You shall not wear a material mixed of wool and linen together.*

Deuteronomy indicates that the two materials which should not be worn together are *wool and linen*. Much speculation about this law in Leviticus and Deuteronomy can be found in most commentaries; however, little modern-day reasoning can be associated between the two. We must leave this verse as a law to be followed without modern-day understanding. Be that as it may, the Jews would have understood the law and the reason.

2. Concerning the Carnal Kinds of Things (19:20-22).

Next, we come to the LORD's statutes concerning the carnal kinds of things. Verse 20. *"Now if a man lies carnally with a woman who is a slave acquired for another man, but who has in no way been redeemed nor given her freedom, there shall be punishment; they shall not, however, be put to death, because she was not free. He shall bring his guilt offering to the LORD to the doorway of the tent of meeting, a ram for a guilt offering. The priest shall also make atonement for him with the ram of the guilt offering before the LORD for his sin which he has committed, and the sin which he has committed will be forgiven him."* (19:20-22).

Two issues need explanation in this passage. First, the sexual intercourse with a woman to whom he is not married. The second is the woman's position as an acquired slave who has not been freed or redeemed.

In the first place, the sexual sin of the man requires the offer of the ram for a guilt offering.

In the second place, the purchase of a slave is not illegal in the LORD's laws; selling a slave is unlawful. Once a Jew purchases a slave, the slave falls under a whole new set of restrictions. She cannot be sold. She must be released at the end of six years, or with the turn of the year of Jubilee, or redeemed by the owner and given freedom. Without these restrictions being met, she is still under the complete control of the one who purchased her. After the woman's purchase, one way or another, at the end of six years, or the year of Jubilee, she will be free. However, this sin does not require the death penalty. It requires the guilt offering. At the point of freedom, she can choose to stay with the owner and become a bondslave. If she makes that choice, a hole will be drilled in her ear to indicate her permanent decision. She does not belong to the man who defiled her.

3. Concerning the Planting Kinds of Things (19:23-25).

When entering the Promised Land, the LORD issues a statute concerning the planting kinds of things. Verse 23. *"When you enter the land and plant all kinds of trees for food, then you shall count their fruit as forbidden. Three years it shall be forbidden to you; it shall not be eaten. But in the fourth year all its fruit shall be holy, an offering of praise to the LORD. In the fifth year you are to eat of its fruit, that its yield may increase for you; I am the LORD your God."* (19:23-25).

Once the plant sprouts, the fruit of the tree must not be taken for food; most likely, the fruit will be discarded as soon as it appears to allow all the energy in the plant to go toward the tree's development rather than the development of the fruit. But in the fourth year, all the fruit belongs to the LORD. In the fifth year, the fruit belongs to the owner.

4. **Concerning the Cultic Kinds of Things (19:26).**

Concerning the cultic kinds of things, the LORD brings us to verse 26. *"You shall not eat anything with the blood, nor practice divination or soothsaying."* (19:26).

Much has been said to this point in Leviticus concerning the LORD's prohibition against blood eating. Here it is tied to cultic practices used by the Canaanites and other nations in divination and soothsaying. The three go together. The three are forbidden.

5. **Concerning the Grooming Kinds of Things (19:27).**

Concerning the grooming kinds of things, we look at verse 27. *"You shall not round off the side-growth of your heads nor harm the edges of your beard."* (19:27).

The LORD gave a statute concerning the appearance of the men in the Nation of Israel. In the rest of the world's religious practices, men shaved the sides of their heads, forming different styles of mohawks. They also shaved the sides of their beards, forming go-tees. The LORD strictly forbids this for the men of Israel.

6. **Concerning the Body Marking Kinds of Things (19:28).**

Concerning the body marking kinds of things, we see in verse 28. *"You shall not make any cuts in your body for the dead nor make any tattoo marks on yourselves: I am the LORD."* (19:28).

The LORD forbids body cuttings and tattoos. Concerning *"cuts in your body for the dead"* and *"tattoo marks,"* both are common practices in cult worship. Both cause the unnatural disfiguration of the body. Both are forbidden.

7. **Concerning the Trafficking Kinds of Things (19:29).**

Then we come to the LORD's statute concerning the trafficking kind of things in verse 29. *"Do not profane your daughter by making her a harlot, so that the land will not fall to harlotry and the land become full of lewdness."* (19:29).

The Scripture uses the word harlot. In a modern translation for today, the better word that matches the context is a *prostitute*. Parents in Israel are not to traffic their daughters into prostitution for income, bargaining, bartering, or favors of any kind.

8. Concerning the Worship Kinds of Things (19:30).

Then comes the statute concerning the worship kinds of things. *"You shall keep My sabbaths and revere My sanctuary; I am the LORD."* (19:30).

The sabbaths and the sanctuary are two of the most important things to the LORD. Both are involved in the worship of the LORD every seven days.

9. Concerning the Defiling Kinds of Things (19:31).

From the worship kinds of things, we come to the defining kings of things. Verse 31. *"Do not turn to mediums or spiritists; do not seek them out to be defiled by them. I am the LORD your God."* (19:31).

What is the difference between the two? A *medium delivers spiritual messages;* a *spiritists* claims to communicate with the dead. Both are fake. Both are idolatry. The LORD forbids both.

10. Concerning the Elderly Kinds of Things (19:32).

Concerning the elderly kind of things, the LORD says in verse 32, *"You shall rise up before the gray-headed and honor the aged, and you shall revere your God; I am the LORD."* (19:32).

Older people are to be honored by the people of the Nation of Israel.

11. Concerning the Foreigner Kind of Things (19:33-34).

Concerning the foreigner kind of things, the passage says in verse 33, *"When a stranger resides with you in your land, you shall not do him wrong. The stranger who resides with you shall be to you as the native among you, and you shall love him as yourself, for you were aliens in the land of Egypt; I am the LORD your God."* (19:33-34).

Foreigners are to be treated with the same love and respect as you have your native tribal friends.

12. Concerning the Commerce Kinds of Things (19:35-36).

Then the LORD states the statutes concerning the commerce kinds of things. Verse 35. *"You shall do no wrong in judgment, in measurement of weight, or capacity. You shall have just balances, just weights, a just ephah, and a just hin; I am the LORD your God, who brought you out from the land of Egypt."* (19:35-36).

All commerce between Jew and Jew, or Jew and foreigner, must be fair in every transaction.

13. Concerning the LORD's Kind of Things (19:37).

Finally, concerning the LORD's kind of things, we hear in verse 37, *"You shall thus observe all My statutes and all My ordinances and do them; I am the LORD."* (19:37).

The Nation of Israel must follow the LORD's statutes precisely.

Chapter 20

XIV. The Law of the Sin Penalty (20:1-27).
  A. The Idolatry Sins (20:1-8).
    1. By Playing the Harlot with Molech (20:1-5).
      a) Those Who Act in the Worship of Molech (20:1-3).

Leaving the law of the ways of life in the Promised Land, we come to the law of the sin penalty. These or idolatry sins. The first is a sin by playing the harlot with Molech. Playing the harlot with a false god addresses those who participate in the worship of Molech. Chapter 20, verse 1. *"Then the LORD spoke to Moses, saying, "You shall also say to the sons of Israel: 'Any man from the sons of Israel or from the aliens sojourning in Israel who gives any of his offspring to Molech, shall surely be put to death; the people of the land shall stone him with stones. 'I will also set My face against that man and will cut him off from among his people, because he has given some of his offspring to Molech, so as to defile My sanctuary and to profane My holy name."* (20:1-3).

In this passage, the LORD speaks again about Molech. We spoke in detail about this sin in chapter 18:21. Here, the penalty is clear. Anyone caught worshiping and making child offerings to Molech was to be put to death by stoning. The worship of false gods is in direct contradiction to the LORD's law found first in the Ten Commandments.

      b) Those Who Disregard the Worship of Molech (20:4-5).

But the LORD does not merely address the worshiper of Molech; He also addresses those who disregard the worshiper of Molech. Verse 4. *"If the people of the land, however, should ever disregard that man when he gives any of his offspring to Molech, so as not to put him to death, then I Myself will set My face against that man and against his family, and I will cut off from among their people both him and all those who play the harlot after him, by playing the harlot after Molech."* (20:4-5).

Sin is sin. Right is right. Wrong is wrong. Those who see the sin must address the sin. The worship of Molech must not be tolerated or ignored in Israel. Why is the LORD giving this law? He knows His creation. He knows His people, Israel. He knows some of them will turn their heads and disregard the sinful worship of Molech, thinking nothing is wrong with the practice. The LORD will punish them also by cutting them off from the Nation of Israel.

   2. By Playing the Harlot with Mediums (20:6-8).

Playing the harlot with Molech is not the only concern of the LORD. He also calls out playing the harlot with mediums. Verse 6. *"As for the person who turns to mediums and to spiritists, to play the harlot after them, I will also set My face against that person and will cut him off from among his people. You shall consecrate yourselves therefore and be holy, for I am the LORD your God. You shall keep My statutes and practice them; I am the LORD who sanctifies you."* (20:6-8).

When Israel takes the Promised Land, the seeking out of mediums and spiritists is strictly forbidden in 19:31. Thirty-nine years after this law is given, with the Nation of Israel stationed in the Plains of Moab, ready to cross over to take the Promised Land, the LORD adds to this law.

> *"When you enter the land which the LORD your God gives you, you shall not learn to imitate the detestable things of those nations. ¹⁰ There shall not be found among you anyone who makes his son or his daughter pass through the fire, one who uses divination, one who practices witchcraft, or one who interprets omens, or a sorcerer, ¹¹ or one who casts a spell, or a medium, or a spiritist, or one who calls up the dead. ¹² For whoever does these things is detestable to the LORD; and because of these detestable things the LORD your*

God will drive them out before you. ¹³ You shall be blameless before the LORD *your God. ¹⁴ For those nations, which you shall dispossess, listen to those who practice witchcraft and to diviners, but as for you, the* LORD *your God has not allowed you to do so."* (Deuteronomy 18:9-14).

If the mediums or spiritists are of Canaanite blood, the nation was to destroy them totally. We know from the story of King Saul found in 1st Samuel that he visited the witch of Endor the night before his death. She knew she was not supposed to be practicing in the land. She also was deathly afraid when she realized her client was King Saul. She knew she should not have been in the land. Saul knew she was in the land. Saul knew she should not have been in the land. Both had defied the LORD's law.

B. The Relationship Sins (20:9-26).
1. The Profanity in Family Relationships (20:9).

From the idolatry sins, we come to the relationship sins with the LORD addressing the profanity in family relationships. Verses 9. *"If there is anyone who curses his father or his mother, he shall surely be put to death; he has cursed his father or his mother, his bloodguiltiness is upon him."* (20:9).

In the retelling of this law in Deuteronomy, Moses will say, *"If any man has a stubborn and rebellious son who will not obey his father or his mother, and when they chastise him, he will not even listen to them, ¹⁹ then his father and mother shall seize him, and bring him out to the elders of his city at the gateway of his hometown. ²⁰ They shall say to the elders of his city, This son of ours is stubborn and rebellious, he will not obey us, he is a glutton and a drunkard." "Then all the men of his city shall stone him to death; so you shall remove the evil from your midst, and all Israel will hear of it and fear."* (Deuteronomy 21:18-21).

Failing to honor parents is directly against the Ten Commandments.

2. The Penalty in Sexual Relationships
a) In Adultery (20:10).

Now we come to the penalty in sexual relationships. Verse 10. *"If there is a man who commits adultery with another man's wife, one who commits adultery with his friend's wife, the adulterer and the adulteress shall surely be put to death."* (20:10).

Often people use adultery as a reason for divorce; however, in the Nation of Israel, adultery was never a reason for divorce. The penalty for adultery is death.

b) In Incest (20:11-12).
(1) With a Father's Wife (20:11).

Until the giving of the laws in Leviticus, the whole world practiced incest. Looking into the book of Genesis and the 2352 years recorded in the book, you will not find one restriction from the LORD concerning incest relationships. They are new for one nation – Israel. Here they are. Verse 11. *"If there is a man who lies with his father's wife, he has uncovered his father's nakedness; both of them shall surely be put to death, their bloodguiltiness is upon them."* (20:11).

You have the same blood as your father. Your father is one flesh with his wife. Therefore, there is a blood relationship with your father's wife, and she is legally off-limits. The penalty is death.

(2) With a Son's Wife (20:12).

Then comes a relationship with a son's wife. Verse 12. *"If there is a man who lies with his daughter-in-law, both of them shall surely be put to death; they have committed incest, their bloodguiltiness is upon them."* (20:12).

You are of the same blood as your son. Your son is one flesh with his wife. Therefore, there is a blood relationship with your son's wife. She is off-limits. The penalty is death.

c) In Homosexuality (20:13).

Next, the LORD addresses homosexuality. Verse 13. *"If there is a man who lies with a male as those who lie with a woman, both of them have committed a detestable act; they shall surely be put to death. Their bloodguiltiness is upon them."* (20:13).

This unnatural union is detestable to the LORD. It is against His natural order in creation. The penalty is death.

d) In Marriage (20:14).

In marriage, a man cannot marry a woman and his mother-in-law. Verse 14. *"If there is a man who marries a woman and her mother, it is immorality; both he and they shall be burned with fire, so that there will be no immorality in your midst."* (20:14).

If you marry a woman, she becomes one flesh with you. Therefore, her mother is off-limits to you because your wife and her mother are blood kin. The penalty is death.

e) In Bestiality (20:15).

Humans cannot mate with animals in bestiality. Verse 15. *"If there is a man who lies with an animal, he shall surely be put to death; you shall also kill the animal. 'If there is a woman who approaches any animal to mate with it, you shall kill the woman and the animal; they shall surely be put to death. Their bloodguiltiness is upon them."* (20:15).

The mating of humans and animals is against the natural order of the LORD's creation. The penalty is death.

f) In Families (20:17-21).
(1) With Sisters (20:17).

In families, we come to incest with sisters. Verse 17. *"If there is a man who takes his sister, his father's daughter or his mother's daughter, so that he sees her nakedness and she sees his nakedness, it is a disgrace; and they shall be cut off in the sight of the sons of their people. He has uncovered his sister's nakedness; he bears his guilt."* (20:17).

Brothers and sisters are of the same blood from at least one parent. They are off-limits to each other. The death penalty is not included here; instead, excommunication from the Nation of Israel is given.

(2) With Menstruous Woman (20:18).

Every month, the body of a woman cleans itself. The LORD's law forbids a sexual relationship with a menstruous woman. Verse 18. *"If there is a man who lies with a menstruous woman and uncovers her nakedness, he has laid bare her flow, and she has exposed the flow of her blood; thus both of them shall be cut off from among their people."* (20:18).

The death penalty is not included here; instead, ex-communication from the Nation of Israel is given.

(3) With Aunts (20:19).

Incestuous relationships with aunts come next. Verse 19. *"You shall also not uncover the nakedness of your mother's sister or of your father's sister, for such a one has made naked his blood relative; they will bear their guilt. (20:20) 'If there is a man who lies with his uncle's wife he has uncovered his uncle's nakedness; they will bear their sin. They will die childless."* (20:19).

Neither the death penalty nor ex-communication from the nation of Israel is indicated here. The penalty is childlessness.

(4) With Sister-in-law (20:21).

Finally, the LORD forbids sexual relationships with a sister-in-law. Verse 21. *"If there is a man who takes his brother's wife, it is abhorrent; he has uncovered his brother's nakedness. They will be childless."* (20:21).

Two brothers are blood kin through their parents. Therefore, the wife of a brother is off-limits. The penalty here is childlessness.

Chapter 20

When we study the book of Deuteronomy, the LORD will address these laws again.

3. The Purpose in Godly Relationships (20:26).
a) To Secure Israel in the Land (20:22-23).
(1) By Following the LORD's Ways (20:22).

From the profanity in family relationships and the penalty in sexual relationships, we come to the purpose of Godly relationships. It is to secure Israel in the land first by following the LORD's way. Verse 22. *"You are therefore to keep all My statutes and all My ordinances and do them, so that the land to which I am bringing you to live will not spew you out."* (20:22).

In chapter 18, we discovered that the Canaanite land was being given to the Nation of Israel because the Canaanites were guilty of doing everything the LORD forbids the Jews to do when they enter the Promised Land. The Canaanites are being spewed out of the land, and if the Israelites break the LORD's law, they will also be spewed out of the land. Here we see that again in the next verse.

(2) By Rejecting the Canaanite's Ways (20:23).

The LORD will secure Israel in the land by rejecting the Canaanite's way. Verse 23. *"Moreover, you shall not follow the customs of the nation which I will drive out before you, for they did all these things, and therefore I have abhorred them."* (20:23).

To fulfill this requirement, the Canaanites must be destroyed. Israel will fail to do so. Long before, the LORD abhorred the Canaanites. He patiently waited until the Nation of Israel was ready to take the land.

b) To Separate Israel in the Land (20:24-25).
(1) By Differentiating Between Israel and Others (20:24).

Having a Godly relationship with the LORD would secure Israel in the land, but it will also separate Israel in the land by differentiating between Israel and others. Verse 24. *"Hence I have said to you, "You are to possess their land, and I Myself will give it to you to possess it, a land flowing with milk and honey." I am the LORD your God, who has separated you from the peoples."* (20:24).

No other nation has these restrictions. Israel is to be a holy nation, separated and different from all the nations.

(2) By Distinguishing Between Clean and Unclean (20:25).

As a unique nation, Israel will do something no other nation will do by distinguishing between the clean and unclean. Verse 25. *'You are therefore to make a distinction between the clean animal and the unclean, and between the unclean bird and the clean; and you shall not make yourselves detestable by animal or by bird or by anything that creeps on the ground, which I have separated for you as unclean.* (20:25).

All the people of the world did not distinguish between clean and unclean animals for food. Every animal was food. The LORD had declared that to be so when Noah departed with his family from the Ark. But for this new nation, there would be a difference between the clean and unclean foods.

c) To Sanctify Israel in the Land (20:26).

First, we saw the purpose of a Godly relationship with the LORD to secure Israel in the land, then to separate Israel in the land, and now to sanctify Israel in the Land. Verse 26. *"Thus you are to be holy to Me, for I the LORD am holy; and I have set you apart from the peoples to be Mine."* (20:26).

The Nation of Israel belongs to the LORD. It is His holy nation. It is His royal priesthood. It is the nation Peter will write two letters to in the New Testament who have trusted in the LORD. But by then, the nation will be in total rebellion against the LORD.

C. The Mediums Sin (20:27).

We looked at the idolatry sins, then the relationship sins, and finally, we come to the medium sins in this section.

Chapter 20

Verse 27. *"Now a man or a woman who is a medium or a spiritist shall surely be put to death. They shall be stoned with stones, their bloodguiltiness is upon them."* (20:27).

The penalty for this occultic activity is death.

As we turn to chapter 21, the LORD will specifically address the law for the life of a priest.

Chapter 21

XV. The Law for the Life of a Priest (21:1-22:14).
  A. To Keep the Priestly Line Holy (21:1-8).
    1. From Defiling Himself by Touching the Dead (21:1).

The LORD turns to address the law for the life of a priest. The purpose of this set of laws is to keep the priestly line holy from birth to death. Every man in the priestly line is to carefully keep from defiling himself by touching the dead. Verse 21. *"Then the LORD said to Moses, "Speak to the priests, the sons of Aaron, and say to them: 'No one shall defile himself for a dead person among his people, except for his relatives who are nearest to him, his mother and his father and his son and his daughter and his brother, also for his virgin sister, who is near to him because she has had no husband; for her he may defile himself."* (21:1).

From the birth to death of aa man in Aaron's priestly line, the man may touch only one category of people who die – his own personal biological blood family unit. If he has married daughters, those daughters are off-limits in the law; he cannot touch them. If they are not married, then he can touch them. Touching the dead defiles the priests and forfeits his right to serve as a priest. In the story of Benaiah, the chief of David's bodyguard, we find that he was the son of the high priest. It meant that Benaiah was in line to serve as a priest beginning at the age of twenty-five and serving for twenty-five years until he turned fifty when he was required to retire. However, the Scripture in 2nd Samuel and 1st Chronicles details the reason Benaiah could not serve as a priest and possibly become the high priest. In his teenage years, Benaiah killed two Moabite men, an Egyptian man, and a lion. His killing of these men and the lion forfeited forever his place to serve as a priest. Touching the dead body of a married daughter would also forfeit the right to be a priest. The only exception for the priest was the dead bodies of his immediate blood family kin.

   2. **From Defiling Himself by the Blood Relationships (21:4).**

In the same light as defiling himself from touching the dead, the priest must carefully keep himself from defiling himself by the blood relationships. Verse 4. *"He shall not defile himself as a relative by marriage among his people, and so profane himself."* (21:4).

We could have included this verse with verse 3, but we needed to discover the critical thought in this passage. The priest *"...shall not defile himself as a relative by marriage among his people...."* The critical thought is *"marriage."* All priests in Aaron's family line are related by marriage. In verses 1-3, a brother, sister, uncle, and aunt were not mentioned because they are not part of a priest's immediate blood family. The dead bodies of the brothers, sisters, uncles, and aunts are off-limits and cannot be touched. So, when priestly brothers leave the family by taking a wife in marriage, the brothers with their own families and wives are off-limits.

   3. **From Defiling Himself by Altering the Flesh (21:5).**

The priest must keep from defiling himself by altering the flesh. Verse 5. *"They shall not make any baldness on their heads, nor shave off the edges of their beards, nor make any cuts in their flesh."* (21:5).

All religions worshiped in all the world at that time required the head's shaving to expose either the whole head or portions of the head. One example would be the baldness of a completely shaved head; another example is the shaving of the head's sides to produce a mohawk. The head of the LORD's priest were to be left to grow naturally. If the head became bald, it was to do so on its own. Cutting the body of the priest was forbidden too. In other religions, tattooing the body with cut designs was common. Not so for the LORD's priests.

4. From Defiling Himself by Profaning the LORD (21:6).

The priest must keep from defiling himself by profaning the LORD. Verse 6. *"They shall be holy to their God and not profane the name of their God, for they present the offerings by fire to the LORD, the food of their God; so they shall be holy."* (21:6).

The Hebrew word for *profane* is *halal*. It means to *open, give access, make common*. The important word in this verse is at the beginning of the sentence and at the end – holy. Holy things were not to become common things. The offerings were holy. The LORD does not allow common people to present His holy offering to Him. Priests were to be holy – not common. If priests begin to do common things, he is no longer holy. He has profaned his office.

5. From Defiling Himself by Women Relationships (21:7).

a) With the Harlot (21:7a).

A priest must keep from defiling himself by women relationships. First, we see the harlot. Verse 7a. *"They shall not take a woman who is profaned by harlotry..."* (21:7a).

Any relationship, of any kind, with a prostitute, was strictly forbidden for a priest.

b) With the Divorced Woman (21:7b).

Second, we see the divorced woman. Verse 7b. *"...nor shall they take a woman divorced from her husband; for he is holy to his God."* (21:7b).

In the Old Testament, when a man decided to divorce a wife, her letter of divorce was proof that she was totally innocent in the divorce and did nothing wrong. That is the reason when Jesus was asked why Moses allowed the divorce, Jesus answered, *"Because of your hardness of heart Moses permitted you to divorce your wives; but from the beginning it has been this way."* (Matthew 19:7-8). In other words, the hearts of the man had shrunk up and become hard toward his wife. But, if the woman was guilty of adultery, divorce was not an option, the death penalty was the only option for the woman. For that reason, when Jesus says, *"It was said, 'Whoever sends his wife away, let him give her a certificate of divorce'"* (Matthew 5:31). Continuing, Jesus says, *"... but I say to you that everyone who divorces his wife, except for the reason of adultery, makes her commit adultery; and whoever marries a divorced woman commits adultery."* (Matthew 5:32). Jesus's word "except" is not a reason for divorce; it explains why adultery is not a reason for divorce. When a woman commits adultery, the penalty is death (20:10). When a certificate of divorce is given, the woman is set free from the man. However, when she marries, she commits adultery against her first husband, who divorced her. Her divorced husband set the path for her sin to possibly occur. Moreover, if a priest married a divorced woman, he would be participating in the act of adultery.

> 6. From Defiling Himself by His Consecration (21:8).

The priest must keep from defiling himself by His consecration. Verse 8. *"You shall consecrate him, therefore, for he offers the food of your God; he shall be holy to you; for I the LORD, who sanctifies you, am holy."* (21:8).

The priest must be holy as the LORD is holy. He is consecrated to the LORD to serve in the Tabernacle complex in the presence of the LORD. Once consecrated, a priest is no longer a common person among the nation.

> B. To Keep the Priestly Family Holy (21:9).

The law for the life of a priest is to keep the priestly line holy and to keep the priestly family holy. Verse 9. *"Also the daughter of any priest, if she profanes herself by harlotry, she profanes her father; she shall be burned with fire."* (21:9).

Because of the bloodline to her father serving as a priest, if she becomes a prostitute, she brings the penalty of death by fire upon herself. But she also profanes her priestly father. He is not put to death, but she has brought dishonor to him by breaking one of the Ten Commandments.

C. To Keep the Highest Priest Holy (21:10-15).
1. His Garments (21:10).

The law for the life of a priest is to keep the priestly line holy, to keep the priestly family holy, and to keep the highest priest holy. First, we see his garments. Verse 10. *"The priest who is the highest among his brothers, on whose head the anointing oil has been poured and who has been consecrated to wear the garments, shall not uncover his head nor tear his clothes;"* (21:10).

The guidelines for the high priest were more stringent than that of all the others. His head was always to be covered, and he was never to tear his clothes. What does this mean? In the high priest's position, few reasons can be given for a priest to think of uncovering his head or tearing his clothes. What is the reason? The death of a loved one. The common practice among men in almost all cultures of the world at the time of a loved one's death is to shave the head and tear the clothing. The high priest is forbidden from shaving or uncovering his head or tearing his dress or the priestly garments when the time of mourning occurs.

2. His Actions (21:11).

Second, we see his actions in his time of mourning. *"...nor shall he approach any dead person, nor defile himself even for his father or his mother; nor shall he go out of the sanctuary nor profane the sanctuary of his God, for the consecration of the anointing oil of his God is on him; I am the LORD."* (21:11).

During the time of the context that this book was given to Moses, Aaron's sons died for offering strange fire on the Altar of Incense on the final day of their ordination in front of Aaron and Moses. If you will remember, Moses told Aaron, the high priest, not to flinch. Relatives would carry the sons out of the Tabernacle and bury them (10:1-7). The high priest was not to carry out the duties of the ordinary people. He was not an ordinary person. His job was to serve the LORD fully.

- 3. His Wife (21:13-15).
  - a) Who He Can Take for a Wife (21:13).

Fourth, we see his wife and who he can take for a wife. Verse 13. *"He shall take a wife in her virginity."* (21:13).

The high priest must be married to a virgin woman.

- b) Who He Cannot Take for a Wife (21:14-15).

Now we come to the women who he cannot take for a wife. Verse 14. *"A widow, or a divorced woman, or one who is profaned by harlotry, these he may not take; but rather he is to marry a virgin of his own people so that he will not profane his offspring among his people; for I am the LORD who sanctifies him."* (21:14-15).

Widows are obviously not virgins. Divorced women are not virgins. Prostitutes are not virgins. By detailing these instructions, the LORD clarifies that the priest must marry a virgin if he wants to be the high priest someday. If his wife were not a virgin, he would have forfeited the right to take office when the opportunity came to be the high priest.

- D. To Keep the Priesthood Holy (21:16-24).
  - 1. The Man with a Physical Defect Cannot Offer the LORD's Food (21:16-21).

The law for the life of a priest is to keep the priestly line holy, to keep the priestly family holy, to keep the highest priest holy, and to keep the priesthood holy. First, we come to the man with a physical defect who cannot offer the

LORD's food. Verse 16. *"Then the LORD spoke to Moses, saying, 'Speak to Aaron, saying, 'No man of your offspring throughout their generations who has a defect shall approach to offer the food of his God. For no one who has a defect shall approach: a blind man, or a lame man, or he who has a disfigured face, or any deformed limb, or a man who has a broken foot or broken hand, or a hunchback or a dwarf, or one who has a defect in his eye or eczema or scabs or crushed testicles. 'No man among the descendants of Aaron the priest who has a defect is to come near to offer the LORD'S offerings by fire; since he has a defect, he shall not come near to offer the food of his God."* (21:16-21).

The priest begins training for the work of the priesthood at the age of twenty-five. At the age of thirty, he can start work as a priest. Sadly, between birth and age twenty-five, many things can happen. Birth defects occur that cause deformities. Accidents happen that cause deformities. Diseases happen that cause deformities. The list in this passage disqualifies a man in Aaron's priestly line from serving as a priest. Factually, this list disqualifies a man from entering the training as a priest, and if any of the accidents or deceases occur during the training, the person will be removed from the school.

2. The Man with a Physical Defect Can Eat the LORD's Food (21:24).

Second, we come to the man with a physical defect who can eat the LORD's food. Verse 24. *"He may eat the food of his God, both of the most holy and of the holy, only he shall not go in to the veil or come near the altar because he has a defect, so that he will not profane My sanctuaries. For I am the LORD who sanctifies them.'" So Moses spoke to Aaron and to his sons and to all the sons of Israel."* (21:24).

A man of the priestly line, forbidden from serving as a priest because of a birth defect, accident, or disease, still remains a part of the priestly family, and the provisions for meals still come in the holy areas of the Tabernacle complex as with the rest of his extended priestly family. Yet, he is never to enter the Tabernacle or approach the Altar of Incense next to the Veil. That is off-limits. However, for his offerings, he would still be required to bring them to the priests serving the LORD at the Tent of Meeting doorway as with all the people of the Nation of Israel.

Chapter 22

E. To Keep the Gifts of Israel Holy (22:1-14).
1. The Purpose of the Holy Gifts (22:1-2).

The law for the life of a priest is to keep the priestly line holy, to keep the priestly family holy, to keep the highest priest holy, to keep the priesthood holy, and to keep the gifts of Israel holy. First, we look at the purpose of the holy gifts. Chapter 22, verse 1. *"Then the LORD spoke to Moses, saying, Tell Aaron and his sons to be careful with the holy gifts of the sons of Israel, which they dedicate to Me, so as not to profane My holy name; I am the LORD."* (22:1-2).

Inside the outer curtain of the Tabernacle complex, everything must be kept holy for the LORD. Every gift that passes through the curtain must be holy. The gifts are the offerings that we studied in chapters 1 through 7 of this book. In those chapters, the LORD made clear that the offerings had to be without blemish.

2. The Prohibited of the Holy Gifts
    a) The Unclean Among the Sons of Israel (22:3).

Second, we look at the prohibited of the holy gifts. Specifically, this is a reference to the unclean among the sons of Israel who bring the gifts. Verse 3. *"Say to them, 'If any man among all your descendants throughout your generations approaches the holy gifts which the sons of Israel dedicate to the LORD, while he has an uncleanness, that person shall be cut off from before Me; I am the LORD."* (22:3).

The gifts for the offering may have been without blemish, but the giver could not come through the curtain if he were blemished in any way. The unclean person could not bring a clean gift to the LORD. Uncleanness was not allowed inside the Tabernacle complex.

b) The Unclean Among the Priests of Israel (22:9).

Third, we look at the unclean among the priests of Israel. Verse 9. *"No man of the descendants of Aaron, who is a leper or who has a discharge, may eat of the holy gifts until he is clean. And if one touches anything made unclean by a corpse or if a man has a seminal emission, or if a man touches any teeming things by which he is made unclean, or any man by whom he is made unclean, whatever his uncleanness; a person who touches any such shall be unclean until evening, and shall not eat of the holy gifts unless he has bathed his body in water. But when the sun sets, he will be clean, and afterward he shall eat of the holy gifts, for it is his food. He shall not eat an animal which dies or is torn by beasts, becoming unclean by it; I am the LORD. 'They shall therefore keep My charge, so that they will not bear sin because of it and die thereby because they profane it; I am the LORD who sanctifies them."* (22:9).

One job of the priest is to determine those who are clean and unclean. Therefore, he is among those who are unclean every day, and that includes the diagnosis of the leper. In order to eat his meals in the Tabernacle complex, if he has been in contact with any unclean and become unclean, he must bathe and wait until evening to be clean and then eat. The Tabernacle complex operated twenty-four hours a day. Priests were always on duty. The meat was constantly being cooked. The process to keep the gifts of the offerings that became the priests' food was in place and had to be followed.

c) The Unclean Among the Layman of Israel
(1) The Sojourner or Employed Cannot Eat the Holy Gifts (22:10).

Fourth, we look at the unclean among the layman of Israel. Specifically, we look at the sojourner or employed who cannot eat the holy gifts. Verse 10. *"No layman, however, is to eat the holy gift; a sojourner with the priest or a hired man shall not eat of the holy gift."* (22:10).

Simply, the gifts of the offerings to the LORD were the food for the priests. People passing through or people hired to work were not to eat the holy gifts' meat because they are considered unclean.

(2) The Purchased Slave Can Eat the Holy Gifts (22:11).

However, if the priest purchased a slave, the purchased slave can eat the holy gifts. Verse 11. *"But if a priest buys a slave as his property with his money, that one may eat of it, and those who are born in his house may eat of his food."* (22:11).

Here is the reason why. The priest has purchased the slave out of slavery and brought him or her to his family. Within the process, the priest will free this purchased slave one day. Once an Israelite bought a slave, the slave could not be sold; he had to be freed. We covered this topic in the commentary of 19:20-22 of this book. Therefore, the purchased slave was part of the priest's family and could eat the Tabernacle food.

d) The Married Daughter to a Layman Cannot Eat the Holy Gifts (22:12).

Being part of a priestly family did not mean that a person could always eat the Tabernacle food. The married daughter to a layman cannot eat the holy gifts. Verse 12. *"If a priest's daughter is married to a layman, she shall not eat of the offering of the gifts."* (22:12).

Why? The priestly family's daughter became part of another tribe when she married someone not of the priestly line. She changed families. Only the priestly line could eat the Tabernacle meat.

e) The Daughter who Returns to the Family Can Eat the Holy Gifts (22:13).

A daughter is always a daughter. If the daughter who married a layman becomes divorced or widowed, she can return to her biological family in the priestly line. Verse 13. *"But if a priest's daughter becomes a widow or divorced, and has no child and returns to her father's house as in her youth, she shall eat of her father's food; but no layman shall eat of it."* (22:13).

The key in this instruction is the words *"no child."* If there is a child, then the daughter with the child will stay in the tribe with whom she married to be cared for by some kinsman-redeemer. But if no child was born, the daughter may choose to return to her father's priestly family and eat meals in the Tabernacle complex.

3. The Punishment of the Holy Gifts (22:14).

From the purpose of the holy gifts to the prohibited of the holy gifts, we come to the punishment of the holy gifts. Verse 14. *"But if a man eats a holy gift unintentionally, then he shall add to it a fifth of it and shall give the holy gift to the priest. They shall not profane the holy gifts of the sons of Israel which they offer to the LORD, and so cause them to bear punishment for guilt by eating their holy gifts; for I am the LORD who sanctifies them."* (22:14).

How could a layman unintentionally eat a holy gift to the LORD? In the offering explained in chapter 3, we learned that certain portions of the meat from the offering could be eaten by any priest or priestly family members in the Tabernacle complex. Still, certain cuts of the meat were given to the priest making the offering to the LORD. That meat could be taken to that priest's home outside the Tabernacle complex to be explicitly eaten by his family. If that meat was eaten by a layman, not knowing that it was part of the holy gifts that had been presented to the LORD, it was eaten unintentionally and fell under this law. All meals of the priestly families prepared in the home were from the animals and grains brought to the complex as tithes. Out of the tithes, a tenth was selected from the best of the best to be part of the required daily offerings, and the remaining ninety percent of the tithes were distributed to the priestly families to supply their needs. Those food supplies could be shared with anyone needing a meal. But as for the offerings required in the first seven chapters of this book, they were holy gifts that were only to be eaten by the priests and their families. At home, a restricted meal could accidentally be eaten by a layman. In that case, the layman was to present an offering at the Tabernacle complex equal to what he had eaten with an additional one-fifth. For example, if he had eaten a pound of holy meat, he would need to offer a pound and a fifth of meat to the LORD.

XVI. The Law of the Animal Offerings (22:17-33).
  A. The Offering Must Be without Defect (22:17-25).
    1. The Burnt Offering (22:17-20).

From the law of the life of a priest, we come to the law of the animal offerings that the priest must oversee. The offerings must be without defect in every case. The priest must make sure they are without blemish. First, we see the burnt offering. Verse 17. *"Then the LORD spoke to Moses, saying, Speak to Aaron and to his sons and to all the sons of Israel and say to them, 'Any man of the house of Israel or of the aliens in Israel who presents his offering, whether it is any of their votive or any of their freewill offerings, which they present to the LORD for a burnt offering— for you to be accepted—it must be a male without defect from the cattle, the sheep, or the goats. 'Whatever has a defect, you shall not offer, for it will not be accepted for you."* (22:17-20).

Burnt offerings were required, as presented in chapter 1. However, vow and freewill offerings were also burnt offerings as part of a *sacrifice of peace offering*, as explained in chapter 7. The two offerings were not required. The people gave them because of a promise they wanted to make to the LORD or in appreciation to the LORD.

2. The Sacrifice of Peace Offering (22:21-25).

Second, we come to the sacrifice of peace offering. Verse 21. *"When a man offers a sacrifice of peace offerings to the LORD to fulfill a special vow or for a freewill offering, of the herd or of the flock, it must be perfect to be accepted; there shall be no defect in it. Those that are blind or fractured or maimed or having a running sore or eczema or scabs, you shall not offer to the LORD, nor make of them an offering by fire on the altar to the LORD. In respect to an ox or a lamb which has an overgrown or stunted member, you may present it for a freewill offering, but for a vow it will not be accepted. Also anything with its testicles bruised or crushed or torn or cut, you shall not offer to the LORD, or sacrifice in your land, nor shall you accept any such from the hand of a foreigner for offering as the food of your God; for their corruption is in them, they have a defect, they shall not be accepted for you."* (22:21-25).

And again, as before, the LORD is making sure the priests and the people understand that the offerings must be without blemishes of any kind.

B. The Offering Must Meet Requirements (22:27-33).
1. The Age of the Animal (22:27).

The offerings must meet requirements to be accepted by the LORD. First, we come to the age of the animal. Verse 27. *"Then the LORD spoke to Moses, saying, When an ox or a sheep or a goat is born, it shall remain seven days with its mother, and from the eighth day on it shall be accepted as a sacrifice of an offering by fire to the LORD."* (22:27).

No animal offering is to be presented before the age of eight days. On the eighth day, the animal can be brought to the Tabernacle as an offering.

2. The Restriction of the Animal (22:28).

Second, the restriction of the animal being offered. Verse 28. *"But, whether it is an ox or a sheep, you shall not kill both it and its young in one day."* (22:28).

A mother ox or sheep cannot be sacrificed on the same day as its offspring.

3. The Presentation of the Animal (22:29).

Third, the presentation of the animal had a purpose. Verse 29. *"When you sacrifice a sacrifice of thanksgiving to the LORD, you shall sacrifice it so that you may be accepted."* (22:29).

Hidden in this verse is the purpose of the sacrifice. It says *"that you may be accepted."* When a *sacrifice of thanksgiving* is presented, it is a free will or vow offering presented totally upon the giver's willingness. It is the same as the *sacrifice of peace offering*. It is not a required offering. However, the LORD did lay the requirements for this offering's presentation in chapters 3 and 7. What is not said here but is within the intent of the passage is the heart of the one bringing the offering. The gift must be given for the right reason, in the right way, and with the right heart. Only with those three requirements met would the LORD, Who sees the heart and mind of man, accept the man and his offering.

4. The Eating of the Animal (22:33).

In the requirements for the animal offerings, we see the age of the animal, the restriction of the animal, the presentation of the animal, and lastly, we come to the eating of the animal. Verse 30. *"It shall be eaten on the same day, you shall leave none of it until morning; I am the LORD. So you shall keep My commandments, and do them; I am the LORD. You shall not profane My holy name, but I will be sanctified among the sons of Israel; I am the LORD who sanctifies you, who brought you out from the land of Egypt, to be your God; I am the LORD."* (22:33).

Chapter 22

Overseeing the offerings presented to the LORD was a detailed job for the priests. From the animals' arrival to the eating of the animals, everything done in the process had to be precise and perfect. That included the consumption of the meat from the offering gifted to the priestly families by the LORD. It could be eaten that day or through that night, but it could not be eaten when morning broke. The meat had to be consumed before the break of the next day.

Chapter 23

Now we come to the law of the appointed times.

XVII. The Law of the Appointed Times and Seasons (23:1-44).
A. The Sabbath Day (23:1-4).

The LORD addresses the law of the appointed times. He begins with the sabbath day. Chapter 23, verse 1. *"The LORD spoke again to Moses, saying, Speak to the sons of Israel and say to them, 'The LORD'S appointed times which you shall proclaim as holy convocations—My appointed times are these: For six days work may be done, but on the seventh day there is a sabbath of complete rest, a holy convocation. You shall not do any work; it is a sabbath to the LORD in all your dwellings. These are the appointed times of the LORD, holy convocations which you shall proclaim at the times appointed for them."* (23:1-4).

What is a *"holy convocation?"* The term appears exclusively in Exodus, Leviticus, and Numbers. We understand that the word *holy* means *sacred*. The word *convocation* means *a meeting of people who have been summoned*. Sometime during each of the appointed times, the LORD summoned His people to a sacred gathering. On the seventh day of every week, the LORD summons His people to rest entirely from their work of the other six days as an assembly.

B. The Passover (23:5).

Each year the LORD calls for the remembrance of the Passover. Verse 5. *"In the first month, on the fourteenth day of the month at twilight is the LORD'S Passover."* (23:5).

The New American Standard Bible that we are using uses the word *"twilight."* It means the light that we see in the thirty minutes before the sun rises or the thirty minutes after the sun has set. It is an incorrect translation because when the sun sets on the Jewish calendar, the new day begins, and the calendar date changes. It should say, as Wycliff's translation, *"in the evening."* However, the *evening* for the Jews in the eastern world is equal to our *afternoon*. The *day* on the Hebrew calendar begins with the setting of the sun. Night follows as the start of the day. When the sun rises, it is *morning*. When the sun reached its peak at high noon and begins to descend, the *evening* starts. For those of us who live in the western world, we call the *evening, afternoon*.

The original meal of the Passover was prepared through the morning and eaten late in the afternoon. When darkness came after sunset, the day changed, the families waited, behind closed doors, for the Passover to occur.

This law in Leviticus was given before the first anniversary of the Passover came on the calendar. It will soon be celebrated.

C. The Feast of Unleavened Bread (23:4-8).

The LORD gives the instruction for the Feast of Unleavened Bread. Verse 4. *"Then on the fifteenth day of the same month there is the Feast of Unleavened Bread to the LORD; for seven days you shall eat unleavened bread. On the first day you shall have a holy convocation; you shall not do any laborious work. 'But for seven days you shall present an offering by fire to the LORD. On the seventh day is a holy convocation; you shall not do any laborious work."* (23:4-8).

The Passover meal occurred in the afternoon on the fourteenth of the first month. The fifteenth of the month began with the setting of the sun on the fourteenth. The Passover deaths occurred, Pharaoh called for Moses, Moses told the people to spread the word to assemble to depart Egypt. The gathering occurred, and as the sun was about to set on the fifteenth of the month, the Nation of Israel took their first step toward freedom from Egypt under the light of a full moon. Within a few minutes of starting the march out of Egypt, the day turned to the sixteen of the month.

Thirty-nine years after this instruction is given, it will be changed for the Passover celebration when the Nation of Israel enters the Promised Land. We find that in the book of Deuteronomy.

> *"... you shall sacrifice the Passover in the evening at sunset, <u>at the time that you came out of Egypt</u>. ⁷ You shall cook and eat it in the place which the LORD your God chooses. In the morning you are to return to your tents. ⁸ Six days you shall eat unleavened bread, and on the seventh day there shall be a solemn assembly to the LORD your God; you shall do no work on it."* (16:1-8).

In Leviticus, the Passover meal began at the same time as it did in Egypt, in the *evening* before sunset. The camp departed Egypt at sunset on the fifteenth of the month. Then, seven days of the Feast of Unleavened Bread took place. On the seventh day, a holy convocation occurred. But entering the Promised Land, with the instruction in Deuteronomy, the Passover meal was moved to the time of the departure from Egypt on the fifteenth with six days for the Feast of Unleavened Bread followed by a holy convocation on the seventh day. In either formula, the seventh-day assembly occurred on the same day.

D. The First Fruits (23:9-14).

The LORD gives the instruction for the First Fruits offering. Verse 9. *"Then the LORD spoke to Moses, saying, Speak to the sons of Israel and say to them, 'When you enter the land which I am going to give to you and reap its harvest, then you shall bring in the sheaf of the first fruits of your harvest to the priest. He shall wave the sheaf before the LORD for you to be accepted; on the day after the sabbath the priest shall wave it. Now on the day when you wave the sheaf, you shall offer a male lamb one year old without defect for a burnt offering to the LORD. Its grain offering shall then be two-tenths of an ephah of fine flour mixed with oil, an offering by fire to the LORD for a soothing aroma, with its drink offering, a fourth of a hin of wine. 'Until this same day, until you have brought in the offering of your God, you shall eat neither bread nor roasted grain nor new growth. It is to be a perpetual statute throughout your generations in all your dwelling places."* (23:9-14).

The celebration of First Fruits occurs only on one day of the week, *"the day after the sabbath."* Saturday is the sabbath, and Sunday is the first day of the week, the day after the sabbath. The names Saturday and Sunday are not found in the Scripture because those were not the name of the days used in that time in history. The days were named by numbers, the first equals our Sunday, the seventh equals our Saturday.

The *sheaf* of grain was not a single stalk; neither was it a bushel basket. It is the number of stalks of grain that a man can carry in the grasp of one hand. It was brought to the Tabernacle complex on the first day of the week at harvest time. The priest offered the sheaf in a wave offering and also processed the lamb burnt offering and the grain and drink offering. The harvested of the grain began on Sunday and could not be used for food until the offering occurred.

Also, notice that there is no set calendar day for the harvest to begin and the first fruit celebration to occur except that the sheaf was brought the on Sunday to the priests when the harvest was ripe. The agrees with Leviticus 16:9, *"You shall count seven weeks for yourself; you shall begin to count seven weeks from the time you begin to put the sickle to the standing grain."* Except in this direction for the appointed times in chapter 23, the countdown begins on Sunday. Then the two are on the same day.

E. The Day of Pentecost (23:15).

The countdown begins on the day of First Fruits to set a date for Pentecost. Verse 15. *"You shall also count for yourselves from the day after the sabbath, from the day when you brought in the sheaf of the wave offering; there shall be seven complete sabbaths."* (23:15).

The Day of Pentecost occurs on the fiftieth day after First Fruits. Seven sabbath days must pass before Pentecost is celebrated on the Sunday following the seventh sabbath. Notice that, like the day of First Fruits, the LORD did not tie Pentecost to a specific calendar day like the Passover and Feast of Unleavened Bread.

As we discover the offerings for the Day of Pentecost, it is essential to know that the priests present the offerings on this day from the best of the best of the tithes already at the Tabernacle complex. This offering is not for every family to bring to the Tabernacle. If that occurred, the sheer volume of animals coming to the Tabernacle complex would have overrun the facility. On the year this instruction was given, only three priests worked the twenty-four-hour shift at the Tabernacle complex, Aaron and his two sons. If 600,000 men of Israel brought a Pentecost offering to the Tabernacle for the three priests to offer, only a few could have been processed that day.

1. **The Offering for Pentecost (23:16-22)**
    a) The Grain (23:16-17)

For the offering for Pentecost, a grain offering is required. Verse 16. *"You shall count fifty days to the day after the seventh sabbath; then you shall present a new grain offering to the LORD. 'You shall bring in from your dwelling places two loaves of bread for a wave offering, made of two-tenths of an ephah; they shall be of a fine flour, baked with leaven as first fruits to the LORD."* (23:16-17).

The verse starts with, *"You shall count fifty days to the day after the seventh sabbath."* It seems to imply that the nation will wait until seven sabbaths pass and then begin to count fifty days until Pentecost. This is not the case nor the meaning. This verse means that from the waving of the sheaf on the first day of the harvest on the first day of the week, forty-nine days are to pass. The forty-ninth day will end on a sabbath. The following day is the fiftieth day, a Sunday, the day of Pentecost.

First, on the fiftieth day, a grain offering is required as a wave offering. It is two loaves of bread made with the ingredients listed in verse 17.

b) The Burnt and Drink (23:18).

With the bread offering, ten animals were offered as a burnt offering. Verse 18. *"Along with the bread you shall present seven one year old male lambs without defect, and a bull of the herd and two rams; they are to be a burnt offering to the LORD, with their grain offering and their drink offerings, an offering by fire of a soothing aroma to the LORD."* (23:18).

Second, the priest offers seven lambs without defect. The second is a bull. The third is two rams. The burnt offering is prescribed in chapter 1. Included with this offering is the drink offering. The drink offering amount is not mentioned here, but if it was the same as with the first fruit offering in verse 13 of this chapter, the drink offering was a fourth of a hin of wine.

c) The Sacrifice of Peace (23:20).

Third, for the sacrifice of peace offering on the Day of Pentecost, three animals are sacrificed. Verse 20. *"You shall also offer one male goat for a sin offering and two male lambs one year old for a sacrifice of peace offerings. The priest shall then wave them with the bread of the first fruits for a wave offering with two lambs before the LORD; they are to be holy to the LORD for the priest."* (23:20).

One male goat and two male lambs are offered for this Sacrifice of Peace Offering. The order of this ceremony was given in chapter 3.

We must not miss an important detail in this verse. The LORD says, *"The priest shall then wave them with the bread of the first fruits for a wave offering."* On the Sunday of First Fruits, each farmer brought a sheaf, a handful of stalks of grain, to the Tabernacle complex. These sheaves were waved above the Brazen Altar but not placed on the Altar. After the sheaves were waved, they were then stored to make bread for the priests. That is where the grain for the bread of the wave offerings came. The grain came from the First Fruit offerings.

d) The Rest (23:21).

The Day of Pentecost included rest from all labor on that day as well as a holy convocation. Verse 21. *"On this same day you shall make a proclamation as well; you are to have a holy convocation. You shall do no laborious work. It is to be a perpetual statute in all your dwelling places throughout your generations."* (23:21).

Some English commentaries call the Day of Pentecost a sabbath. It is as a day of rest, but it is not the seventh day of the week. The Day of Pentecost occurs on the first day of the week – Sunday. The reason for calling this a sabbath is because of the words *"You shall do no laborious work."* However, the Hebrew word for sabbath is not found in this verse. Therefore, on Sunday, the Day of Pentecost, a service was held, and anyone except the priest did no regular work.

Chapter 23

e) The Gift (23:22).

The Day of Pentecost is tied to the spring harvest of the grain. It is connected to the season, not a calendar day. Concluding the instruction for the harvest and Pentecost, the requires the gift for the needy. Verse 22. *"When you reap the harvest of your land, moreover, you shall not reap to the very corners of your field nor gather the gleaning of your harvest; you are to leave them for the needy and the alien. I am the LORD your God."* (23:22).

Naturally, roads or paths surrounded the fields. At each of the four corners of each field, the LORD instructed the owners to leave the corners for the poor and needy and those traveling through the country with no home of their own in the land.

F. The Day of the New Year (23:23-25).

Returning to a day on the calendar, the LORD gives instructions for the day of the New Year. Verse 23. *"Again the LORD spoke to Moses, saying, Speak to the sons of Israel, saying, 'In the seventh month on the first of the month you shall have a rest, a reminder by blowing of trumpets, a holy convocation. 'You shall not do any laborious work, but you shall present an offering by fire to the LORD."* (23:23-25).

The first day of the seventh month is the day of the civil New Year for the Jews. It is the first month on the Egyptian calendar and many other nations worldwide. Earlier in the year, the laws of this book were given to Moses, the LORD changed the Jewish calendar. The Jews left Egypt on the fifteenth of the seventh month of the Egyptian calendar. The LORD made the seventh month of the Egyptian calendar the first month on the Jewish religious calendar. However, the Jew celebrate a new year on the religious calendar and the new year on the civil calendar. This day, in this verse, is the celebration of the civil calendar. In

Jewish life, the day is called Rosh Hashanah, which means *the head of the year.* Two more special events will occur in this seventh month.

The passage uses the word *rest,* and it is the Hebrew word *sabbath.* The day is not a sabbath day, meaning *the seventh day of the week;* it is a day of rest in the sense of suspending *"any laborious work.* The priest is required to present an offering on that day as a holy convocation. But the kind of offering is not specified here.

G. The Day of Atonement (23:26-28).

The second special event of the seventh month is the Day of Atonement. Verse 26. *"The LORD spoke to Moses, saying, On exactly the tenth day of this seventh month is the day of atonement; it shall be a holy convocation for you, and you shall humble your souls and present an offering by fire to the LORD. "You shall not do any work on this same day, for it is a day of atonement, to make atonement on your behalf before the LORD your God.* (23:26-28).

What is special about the Day of Atonement? You may have heard it called Yom Kippur. It is a day on which Israel cleansed the sanctuary of impurity and dealt with their sin through blood rituals and sending a goat into the wilderness.

The full order from the LORD concerning the activities was given in detail in chapter 16 for the Day of Atonement. In that chapter, we discovered that the LORD put a restriction in place limiting the entrance into the Holy of Holies to one day a year, and only by the High Priest. It was the day when the priest offered offerings for his sins, his family's sins, and the sins of the nation. The bull of the sin offering is presented first. Second, a goat for a sin offering is presented. Finally, a goat is loosed into the wild as a scapegoat.

1. The Restriction (23:29-32).
    a) The Unfaithful (23:29-31).

Here in chapter 23, the LORD places restrictions on the events of the Day of Atonement. First, the LORD addresses the unfaithful. Verse 29. *"If there is any person who will not humble himself on this same day, he shall be cut off from his people. As for any person who does any work on this same day, that person I will destroy from among his people. "You shall do no work at all. It is to be a perpetual statute throughout your generations in all your dwelling places."* (23:29-31).

For the first time, we see the word *humble* attached to the day. What does that mean? It means to be respectful of the requirements of the day. Even though the day's events are the priest's responsibility, the whole nation must observe the day with reverence. Failing to do so means excommunication. Working on the day garners the death penalty.

   b) The Ninth Day (23:32).

When does the work and humility start for the Day of Atonement? On the ninth day. Verse 32. *"It is to be a sabbath of complete rest to you, and you shall humble your souls; on the ninth of the month at evening, from evening until evening you shall keep your sabbath."* (23:32).

Remember, the word *sabbath* means *rest;* it does not automatically mean the seventh day. The seventh day is called the sabbath because it is the weekly day of rest for the nation. For the Day of Atonement, the complete rest begins on the evening of the ninth day and continues through the evening of the tenth day. Remember, the Old Testament's word *evening* meant the time of day from high noon until the sun's setting. Therefore, at high noon on the ninth day of the month until the end of the evening at sunset on the tenth, complete rest and respect are required by the LORD.

H. The Feast of Booths (23:33-24).

The third special event in the seventh month of every year is the Feast of Booths, also called the Feast of Tabernacles. Verse 33. *"Again, the LORD spoke to Moses, saying, "Speak to the sons of Israel, saying, 'On the fifteenth of this seventh month is the Feast of Booths for seven days to the LORD."* (23:33-24).

The Feast of Booths began on the fifteenth day, which is always a full moon, and continued for seven days until the twenty-second of the month. For the next thirty-nine years, the Feast of Booths will be tied to the calendar. The instruction for this Feast of Booths will change when the nation enters the Promised Land. Here we will follow the instruction given in this Leviticus passage.

1. The First of the Seven Days (23:35).

Special instructions were given for the first of the seven days. Verse 35. *"On the first day is a holy convocation; you shall do no laborious work of any kind."* (23:35).

While in the wilderness, regardless of the day of the week on which the fifteenth fell in the week, the nation was to observe the holy convocation, and no *laborious work* was done. It is the same for all the appointed times and seasons requiring a holy convocation.

2. The Days of the Seven Days (23:36).

On each of the days of the seven days, the priest presents offering to the LORD. Verse 36. *"For seven days you shall present an offering by fire to the LORD."* (23:36).

We are not told the requirements for this daily offering here. It will come in the following verses.

3. The Eighth Day after the Seven Days (23:37-38).

On the eighth day after the seven days are completed, the LORD prescribes the events. Verse 37. *"On the eighth*

Chapter 23

day, you shall have a holy convocation and present an offering by fire to the LORD; it is an assembly. You shall do no laborious work. These are the appointed times of the LORD which you shall proclaim as holy convocations, to present offerings by fire to the LORD—burnt offerings and grain offerings, sacrifices and drink offerings, each day's matter on its own day—besides those of the sabbaths of the LORD, and besides your gifts and besides all your votive and freewill offerings, which you give to the LORD." (23:37-38).

The offerings for each day are given as *"burnt offerings and grain offerings, sacrifices and drink offerings, each day's matter on its own day."* The LORD makes no changes from the original instructions for these offerings as found in chapters 1 through 7. These are presented by the priests from animals, grains, and juices brought as tithes from the nation's people.

The LORD continues to say concerning these daily offerings, *"besides those of the sabbaths of the LORD, and besides your gifts and besides all your votive and freewill offerings."* This means that all the regular daily offerings continue at their appointed times, and the Feast of Booths' offerings are in addition to the regular daily offerings.

4. The Events of the Seven Days (23:39).

The LORD now turns to the events of the seven days giving instruction for the people and what they are to do each day. Verse 23. *"On exactly the fifteenth day of the seventh month, when you have gathered in the crops of the land, you shall celebrate the feast of the LORD for seven days, with a rest on the first day and a rest on the eighth day."* (23:39).

The feast is tied to the gathering of the crop. Then, on the fifteenth of the seventh month, the celebration begins with a rest and ends eight days later with a rest. Here is an interesting phenomenon. Deuteronomy 16 says the following about these feasts.

"Three times in a year all your males shall appear before the LORD your God in the place which He chooses, at the Feast of Unleavened Bread and at the Feast of Weeks and at the Feast of Booths, and they shall not appear before the LORD empty-handed. ¹⁷ Every man shall give as he is able, according to the blessing of the LORD your God which He has given you." (16:16-17).

All three are associated with a seasonal harvest. Because the calendar of the Jews was lunar, based on twelve months that start with a new moon, and consists of three-hundred and fifty-four days each year, every year, New Year's Day falls eleven days ahead of the solar year. Therefore, New Year's Day moves backward through all the seasons and arrives back at the same time and season thirty-two years later. Because of the month's movement through all the seasons of the year, the LORD gives specific instructions for the seven days. However, where were the people going to harvest the grains for the three seasons while living in the wilderness? The people could not feed themselves. They were being fed by the LORD with manna each day. Where were the fields around Mount Sinai to plant grains for over 600,000 men and their families? In addition, this instruction was given for the remembrance of living in booths while at Mount Sinai. Why would the people need to remember their time in the booths while they were still living in the booths at Mount Sinai? These instructions are for after the Jews enter the Promised Land. That will be thirty-nine years away.

a) On the First Day of the Celebration (23:40).

On the first day of the celebration, the fifteenth of the month, the LORD says in verse 40, *"Now on the first day you shall take for yourselves the foliage of beautiful trees, palm branches and boughs of leafy trees and willows of the brook, and you shall rejoice before the LORD your God for seven days."* (23:40).

All the supplies listed in this verse are used to build a temporary living quarter outside of the regular home in the Promised Land.

b) For Seven Days of the Celebration (23:41).

For seven days of the celebration of booths, the LORD says in verse 41, *"You shall thus celebrate it as a feast to the LORD for seven days in the year. It shall be a perpetual statute throughout your generations; you shall celebrate it in the seventh month."* (23:41).

The booths celebration is locked into the seventh month by the LORD, regardless of the season it falls in. Because three crops are harvested each year, the seventh month will fall after one of the three harvests.

c) The Living Quarters for the Celebration (23:42-44).

The supplies listed in verse 40 will be used to create the living quarters for the celebration. Verse 42. *"You shall live in booths for seven days; all the native-born in Israel shall live in booths, so that your generations may know that I had the sons of Israel live in booths when I brought them out from the land of Egypt. I am the LORD your God.'" So Moses declared to the sons of Israel the appointed times of the LORD."* (23:42-44).

We must make an interesting point as we conclude the end of the instructions for this feast. The Jews did not leave Egypt in the seventh month on the religious calendar; the Jews left Egypt in the first month. Therefore, the Feast of Booths is celebrated six months out of sync with the actual time the Jews left Egypt. The feast is a yearly reminder of the temporary structures the Nation of Israel's people lived in during their time in the wilderness.

Chapter 24

XVIII. The Law for the Tabernacle Objects (24:1-9).
A. The Menorah (24:1-4).

Now we come to the law for the Tabernacle objects, and we start with Menorah. Chapter 24, verse 1. *"Then the LORD spoke to Moses, saying, Command the sons of Israel that they bring to you clear oil from beaten olives for the light, to make a lamp burn continually. "Outside the veil of testimony in the tent of meeting, Aaron shall keep it in order from evening to morning before the LORD continually; it shall be a perpetual statute throughout your generations. "He shall keep the lamps in order on the pure gold lampstand before the LORD continually."* (24:1-4).

The duties in the Tabernacle complex ran twenty-four hours a day. From evening until morning, the priest kept the Tabernacle in order and tended the golden lampstand. Today, we call the golden lampstand the Menorah. As we have mentioned several times in this study, the evening of the Jewish day began at high noon and lasted until sunset, when the new day started with the dark of the night. Morning, as spoken here, started at the break of day, and ended at high noon. When the LORD says, *"Aaron shall keep it in order from evening to morning before the LORD continually…"* it means twenty-four hours a day. We find this exact wording in the first verse in the book of Genesis. *"And there was evening, and there was morning, one day."* (Genesis 1:5). It means the same in Genesis, twenty-four hours. The light of the Menorah was never to go dim.

The Menorah was to be fed with clear olive oil. A clear oil is pressed from the olives at the beginning of the harvest season. The oil is not clear like water. It still has a green tint, but it is completely see-through because no olive particles are in the oil. If particles are found in the new oil, the producer will strain the oil through a rag to remove all impurities. However, if the oil is pressed at the end of the production season with older olives, the oil will be thicker and cloudy. Therefore, the clear oil must be taken of the freshest new olives. The people of the nation were instructed to bring this oil as an offering every olive season. The same instruction is given in Exodus 27:20.

> B. The Table of Showbread (24:5-9).

Next, the LORD instructs the details for the Table of Showbread. Verse 5. *"Then you shall take fine flour and bake twelve cakes with it; two-tenths of an ephah shall be in each cake. You shall set them in two rows, six to a row, on the pure gold table before the LORD. You shall put pure frankincense on each row that it may be a memorial portion for the bread, even an offering by fire to the LORD. Every sabbath day he shall set it in order before the LORD continually; it is an everlasting covenant for the sons of Israel. "It shall be for Aaron and his sons, and they shall eat it in a holy place; for it is most holy to him from the LORD'S offerings by fire, his portion forever."* (24:5-9).

We often see pictures of the Table of Showbread with the bread stacked in columns, not rows. The tables in the photos are not to scale, and the only way to space the twelves loaves of bread on the table is to stack them. However, the table is larger than normally pictured. It is about three feet long and eighteen inches wide, standing twenty-seven inches high. Each of the loaves was made from two-tenths of an ephah of flour, or 88% of a gallon of flour. Today, a gallon of flour is used to make a pound loaf of bread. When yeast is used, a pound loaf is a good size loaf, but these loaves are made without yeast, causing them to be extremely dense and small. The loaves made for the table were about 12% smaller than a one-pound loaf. Twelve loaves of bread could easily be placed on the table in two rows of six loaves with room to spare.

These loaves were seasoned with *pure frankincense,* which is a spice. All incenses used in that day were simply spices or herbs used in cooking. Can you eat frankincense? We find it in the supplement sections of our drug stores under the name Boswellia, and it is consumed to help with osteoarthritis, rheumatoid arthritis, asthma, and inflammatory bowel disease. It is called *frank* because of the freeness with which the odor goes forth from the substance. It is a resin from a tree, and it is eatable.

The twelve loaves represent a *"memorial portion for the bread."* The English word *memorial* is our attempt to translate the Hebrew word that means *to remember.* The smell of the bread with the frankincense is a reminder of the LORD's goodness to His people. The twelve loaves of bread sat on the table for seven days. They were replaced every seventh day. After that, the priests would be allowed to eat the bread with the meats they were required to eat from some of the offerings.

XIX. The Law for Those Who Fight (24:10-23).
A. The Example of the Israelite Who Blasphemes (24:10-12).

Now the LORD delivers the law for those who fight. He gives the example of the Israelite who blasphemes. Verse 10. *"Now the son of an Israelite woman, whose father was an Egyptian, went out among the sons of Israel; and the Israelite woman's son and a man of Israel struggled with each other in the camp. The son of the Israelite woman blasphemed the Name and cursed. So they brought him to Moses.* ~~(Now his mother's name was Shelomith, the daughter of Dibri, of the tribe of Dan.)~~ *They put him in custody so that the command of the LORD might be made clear to them."* (24:10-12).

During the giving of this law, a quarrel broke out in the camp. The son had an Egyptian father and an Israelite mother. He *"blasphemed the Name and cursed."* By telling us that the son had an Egyptian father tells us that the Egyptian culture still influenced the son. In Egyptian culture, it was common to curse their idols when petitions were not answered. For this son, he thought he could inflict the greatest insult by blaspheming the LORD – a grave sin brought to the camp from the Egyptian culture.

1. **The Consequence (24:13).**

The sin of the son brings us to the consequence. Verse 13. *"Then the LORD spoke to Moses, saying, Bring the one who has cursed outside the camp, and let all who heard him lay their hands on his head; then let all the congregation stone him."* (24:13).

In the Nation of Israel, no one is to curse the Name of the LORD. Those who do are to be stoned.

2. **The Communication (24:16).**

After giving the penalty for cursing the LORD, He provides the communication with the reason for the stoning. Verse 16. *"You shall speak to the sons of Israel, saying, 'If anyone curses his God, then he will bear his sin. 'Moreover, the one who blasphemes the name of the LORD shall surely be put to death; all the congregation shall certainly stone him. The alien as well as the native, when he blasphemes the Name, shall be put to death."* (24:16).

No one, Israelite or alien, will ever get away with cursing the LORD. He will have them put to death by stoning.

B. The Example of the Difference between Man and Beast (24:17-23).

1. The Story (24:17-21).

When the fight between men and an animal is involved, the LORD gives the example of the difference between man and beast. He starts with a story. Verse 17. *"If a man takes the life of any human being, he shall surely be put to death. 'The one who takes the life of an animal shall make it good, life for life. 'If a man injures his neighbor, just as he has done, so it shall be done to him: fracture for fracture, eye for eye, tooth for tooth; just as he has injured a man, so it shall be inflicted on him. 'Thus the one who kills an animal shall make it good, but the one who kills a man shall be put to death.* (24:17-21).

It is clear that the LORD places a different value on a man's life and the life of an animal. For killing a man, the penalty is death. For injuring a man, the penalty is to have done unto him what he did to the man. For killing an animal, a substitute animal was given to replace it.

2. The Standard (24:22).

From the story, we come to the standard. Verse 22. *"There shall be one standard for you; it shall be for the stranger as well as the native, for I am the LORD your God."* (24:22).

The Nation of Israel consisted primarily of descendants of Jacob. However, others married into the Jewish families, and foreigners would come to live with the camp. This law for those who fight is the same for all living in the Nation of Israel regardless of the nationality of the blood in their veins. If a man kills a man, the death penalty is required. If a man kills an animal, a replacement animal is required. If a man injures a man, that same injury is to be inflicted on the man. The standard applies to everyone in the Nation of Israel and living with the Nation of Israel.

Chapter 24

3. The Stoning (24:23).

From the story to the standard, we now come to the stoning. Verse 23. *"Then Moses spoke to the sons of Israel, and they brought the one who had cursed outside the camp and stoned him with stones. Thus the sons of Israel did, just as the LORD had commanded Moses."* (24:23).

The son of the Egyptian man and the Israelite woman was stoned, not inside the camp, but outside the camp. No doubt, the carrying out of the death penalty on this son was a terrific example to all the people so that no one should ever curse the Name of the LORD.

We now turn to the law of the years of rest.

Chapter 25

XX. The Law of the Years of Rest (25:1-22).
   A. The Rest of the Fields in the Seventh Year (25:1-7).

Moving into chapter 25, the LORD presents the law of the years of rest. He begins with the rest of the fields in the seventh year. Chapter 25, verse 1. *"The LORD then spoke to Moses at Mount Sinai, saying, "Speak to the sons of Israel and say to them, 'When you come into the land which I shall give you, then the land shall have a sabbath to the LORD. Six years you shall sow your field, and six years you shall prune your vineyard and gather in its crop, but during the seventh year the land shall have a sabbath rest, a sabbath to the LORD; you shall not sow your field nor prune your vineyard. Your harvest's aftergrowth you shall not reap, and your grapes of untrimmed vines you shall not gather; the land shall have a sabbatical year. All of you shall have the sabbath products of the land for food; yourself, and your male and female slaves, and your hired man and your foreign resident, those who live as aliens with you. Even your cattle and the animals that are in your land shall have all its crops to eat."* (25:1-7).

In chapter 1, verse 1, the LORD called Moses from the Tent of Meeting to give the laws presented in this book. It was not until the end of chapter 7 and the completion of the laws for the offerings that the Scripture says *the LORD commanded at Mount Sinai in the day that He commanded the sons of Israel to present their offerings to the LORD in the wilderness of Sinai."* (7:38). We must notice that the commands were given at Mount Sinai, not on Mount Sinai. They were given in the camp at the foot of Mount Sinai *"from the Tent of Meeting."* (1:1). Once the Tent of Meeting was constructed and ready for the Tabernacle to be erected and dedicated under its shelter, the LORD began to speak to Moses "from the Tent of Meeting," and the LORD moved from the burning fire on Mount Sinai. Here in chapter 25, verse 1, we come to the second reference when the LORD is speaking with Moses *at Mount Sinai* but not on Mount Sinai. The last reference will come at the end of the book with the same wording. Moses will not climb up Mount Sinai again. This wording simply means the camp of the Nation of Israel is still at the foot of Mount Sinai where it will live for one year after leaving Egypt, spend a year on a journey from Mount Sinai to Kadesh-barnea, and back to Mount Sinai where it will remain for thirty-eight more years. For now, the nation is near the end of the first year out of Egypt as the LORD is giving the laws recorded in this book.

In verses 1 – 7, the LORD instructs for what is commonly called a sabbatical year. Just as the workweek runs from the first day (Sunday) until the sixth day (Friday) and is followed by a day of rest (Saturday), so, too, the LORD requires a seven-year cycle for the planting and harvesting of crops in the Promised Land for six years, then the land must rest entirely on the seventh year of each cycle.

During the seventh year, no seed is planted, no formal harvest is scheduled. The land is allowed to sprout on its own and grow wild from the seeds left on the ground the year before. The passage calls it *"aftergrowth."* No matter who owned the fields, anyone of any nationality and any animal could come and graze as needed from the fruit and grain that grew on the aftergrowth. No formal reaping or harvesting was allowed. No crops were gathered or placed in the barns. The same occurred every seventh year.

B. The Rest of the Jubilee in the Fiftieth Year (25:8-13).

After the forty-nine sabbaths comes the fiftieth year, the LORD requires the rest of the Jubilee in the fiftieth year.

Verse 8. *"You are also to count off seven sabbaths of years for yourself, seven times seven years, so that you have the time of the seven sabbaths of years, namely, forty-nine years. You shall then sound a ram's horn abroad on the tenth day of the seventh month; on the day of atonement you shall sound a horn all through your land. You shall thus consecrate the fiftieth year and proclaim a release through the land to all its inhabitants. It shall be a jubilee for you, and each of you shall return to his own property, and each of you shall return to his family. You shall have the fiftieth year as a jubilee; you shall not sow, nor reap its aftergrowth, nor gather in from its untrimmed vines. For it is a jubilee; it shall be holy to you. You shall eat its crops out of the field. On this year of jubilee each of you shall return to his own property."* (25:8-13).

Three important things occur in the fiftieth Jubilee year. First, except under one exception, all property sold or traded during the forty-nine years will revert to its original family unit. We will see the exception later in this book. The families will acquire the property at the Promised Land division under Joshua's direction, the new leader after Moses's death. As a reminder, at this point in the storyline with the giving of the book of Leviticus, Moses is still in charge of the nation and will be for thirty-nine more years.

Second, all loans or debts were forgiven.

Third, the land was to rest from planting and harvesting in the same way it rested every seventh year. The owners will allow the wild growth of the land to occur, and any one of any nationality and any animal can come and graze as needed from the fruit and grain that grows on the aftergrowth. In this passage, it is not said but can be deduced from the instruction, the forty-ninth and the fiftieth years the land would be allowed to grow wild with no formal planting or harvesting.

At the end of Leviticus, the LORD provides a valuation for the important things in Israel's care. From Jubilee to Jubilee, the valuations control the buying, selling, and trading of most things, but it also controls the redemption of those things as we will see shortly.

C. The Rest of the Property in the Seventh Year
1. Establish the Value of the Crops (25:14-17).

Concerning the rest of the property in the seventh year, the LORD instructs the people to establish the value of the crops. Verse 14. *"If you make a sale, moreover, to your friend or buy from your friend's hand, you shall not wrong one another. Corresponding to the number of years after the jubilee, you shall buy from your friend; he is to sell to you according to the number of years of crops. In proportion to the extent of the years you shall increase its price, and in proportion to the fewness of the years you shall diminish its price, for it is a number of crops he is selling to you. So you shall not wrong one another, but you shall fear your God; for I am the LORD your God."* (25:14-17).

This passage seems difficult to understand in this place in the story. Why? We do not yet know the value of crops; however, this passage is just the beginning of the instruction that will make perfect sense once we complete the information in the rest of the book. For instance, later, in chapter 27, the LORD will give the valuations for people and property. Because the LORD is speaking of crops in this passage, we will bring in the value of barley seed at this point. *"Again, if a man consecrates to the LORD part of the fields of his own property, then your valuation shall be proportionate to the seed needed for it: a homer of barley seed at fifty shekels of silver."* (27:16).

A homer of barley will be worth fifty shekels. To understand the LORD's instruction in verses 14-17, we can use the barley seed's value as an example. On year one, after the year of Jubilee is complete, a man sells a homer of barley seed from his field for every year a crop is harvested, for forty-nine years, until the next Jubilee. But the man cannot charge him fifty shekels times forty-nine years because in seven of those years the land will rest and cannot be harvested. Forty-nine minus seven is forty-two. Therefore, the man can pre-sell a homer of barley seed for forty-two years at fifty shekels per year. The seller will receive 2100 shekels, and he must deliver a homer of barley seed to the purchaser every harvest year until the next Jubilee, when the contract will end.

Now suppose that a man wants to pre-sale a homer of barley seed in the forty-fifth year of the forty-nine-year cycle. The forty-ninth year will not have a harvest, so the man can only sell three years of seed because he must pro-rate the seed's value for the number of crops left in the cycle. For the remaining three years, the man will receive 150 shekels on the contract before it is canceled by the year of Jubilee.

2. Establish the Blessing of the Crops (25:18-21).

Skipping a planting season, and allowing the fields to grow wild, could be troubling for the nation. However, the LORD has established the blessing of the crops in advance for the Nation of Israel. Verse 18. *"You shall thus observe My statutes and keep My judgments, so as to carry them out, that you may live securely on the land. Then the land will yield its produce, so that you can eat your fill and live securely on it. But if you say, "What are we going to eat on the seventh year if we do not sow or gather in our crops?" then I will so order My blessing for you in the sixth year that it will bring forth the crop for three years."* (25:18-21).

In this passage, the LORD promises that the harvest's blessing in the sixth year will provide all that is needed until the yield of the ninth year is ready. For instance, after the

Chapter 25

seventh year's rest, barley will be planted at the appropriate time in the eighth year, but it will not be ready to harvest until the ninth yard.

3. Establish the Consumption of the Crops (25:22).

Finally, the LORD establishes the consumption of the crops. Verse 22. *"When you are sowing the eighth year, you can still eat old things from the crop, eating the old until the ninth year when its crop comes in."* (25:22).

The crop of planting in the sixth year will be harvested on time; however, no planting will occur in the seventh year. Therefore, there will not be a harvest in the eighth year. To provide for the people, the yield of the seeding from the sixth year will be so bountiful that the grain will last until the harvest of the ninth years. Later in Leviticus, we will learn that the crops' bounty will be so great that the yields of each year will take a long time to complete. *"Indeed, your threshing will last for you until grape gathering, and grape gathering will last until sowing time."* (26:5). In other words, harvesting, gathering, and sowing will be a continual process in the Promised Land, which means the maturing of the crops will occur in succession according to when the seeds were planted. Knowing that, we understand that new products will arrive in storage every day. The LORD wants the product to be eaten in a certain order. The first product in the warehouse is always eaten first. The last-placed in storage is eaten last.

XXI. The Law of the Redemption (25:23-26:46).
A. The Land (25:23-34).
1. Redemption Rights of the Land (25:23).

The LORD addressed the topic of the law of redemption. He begins with the land and the redemption rights of the land. Verse 23. *"The land, moreover, shall not be sold permanently, for the land is Mine; for you are but aliens and sojourners with Me. Thus for every piece of your property, you are to provide for the redemption of the land."* (25:23).

Every inch of the Promised Land belongs to the LORD, and He is allotting a portion of the land to each initial family unit. The taking of the Promise Land is thirty-nine years away. Be that as it may, when the time comes to cross the Jordan and take the land, a census will be made of every man within every tribe. For a complete commentary on the Promised Land's boundaries and the square miles allotted by the LORD to the people, see my lesson in the Book of Numbers, chapters 26:1-27:11. In the book of Numbers, we learn that the family of each man was allotted about twelve acres of land. It was a gift from the LORD to provide food for each family. The land was never to be *"sold permanently."* The keyword is *"permanently."* The Jewish families could sell all or a portion of their allotted land, but only temporarily. The buyer knew that all sold property returned to the original family ownership on the year of Jubilee. Also, as stated in this passage, the sold portion of land could be redeemed by the original owner for a price equal to the remaining years until the Jubilee.

Suppose an original family sold six acres of land in year forty; ten years remain. The new buyer will only own the land for ten years; then, it will revert to the original family. Here the LORD says, *Thus for every piece of your property, you are to provide for the redemption of the land."* In other words, in every sales contract, a redemption clause is to be added. If it is not added, the LORD has placed it in the law found here in the book, as we will soon see. If the land is sold for ten years and the original owner wants to repurchase the land on the fifth year of the contract, the original owner must pay back or refund five years of the value paid for the land and add a fifth to the value. Otherwise, he must wait until the Jubilee which cancels the contract and reverts the land. We will see this law from the LORD in chapter 27.

2. Redemption Rights of Sold Land (25:25-28).

Continuing with the redemption rights of sold land, the LORD says in verse 25, *"If a fellow countryman of yours becomes so poor he has to sell part of his property, then his nearest kinsman is to come and buy back what his relative has sold. Or in case a man has no kinsman, but so recovers his means as to find sufficient for its redemption, then he shall calculate the years since its sale and refund the balance to the man to whom he sold it, and so return to his property. 'But if he has not found sufficient means to get it back for himself, then what he has sold shall remain in the hands of its purchaser until the year of jubilee; but at the jubilee it shall revert, that he may return to his property."* (25:25-28).

The LORD writes into the law this provision allowing the nearest relative or the seller to redeem the sold land and return the original family to the land. If the land is not redeemed by a relative or the seller, it will return on the year of Jubilee.

3. Redemption Rights in Walled Cities (25:29-30).

The LORD makes an exemption on the redemption rights in walled cities. Verse 29. *"Likewise, if a man sells a dwelling house in a walled city, then his redemption right remains valid until a full year from its sale; his right of redemption lasts a full year. But if it is not bought back for him within the space of a full year, then the house that is in the walled city passes permanently to its purchaser throughout his generations; it does not revert in the jubilee."* (25:29-30).

When a home that resides within a walled city is sold, the seller has one year to redeem the property. If the home is not redeemed within the year, the home is permanently sold, and the year of Jubilee does not transfer the home to the original owner.

4. Redemption Rights in Unwalled Villages (25:31).

The then LORD writes the law for the redemption rights in unwalled villages. Verse 31. *"The houses of the villages, however, which have no surrounding wall shall be considered as open fields; they have redemption rights and revert in the jubilee."* (25:31).

Homes in unwalled villages have the same redemption rights as a parcel of land. The home can be sold, change owners until the year of Jubilee when it reverts. If the seller desires to redeem the land, he must refund the unused portion, and as we will see, add one-fifth of the value to the redemption price.

5. Redemption Rights for Levite Cities (25:32-34).

The LORD provides a special law for the redemption rights for Levite cities. Verse 32. *"As for cities of the Levites, the Levites have a permanent right of redemption for the houses of the cities which are their possession. What, therefore, belongs to the Levites may be redeemed and a house sale in the city of this possession reverts in the jubilee, for the houses of the cities of the Levites are their possession among the sons of Israel. But pasture fields of their cities shall not be sold, for that is their perpetual possession."* (25:32-34).

The Levitical cities are the places chosen by the LORD where the tribes were to bring their offerings. The LORD designated four cities in each tribal area, forty-eight cities in all. We find the instruction for these cities in the book of Numbers.

> *[1] Now the LORD spoke to Moses in the plains of Moab by the Jordan opposite Jericho, saying, [2] "Command the sons of Israel that they give to the Levites from the inheritance of their possession cities to live in; and you shall give to the Levites pasture lands around the cities. [3] The cities shall be theirs to live in; and their pasture lands shall be for their cattle and for their herds and for all their beasts. [4] "The pasture lands of the cities which you shall give to the Levites shall extend from the*

wall of the city outward a thousand cubits around. ⁵ You shall also measure outside the city on the east side two thousand cubits, and on the south side two thousand cubits, and on the west side two thousand cubits, and on the north side two thousand cubits, with the city in the center. This shall become theirs as pasture lands for the cities.⁶ "The cities which you shall give to the Levites shall be the six cities of refuge, which you shall give for the manslayer to flee to; and in addition to them you shall give forty-two cities. ⁷ All the cities which you shall give to the Levites shall be forty-eight cities, together with their pasture lands. ⁸ As for the cities which you shall give from the possession of the sons of Israel, you shall take more from the larger and you shall take less from the smaller; each shall give some of his cities to the Levites in proportion to his possession which he inherits." (Numbers 35:1-8).

The Levites did not receive land in the Promised Land, yet, it was necessary that they live on land to tend the flocks that came from their work in the service of the LORD, and, also have a place to live. According to Leviticus 25:32-34, their land was to be the first section on the east and west sides of the city lines out about fifteen hundred feet. This command restricted the forty-eight cities in the Promised Land designated by the LORD for the Levites to live. The land was to be theirs for 50 years and then revert to the tribe. It would then be given again to the Levites for another 50 years. In addition to the first fifteen hundred feet from the city, another fifteen hundred feet were given to the Levites for their pastures. That means that the first three thousand feet from the center of the city of each of these forty-eight cities were living and pasture land for the Levites to use, not own. The owners of the land who designated the land as gifts to the Levites could not sell the land around these cities. To do so might force the eviction of the Levites. The LORD would not allow that to happen. Even though the

Levites did not own the land around these cities, it was permanently theirs to use.

B. The People (25:35-55).
1. Provisions for the Poor (25:35-44).
a) The Gifts of the Poor (25:35-38).

In the topic of the law of redemption, we now come to the people and the provisions for the poor. First, the gifts for the poor. Verse 35. *"Now in case a countryman of yours becomes poor and his means with regard to you falter, then you are to sustain him, like a stranger or a sojourner, that he may live with you. Do not take usurious interest from him, but revere your God, that your countryman may live with you. You shall not give him your silver at interest, nor your food for gain. I am the LORD your God, who brought you out of the land of Egypt to give you the land of Canaan and to be your God."* (25:35-38).

When the LORD says, *"You shall not give him your silver at interest, nor your food for gain,"* He means what you give to the poor person is a gift; it is not a loan. No interest is to be charged or a gain of any kind to be expected. It is a gift like the gift of the Promised Land to the people of the nation of Israel. The LORD gave it to Israel and did not expect a payment for the land.

b) The Work of the Poor (25:39-44).

Second, we come to the work of the poor. Verse 39. *"If a countryman of yours becomes so poor with regard to you that he sells himself to you, you shall not subject him to a slave's service. He shall be with you as a hired man, as if he were a sojourner; he shall serve with you until the year of jubilee. He shall then go out from you, he and his sons with him, and shall go back to his family, that he may return to the property of his forefathers. For they are My servants whom I brought out from the land of Egypt; they are not to be sold in a slave sale. You shall not rule over him with severity, but are to revere your God."* (25:39-44).

Here we see the LORD presenting the idea of a bondservant. A poor person could sell his services as a worker to another Jew for up to fifty years. He is not to be treated like a slave but like a hired hand. He lives on his property with his family but arrives to work six days of the week as an employee. He cannot be sold like a slave. The point is made purposefully. The LORD forbids a Jew from selling anyone as a slave; however, Jews could go to the slave sale and purchase slaves out of the slave market. As we will see next, the slaves become a permanent part of the Jew's family, they must be treated with respect, and they can be redeemed and set free.

    2. Provisions for the Slaves (25:44-55).
      a) The Purchased Must Be Respected (25:44-46).

At the slave market, the Jewish man can purchase slaves from the pagans. Here the LORD makes the provisions for the slaves. The purchased slave must be respected. Verse 44. *"As for your male and female slaves whom you may have—you may acquire male and female slaves from the pagan nations that are around you. Then, too, it is out of the sons of the sojourners who live as aliens among you that you may gain acquisition, and out of their families who are with you, whom they will have produced in your land; they also may become your possession. You may even bequeath them to your sons after you, to receive as a possession; you can use them as permanent slaves. But in respect to your countrymen, the sons of Israel, you shall not rule with severity over one another."* (25:44-46).

First, purchased slaves and their offspring become part of the property of the purchaser. Before we chastise the LORD for this provision, we must remember that in the world at that time, the patriarchal father of the family owned everything, wife, sons, daughters, houses, lands, and equipment. The more family a man possessed, the wealthier the man was considered. When an owner died, the purchased slaves pass to the son responsible for the family for the rest of his life. The slaves become part of the inherited package as permanent slaves or workers. They must be treated right no matter who inherited them. However, a slave can be redeemed, as we will see next.

b) The Purchased May Be Redeemed (25:47-55).
(1) A Man Who Sells Himself (25:47-49).

The LORD makes a provision for the slave. The purchased may be redeemed. The Jews must always provide a redemption right. First, we see the man who sells himself. Verse 47. *"Now if the means of a stranger or of a sojourner with you becomes sufficient, and a countryman of yours becomes so poor with regard to him as to sell himself to a stranger who is sojourning with you, or to the descendants of a stranger's family, then he shall have redemption right after he has been sold. One of his brothers may redeem him, or his uncle, or his uncle's son, may redeem him, or one of his blood relatives from his family may redeem him; or if he prospers, he may redeem himself."* (25:47-49).

Any relative who has the money, or if the person who sold himself into slavery acquires the money, can use the money to redeem the poor person. As for the relatives who redeem the poor person, it does not matter if the redeemer is Jewish or pagan; the purchased person can be redeemed out of the contract.

(2) A Man Who Redeems Himself (25:50-555).
(a) The Sell Price Prorated by Years Left (25:50-51).

For a man who redeems himself, the sell price must be prorated based on the years left until the year of Jubilee. The year of Jubilee is the key here. Any Jew who sells himself into this employment kind of slavery can only sell himself for the remaining years left until the year of Jubilee. Even a slave purchased at the slave market can be redeemed for a prorated amount based on the purchase price and the number of years until the year of Jubilee. Verse 50. *"He then with his purchaser shall calculate from the year when he sold himself to him up to the year of jubilee; and the price of his sale shall correspond to the number of years. It is like the days of a hired man that he shall be with him. If there are still many years, he shall refund part of his purchase price in proportion to them for his own redemption; and if few years remain until the year of jubilee, he shall so calculate with him. In proportion to his years he is to refund the amount for his redemption."* (25:50-51).

(b) The Purchase Price Prorated by Years Left (25:53-55).

The redemption price is the purchase price prorated by the years left until the year of Jubilee. Verse 25. *"Like a man hired year by year he shall be with him; he shall not rule over him with severity in your sight. Even if he is not redeemed by these means, he shall still go out in the year of jubilee, he and his sons with him. For the sons of Israel are My servants; they are My servants whom I brought out from the land of Egypt. I am the LORD your God."* (25:53-55).

The year of Jubilee allows all slaves and people who have pre-sold their labor to be freed from that contract. Why would the LORD do this for those purchased into slavery? He does it for the same reason He redeemed Israel out of Egypt. Israel did not deserve it, it was a gift from the LORD. Israel was forever to treat all people with the same respect as they received from the LORD.

Chapter 26

C. The Law of the Servants of the LORD (26:1-46).
1. Laws for the Faithful Servants (26:1-13).
   a) The Commandments Concerning the Idols (26:1).

Only two laws remain in the LORD's commandments found in the book of Leviticus. Here we come to the law of the servants of the LORD, and the last will be the law of the valuation. The LORD begins with the laws for the faithful servants, and He addresses the commandments concerning the idols. Chapter 26, verse 1. *"You shall not make for yourselves idols, nor shall you set up for yourselves an image or a sacred pillar, nor shall you place a figured stone in your land to bow down to it; for I am the LORD your God."* (26:1).

The Promised Land will be filled with idols, images dedicated to idols, and carved stones as monuments to pagan gods. The LORD knew this. Long before the LORD decided to take Canaan's land because the descendants of Canaan had abandoned the LORD, the GOD of his grandfather, Noah. In chapter 18, we learned the following.

> *"But as for you, you are to keep My statutes and My judgments and shall not do any of these abominations, neither the native, nor the alien who sojourns among you ... so that the land will not spew you out, should you defile it, as it has spewed out the nation which has been before you. For whoever does any of these abominations, those persons who do so shall be cut off from among their people. Thus you are to keep My charge, that you do not practice any of the abominable customs which have been practiced before you, so as not to defile yourselves with them; I am the LORD your God."* (18:24-30).

Chapter 26

In giving the Canaanite land to the Israelites, the LORD spewed the Canaanites out of the land in order for the Israelites to possess the land. However, the Israelites were not to repeat the same sins of the Canaanites. These commandments were the first given to Israel at Mount Sinai when they arrived nine months before as the first part of the Ten Commandments.

b) The Commandments Concerning the Sabbath (26:2).

Then the LORD reminds the faithful servants of Israel of the commandments concerning the sabbath. Verse 2. *"You shall keep My sabbaths and reverence My sanctuary; I am the LORD."* (26:2).

This command is part of the Ten Commandments that every Jew should know by heart.

c) The Commandments Concerning the Walk (26:4)

Next, the LORD reminds His faithful of the commandments concerning the walk. Verse 4. *"If you walk in My statutes and keep My commandments so as to carry them out,* (26:4)

The whole point of giving the people of the Nation of Israel these commandments and statutes in Leviticus is to allow the people to know what He expects them to do to be His faithful servants when they enter the Promised Land.

(1) The Rains of the Seasons (26:3).

As faithful servants of the LORD, He promises wonderful things for the people. First, He speaks of the rains of the seasons. Verse 3. *"... then I shall give you rains in their season, so that the land will yield its produce and the trees of the field will bear their fruit."* (26:3).

Without rain, all plants die. With water, all plants thrive. Rains carry more than just water to the plants; they bring salt-free, soft water the contains much oxygen and nitrates – important nutrients.

(2) The Crops of the Seasons (26:5).

The rains of the seasons bring the crops of the seasons. Verse 5. *"Indeed, your threshing will last for you until grape gathering, and grape gathering will last until sowing time. You will thus eat your food to the full and live securely in your land."* (26:5).

Look how large the crops will be for Israel. It will take from season to season to harvest the crops because the produce will be so great. The Israelites will not have a want for food at all and will live securely and independently with the LORD's provisions.

(a) A Peace in the Land (26:6).

The first of the LORD's provisions will be a peace in the land. Verse 6. *"I shall also grant peace in the land, so that you may lie down with no one making you tremble. I shall also eliminate harmful beasts from the land, and no sword will pass through your land."* (26:6).

Being a faithful servant of the LORD, His protection from enemies and peace in the land is promised.

(b) A Protection in the Land (26:7-8).

The LORD speaks of a protection in the land. Verse 7. *"But you will chase your enemies and they will fall before you by the sword; five of you will chase a hundred, and a hundred of you will chase ten thousand, and your enemies will fall before you by the sword."* (26:7-8).

The LORD does not promise the absence of enemies attacking the nation; He promises the victory over that enemies when they attack.

(c) A Population in the Land (26:9).

The LORD promises an expanding population in the land. Verse 9. *"So I will turn toward you and make you fruitful and multiply you, and I will confirm My covenant with you."* (26:9).

When the people of Israel are faithful to the LORD, He will enlarge the population and provide bountifully for all. The converse may be assumed here if the people are unfaithful, but the LORD will address that soon.

(d) A Produce in the Land (26:10).

The LORD promises a produce for the faithful in the land. Verse 10. *"You will eat the old supply and clear out the old because of the new."* (26:10).

The food will be so bountiful that Israel may have trouble consuming the supply. To ensure the food remains good, the oldest food in the storehouse must be eaten before the newest food is used.

(e) A Promise in the Land (26:12-13).

The LORD finally promises a promise in the land for His faithful servants. Verse 12. *"Moreover, I will make My dwelling among you, and My soul will not reject you. I will also walk among you and be your God, and you shall be My people. 'I am the LORD your God, who brought you out of the land of Egypt so that you would not be their slaves, and I broke the bars of your yoke and made you walk erect."* (26:12-13).

In the passage, the LORD makes the best promise of all – His presences living among His people. What could be better than that?

We now come to the LORD's law for the unfaithful servants.

2. Laws for the Unfaithful Servants (26:14-39).
   a) Appointed Enemies (26:14).

His first section covered the laws for the faithful servants, which include the keeping of the commandments concerning idols, sabbaths, and the daily walk in Jewish life. Now we come to the laws for the unfaithful servants. First, we see the appointed enemies. Chapter 26, verse 14. *"But if you do not obey Me and do not carry out all these commandments, if, instead, you reject My statutes, and if your soul abhors My ordinances so as not to carry out all My commandments, and so break My covenant, I, in turn, will do this to you: I will appoint over you a sudden terror, consumption and fever that will waste away the eyes and cause the soul to pine away; also, you will sow your seed uselessly, for your enemies will eat it up."* (26:14).

When Israel fails to keep the commandments, the statutes, and breaks the LORD's covenant, the LORD makes three serious promises. The promises are prophecies that will come true because the LORD knows the future of His nation; His nation will turn from Him.

First, *"sudden terror"* will come on the unfaithful servants. *"Sudden"* means *immediate, without warning*. The penalty for being unfaithful servants has been spoken by the LORD. The people of the Nation of Israel are without excuse. He will bring upon the unfaithful a *"sudden terror."* *"Terror"* means *something that intimidates, filled with great fear*.

Second, *"consumption and fever that will waste away the eyes and cause the soul to pine away."* *"Consumption"* means *wasting of the body by disease*. *"Fever"* means *the unusual heating of the body by illness*. To *"pine"* means to *cause to starve*.

Third, *"sow ... seed uselessly"* means the nation of Israel will not reap a reward from the seeds they have planted. The enemies of Israel will reap the reward.

The LORD will not forget these three promises. They will come upon the nation at the LORD's order. We will see the fulfillment of these prophecies in Second Kings and many of the Old Testament prophecy books with the LORD's sending of Assyria and Babylon to take a ten percent remnant of faithful Israel away from the Promised Land and bless them while killing the remaining ninety percent of unfaithful and burying them in the dirt of the land.

b) Appointed Punishments (26:17-18).

Continuing, the LORD states His appointed punishments for the unfaithful Nation of Israel. Verse 17. *"I will set My face against you so that you will be struck down before your enemies; and those who hate you will rule over you, and you will flee when no one is pursuing you. If also after these things you do not obey Me, then I will punish you seven times more for your sins."* (26:17-18).

We have the unique blessing of having the whole Bible that tells of the fulfillment of these punishments. The LORD will use Assyria and Babylon as Israel's enemies. Interestingly, these two nations were the closest known relatives of Abraham's family from the Tower of Babel area. Both were descendants of Noah's son, Shem, and so is the Nation of Israel. Cousins against cousins. In 722 BC, Assyria will finish taking over the Northern Kingdom of Israel. In 586 BC, Babylon will finish taking over the Southern Kingdom of Judah. The two will rule over the Jews and fulfill this promise.

In this passage, the LORD says, *"and you will flee when no one is pursuing you."* If Assyria and Babylon are being sent by the LORD as Israel's enemies, how can the LORD say the Jews will flee with no one pursuing them. The answer with both nations is the same and clearly revealed in Second

Kings and the Old Testament prophecy books. Both nations came to take the people away, but the people of Israel did not want to be taken away. Jeremiah, living in the city of Jerusalem, begged the Jews to open the gates and go to Babylon with Nebuchadnezzar, but they refused. Many Jews ran to Egypt and other nations instead of following the LORD's instruction through Jeremiah to go with Nebuchadnezzar. Here is what the LORD said to the Jews about that through Jeremiah.

> *"The LORD has spoken to you, O remnant of Judah, "Do not go into Egypt!" You should clearly understand that today I have testified against you. [20] For you have only deceived yourselves; for it is you who sent me to the LORD your God, saying, "Pray for us to the LORD our God; and whatever the LORD our God says, tell us so, and we will do it." [21] So I have told you today, but you have not obeyed the LORD your God, even in whatever He has sent me to tell you. [22] Therefore you should now clearly understand that you will die by the sword, by famine and by pestilence, in the place where you wish to go to reside."* (Jeremiah 42:19-22).

c) Appointed Plagues (26:19-21).

The LORD promises the appointed plagues. Verse 19. *"I will also break down your pride of power; I will also make your sky like iron and your earth like bronze. Your strength will be spent uselessly, for your land will not yield its produce and the trees of the land will not yield their fruit. If then, you act with hostility against Me and are unwilling to obey Me, I will increase the plague on you seven times according to your sins."* (26:19-21).

When famine came upon the Jews, it was because of their unfaithfulness to the LORD and His commandments and statutes. One example found in Second Kings among the many is as follows.

> [25] *There was a great famine in Samaria; and behold, they besieged it, until a donkey's head was sold for eighty shekels of silver, and*

a fourth of a kab of dove's dung for five shekels of silver. ²⁶ *As the king of Israel was passing by on the wall a woman cried out to him, saying, "Help, my lord, O king!"* ²⁷ *He said, "If the* LORD *does not help you, from where shall I help you? From the threshing floor, or from the wine press?"* ²⁸ *And the king said to her, "What is the matter with you?" And she answered, "This woman said to me, 'Give your son that we may eat him today, and we will eat my son tomorrow.'* ²⁹ *So we boiled my son and ate him . . . ."* (2 Kings 6:25-29).

d) Appointed Hostilities (26:22-24).

The LORD promises his appointed hostilities against the unfaithful servants. Verse 22. *"I will let loose among you the beasts of the field, which will bereave you of your children and destroy your cattle and reduce your number so that your roads lie deserted. And if by these things you are not turned to Me, but act with hostility against Me, then I will act with hostility against you; and I, even I, will strike you seven times for your sins."* (26:22-24).

An example of the LORD fulfilling this promise is found in Second Kings.

"The king of Assyria brought men from Babylon and from Cuthah and from ᵇ*Avva and from Hamath and Sephar-vaim, and settled them in the cities of Samaria in place of the sons of Israel. So they possessed Samaria and lived in its cities.* ²⁵ *At the beginning of their living there, they did not fear the* LORD; *therefore the* LORD *sent lions among them which killed some of them."* (2 Kings 17:24–25).

e) Appointed Vengeance (26:25-28).

The LORD promises appointed vengeance for the unfaithful servants. Verse 25. *"I will also bring upon you a sword which will execute vengeance for the covenant; and when you gather together into your cities, I will send pestilence among you, so that you shall be delivered into enemy hands. When I break your staff of bread, ten women will bake your bread in one oven, and they will bring back your bread in rationed amounts, so that you will eat and not be satisfied. Yet if in spite of this you do not obey Me, but act with hostility against Me, then I will act with wrathful hostility against you, and I, even I, will punish you seven times for your sins."* (26:25-28).

This promise was brought against the Jews, as told by Isaiah.

"For behold, the Lord GOD of hosts is going to remove from Jerusalem and Judah Both supply and support, the whole supply of bread And the whole supply of water..." (Isaiah 3:1-2).

"Moreover, He said to me, "Son of man, behold, I am going to break the staff of bread in Jerusalem, and they will eat bread by weight and with anxiety, and drink water by measure and in horror, [17] because bread and water will be scarce; and they will be appalled with one another and waste away in their iniquity." (Isaiah 4:16-17).

f) **Appointed Desolation (26:29-33).**

Then the LORD promises the appointed desolation. Verse 29. *"Further, you will eat the flesh of your sons and the flesh of your daughters you will eat. I then will destroy your high places, and cut down your incense altars, and heap your remains on the remains of your idols, for My soul shall abhor you. I will lay waste your cities as well and will make your sanctuaries desolate, and I will not smell your soothing aromas. I will make the land desolate so that your enemies who settle in it will be appalled over it. You, however, I will scatter among the nations and will draw out a sword after you, as your land becomes desolate and your cities become waste."* (26:29-33).

We have already seen an example for the eating of children. Let us focus here on the scattering of the Jews among the nations and the Promised Land's desolation. Zechariah tells the fulfillment of this promise.

> *"Then the word of the* LORD *came to Zechariah saying,* [9] *"Thus has the* LORD *of hosts said, 'Dispense true justice and practice kindness and compassion each to his brother;* [10] *and do not oppress the widow or the orphan, the stranger or the poor; and do not devise evil in your hearts against one another.'* [11] *But they refused to pay attention and turned a stubborn shoulder and stopped their ears from hearing.* [12] *They made their hearts like flint so that they could not hear the law and the words which the* LORD *of hosts had sent by His Spirit through the former prophets; therefore great wrath came from the* LORD *of hosts.* [13] *And just as He called and they would not listen, so they called and I would not listen," says the* LORD *of hosts;* [14] *"but I scattered them with a storm wind among all the nations whom they have not known. Thus the land is desolated behind them so that no one went back and forth, for they made the pleasant land desolate."* (Zechariah 7:8-14).

Zechariah is not prophesying at this point; he is reporting what has already occurred. The Jews had become unfaithful to the LORD, breaking His commandments and statutes.

g) Appointed Sabbaths (26:34-35)

The LORD promises the appointed sabbaths. Verse 34. *"Then the land will enjoy its sabbaths all the days of the desolation, while you are in your enemies' land; then the land will rest and enjoy its sabbaths. All the days of its desolation it will observe the rest which it did not observe on your sabbaths, while you were living on it."* (26:34-35).

The story of the fulfillment of this promise began with the death of Solomon. At his death, his son became king. Within the year, the United Kingdom of Israel was divided into the Northern Kingdom of Israel and the Southern Kingdom of Judah. They would remain separate until both were carried away into exile to fulfill the sabbaths' appointed times according to the years of their unfaithfulness. The

Northern Kingdom will immediately become unfaithful to the LORD upon her separation from the southern king. She will change the feast days and holy days in defiance of the LORD's commands and statutes. From Solomon's death to the Northern Kingdom's fall, three-hundred and ninety unfaithful years will pass (Ezekiel 4:5). The land will be desolate for that time in sabbath rest. For the Southern Kingdom, it was unfaithful for forty years and remain desolate for forty years of sabbaths rest (Ezekiel 4:6). With the fall of the Northern and Southern Kingdoms, these promises will be fulfilled against unfaithful Israel.

h) Appointed Decay (26:36-39).

The LORD ends His promises to the unfaithful servants by announcing the appointed decay. Verse 36. *"As for those of you who may be left, I will also bring weakness into their hearts in the lands of their enemies. And the sound of a driven leaf will chase them, and even when no one is pursuing they will flee as though from the sword, and they will fall. They will therefore stumble over each other as if running from the sword, although no one is pursuing; and you will have no strength to stand up before your enemies. But you will perish among the nations, and your enemies' land will consume you. So those of you who may be left will rot away because of their iniquity in the lands of your enemies; and also because of the iniquities of their forefathers they will rot away with them."* (26:36-39).

Ezekiel foretells this when he says, *"Son of man, behold, I am going to break the staff of bread in Jerusalem, and they will eat bread by weight and with anxiety, and drink water by measure and in horror, [17] because bread and water will be scarce; and they will be appalled with one another and waste away in their iniquity."* (Ezekiel 4:16-17).

Ezekiel goes on to report the word of the people in Jerusalem at the time of the fall. *"... Thus you have spoken, saying, "Surely our transgressions and our sins are upon us, and we are rotting away in them; how then can we survive?"* (Ezekiel 33:10).

Those who are unfaithful to the LORD and ignore His commands will rot away in their sin the Promised Land and die.

3. Laws for the Repentant Servants (26:40-46).
a) The One Who Confess – Remembered (26:40-42).

But the LORD is good all the time. He is always willing to accept and protect those who repent. The LORD gives the laws for the repentant servants. First, the LORD addresses the one who confesses will be remembered. Verse 40. *"If they confess their iniquity and the iniquity of their forefathers, in their unfaithfulness which they committed against Me, and also in their acting with hostility against Me— I also was acting with hostility against them, to bring them into the land of their enemies—or if their uncircumcised heart becomes humbled so that they then make amends for their iniquity, then I will remember My covenant with Jacob, and I will remember also My covenant with Isaac, and My covenant with Abraham as well, and I will remember the land.* (26:40-42).

Simply, for those who confess their sins against the LORD, He will remember them, and He will remember His original covenant, which made allowances for their confessed sins, and He will protect the land.

b) The One Who Amends – Remembered (26:43-44).

Second, the LORD addresses the one who amends will be remembered. Verse 43. *"For the land will be abandoned by them, and will make up for its sabbaths while it is made desolate without them. They, meanwhile, will be making amends for their iniquity, because they rejected My ordinances and their soul abhorred My statutes. Yet in spite of this, when they are in the land of their enemies, I will not reject them, nor will I so abhor them as to destroy them, breaking My covenant with them; for I am the LORD their God.* (26:43-44).

Sins against the LORD must be confessed, but they also must be amended. Unfaithfulness must be changed to faithfulness. Rebellion against the commands and statutes of the LORD must be changed to total acceptance of the commands and statutes of the LORD. Faithfulness brings the LORD forgiveness. With forgiveness, the LORD remembers the promises He made in His covenant.

c) The One Who Establishes – Remembered (26:45-46).

The LORD is the one who establishes. He is the One who remembered His covenant. Verse 45. *"But I will remember for them the covenant with their ancestors, whom I brought out of the land of Egypt in the sight of the nations, that I might be their God. I am the LORD. These are the statutes and ordinances and laws which the LORD established between Himself and the sons of Israel through Moses at Mount Sinai."* (26:45-46).

The LORD established the promise for the Nation of Israel, first with Abraham, then with Isaac, and finally with Jacob. Had Israel remained true and faithful to these commandments, ordinances, statutes, and laws given in this book, Israel would have been protected by the LORD from the day they entered the Promised Land until today. The rest of the history concerning Israel found in the Bible records the unfortunate truth, Israel did not remain faithful. All the warnings and promises in this book of what the LORD will do to Israel if she became unfaithful have come true. Israel knew better. Still, today, Israel is in rebellion against the LORD, and He is allowing her enemies to encroach on her land. Yet, Israel is without excuse. In verse 46 of this chapter, the LORD says, *"These are the statutes and ordinances and laws which the LORD established between Himself and the sons of Israel through Moses at Mount Sinai."* From chapter 1, verse 1 through chapter 26, verse 46, all Israel had to do to be blessed beyond all comprehension was to stay faithful to the LORD's words within the book. The words are not difficult. Neither are the commands, statutes, ordinances, or laws. Only one more thing needs to be added to everything that has been said in this book - the law of the valuation of everything in Jewish life.

Chapter 27

XXII. The Law of the Valuation (27:1-33).

 A. The Valuation of Persons for Redemption (27:1-2).

 In this final chapter of Leviticus, the LORD gives the law of the valuation of all things important to Him. Throughout the book, the LORD speaks of the redemption of this or that, the firstborn, the slave for release, the refund of sold property, and more. But what were those values to be? In chapter 27, the LORD provides the list of those values that could be applied when following the laws presented previously in the book. First, we come to the valuation of persons for redemption. Chapter 27, verse 1. *"Again, the LORD spoke to Moses, saying, Speak to the sons of Israel and say to them, 'When a man makes a difficult vow, he shall be valued according to your valuation of persons belonging to the LORD."*

 Dealing with people presents the necessity to make difficult decisions. When money is involved, the decision becomes especially difficult. The LORD does not leave the valuation for man to decide; the LORD tells the value so Israel will be fair and never wrong anyone.

 1. The Male Twenty to Sixty (27:3).

 In verse 3, the LORD tells the value of the male between twenty and sixty years of age. *"If your valuation is of the male from twenty years even to sixty years old, then your valuation shall be fifty shekels of silver, after the shekel of the sanctuary."* (27:3).

 2. The Female Twenty to Sixty (27:4).

Verse 4 gives the value of a female between twenty and sixty years of age. *"Or if it is a female, then your valuation shall be thirty shekels."* (27:4).

3. The Male Five to Twenty (27:5a).

In verse 5a, we see the value of a male between five and twenty years of age. *"If it be from five years even to twenty years old then your valuation for the male shall be twenty shekels…"* (27:5a).

4. The Female Five to Twenty (27:5b).

In verse 5b, we see the value of a female between five and twenty years of age. *"…and for the female ten shekels."* (27:5b).

5. The Male One Month to Five (27:6a).

Verse 6a tells the value of a male between one month and five years of age. *"But if they are from a month even up to five years old, then your valuation shall be five shekels of silver for the male,"* (27:6a).

6. The Female One Month to Five (27:6b).

Verse 6b tells the value of a female between one month and five years of age. *"… and for the female your valuation shall be three shekels of silver."* (27:6b).

7. The Male Sixty and Upward (27:7a).

Verse 7a indicates the value of a male older than sixty years of age. *"If they are from sixty years old and upward, if it is a male, then your valuation shall be fifteen shekels …"* (27:7a).

8. The Female Sixty and Upward (27:7b).

Verse 7b indicates the value of a female older than sixty years of age. *"… and for the female ten shekels."* (27:7b).

9. The Poor (27:8).

The LORD does not give the value of a poor man. He allows the priests to determine the value. Verse 8. *"But if he is poorer than your valuation, then he shall be placed before the priest and the priest shall value him; according to the means of the one who vowed, the priest shall value him."* (27:8).

When the LORD says, *"according to the means of the one who vowed,"* this is a reference to the price the poor man accepted to sell himself as a hired man. The priest would use the purchase price and calculated the years until the Jubilee determined the refund amount to redeem the man and give him freedom.

  B. The Valuation of Animal for Redemption (27:9-13).
   1. The Clean Animals (27:9-10).

Then the LORD turns to the valuation of animals for redemption. He begins with the clean animals. Verse 9. *"Now if it is an animal of the kind which men can present as an offering to the LORD, any such that one gives to the LORD shall be holy. He shall not replace it or exchange it, a good for a bad, or a bad for a good; or if he does exchange animal for animal, then both it and its substitute shall become holy."* (27:9-10).

The redemption of a clean animal must be with another clean animal. Both are holy because they can be offered as offerings on the Brazen Altar if desired.

   2. The Unclean Animals (27:11-13).

Unclean animals can be redeemed. Verse 11. *"If, however, it is any unclean animal of the kind which men do not present as an offering to the LORD, then he shall place the animal before the priest. The priest shall value it as either good or bad; as you, the priest, value it, so it shall be. But if he should ever wish to redeem it, then he shall add one-fifth of it to your valuation.* (27:11-13).

The LORD allows the priest to put a value on an unclean animal. Once the value is set, the redemption value must be paid with a one-fifth bonus added to the price.

Chapter 27

C. The Valuation of Property for Redemption (27:14-24).
1. The Consecrated Home (27:14-15).

Now the LORD turns to the valuation of property for redemption. The consecrated home comes first. Verse 14. *"Now if a man consecrates his house as holy to the LORD, then the priest shall value it as either good or bad; as the priest values it, so it shall stand. Yet if the one who consecrates it should wish to redeem his house, then he shall add one-fifth of your valuation price to it, so that it may be his."* (27:14-15).

One-fifth of the priest's value must be added to the redemption price. This valuation is especially important in one of the forty-eight Levitical cities when the year of Jubilee occurs.

2. The Consecrated Fields (27:16-18).
a) The Homer of Barley (27:16).

The LORD moves to the consecrated fields. An example is the homer of barley. Verse 16. *"Again, if a man consecrates to the LORD part of the fields of his own property, then your valuation shall be proportionate to the seed needed for it: a homer of barley seed at fifty shekels of silver."* (27:16).

Once again, when part of the field is consecrated to the LORD, it means it is set aside to use the Levites. To redeem the field, the value is prorated based on the number of years until the year of Jubilee. In the case of a homer of barley seed, it is fifty shekels of silver.

b) The Year of Jubilee (27:17-18).
(1) For the First Year (27:17).

The LORD is more specific with the valuations of the field and sets limits. He speaks of the Year of Jubilee and addresses the value for the first year. Verse 17. *"If he consecrates his field as of the year of jubilee, according to your valuation it shall stand."* (27:17).

In the year of Jubilee, when all property reverts to its original family owners, the owner can set the price for the sale of the grain of the fields per year, and that value will stand until the following Jubilee.

(2) For Forty-Nine Years (27:18).

But what happens if the owner wants to end the grain contract sometime in the next forty-nine years and make it his own. The priest will calculate to prorate the refund. Verse 18. *"If he consecrates his field after the jubilee, however, then the priest shall calculate the price for him proportionate to the years that are left until the year of jubilee; and it shall be deducted from your valuation."* (27:18).

3. The Redeemed Fields (27:19-21).
a) The Value of the Field (27:19).

Things become more expensive if the owner wants to redeem the field that has been set aside for use by the Levites. Verse 19. *"If the one who consecrates it should ever wish to redeem the field, then he shall add one-fifth of your valuation price to it, so that it may pass to him."* (27:19).

The original price is set in the Year of Jubilee, and the refund will be prorated based on the number of years until the next Jubilee. The redemption will be required one-fifth of the value remaining to be added to the price.

b) The Restriction on the Field (27:20).

The LORD places a restriction on the field. Verse 20. *"Yet if he will not redeem the field, but has sold the field to another man, it may no longer be redeemed..."* (27:20).

Only the selling of the produce of the field can be redeemed. If the land has been sold, and not just the grain that is expected to grow on the land, the land cannot be redeemed.

c) The Return of the Field (27:21).

All is not lost for the man who sold the field and wants it back. The return of the field will come, but with a caveat. Verse 21. *"... and when it reverts in the jubilee, the field shall be holy to the LORD, like a field set apart; it shall be for the priest as his property."* (27:21).

The sold property will revert to the original owner in the year of Jubilee; however, the original owner will be required to allow the Levites to use the field for their food needs.

4. The Purchased Fields (27:22-24).
a) The Valuation of the Field (27:22-23).

What happens if a man purchases a field from another Jew and then consecrated that land to use the Levites. How will the valuation of the field be made? Verse 22. *"Or if he consecrates to the LORD a field which he has bought, which is not a part of the field of his own property, then the priest shall calculate for him the amount of your valuation up to the year of jubilee; and he shall on that day give your valuation as holy to the LORD."* (27:22-23).

The LORD will allow the priest to value the land based on the value established in the Jubilee year. Then, upon setting it aside for the Levitical use, the priest will prorate the cost based on the Jubilee value, and that will be the price until the next Jubilee year when all things are once again valued anew.

b) The Return of the Field (27:24).

In the Year of Jubilee, the return of the field occurs to the original owner. Verse 24. *"In the year of jubilee the field shall return to the one from whom he bought it, to whom the possession of the land belongs."* (27:24).

D. The Value of the Valuations for Redemption (27:25-33).
1. The Shekel (27:25).

How will all the valuations be determined? In what currency will the value of the valuations for redemptions be placed? Verse 25. *"Every valuation of yours, moreover, shall be after the shekel of the sanctuary. The shekel shall be twenty gerahs."* (27:25).

The shekel of the holy sanctuary is the currency used for all valuations.

a) The Firstborn Clean Which Cannot Be Redeemed (27:26).

However, some animals cannot be redeemed. Specifically, the firstborn of clean animals that belong to the LORD. Verse 26. *"However, a firstborn among animals, which as a firstborn belongs to the LORD, no man may consecrate it; whether ox or sheep, it is the LORD'S."* (27:26).

Because the firstborn of all clean animals belongs to the LORD, they must be given to the LORD. The LORD will give them as food to the Levites.

b) The Firstborn Unclean Which Can be Redeemed (27:27).

The LORD allows for unclean animals to be redeemed. Verse 27. *"But if it is among the unclean animals, then he shall redeem it according to your valuation and add to it one-fifth of it; and if it is not redeemed, then it shall be sold according to your valuation."* (27:27).

Every firstborn animal belongs to the LORD of the clean and unclean. The firstborn clean animals cannot be redeemed; the firstborn unclean must be redeemed. To redeem the firstborn unclean animal, the value of the animal is set. One-fifth of the value is added to the price. The unclean animal can then be set for the adjusted price to anyone who wants to purchase the animal.

c) The Devoted for Destruction Cannot be Sold or Redeemed (27:30).

That which is devoted for destruction cannot be sold or redeemed. Verse 28. *"Nevertheless, anything which a man sets apart to the LORD out of all that he has, of man or animal or of the fields of his own property, shall not be sold or redeemed. Anything devoted to destruction is most holy to the LORD. No one who may have been set apart among men shall be ransomed; he shall surely be put to death."* (27:28-29).

What does this mean? How can a man be set apart for destruction and not be redeemed or ransomed? This instruction is for the persons who have broken the law of the LORD and must face the penalty of death. What are some examples of those who face the death penalty? The idolator, the child who curses his parents, and the adulterers cannot escape death's penalty. They cannot be redeemed or ransomed from the penalty. When the nation enters the Promised Land to take for their own, the LORD has set aside all the Canaanites for a penalty of death. They cannot be ransomed or redeemed. They must die.

2. The Tithe (27:30-33)
a) The Owner of the Tithe (27:30)

Lastly, the LORD addresses the tithe and, specifically, the owner of the tithe. Verse 30. *"Thus all the tithe of the land, of the seed of the land or of the fruit of the tree, is the LORD'S; it is holy to the LORD."* (27:30).

The word *"tithe"* means *one-tenth of the persons goods*. As the LORD blesses in each family, a tithe is to be given to the LORD. When the increase comes, the tithe is to be given. The tithe is different from the offerings. The tithe is required, the offerings for sin are required, the offerings for thanks are voluntary. The offerings for sin are prescribed in the first seven chapters of Leviticus. They are not based on ten percent of anything. The offerings for thanks are also prescribe in Leviticus and not based on the ten percent. The tithe is based on a person's increase.

b) The Redemption of the Tithe (27:31)

Can any portion of the tithe be redeemed? Yes. Verse 31. *"If, therefore, a man wishes to redeem part of his tithe, he shall add to it one-fifth of it."* (27:31).

Suppose a man wants to redeem some of the sheep that are part of the required tithe; he can do so by offering the sheep's value with an additional one-fifth of the value.

c) The Tenth of the Herd or Flock (27:32-33)

As an example of why the situation may come that a person would want to redeem an animal that he is required to tithe to the LORD, He offers the following in the selection of the tenth of the herd or flock. Verse 32. *"For every tenth part of herd or flock, whatever passes under the rod, the tenth one shall be holy to the LORD. He is not to be concerned whether it is good or bad, nor shall he exchange it; or if he does exchange it, then both it and its substitute shall become holy. It shall not be redeemed."* (27:32-33).

The way the tithe of animals is determined is interesting. The herdsmen or shepherds would surround the herd or flock and begin to move toward the animals. An opening is made in the circle where the animals could begin to run out. The owner would stand at the opening with a rod. The tip of the rod had a red dye on the end. The owner would count the animals as they exited the circle, and every tenth animal he would mark with the rod and the red dye. The process was totally random based on how the animals left the circle. All the marked animals would then be gathered and taken as a tithe to the Levites regardless of being perfect or imperfect. If the owner decides to substitute a marked animal for a different one, both are holy to the LORD. The replacement animal must be given as the tithe. The substituted animal cannot be redeemed.

XXIII. The Law of the Conclusion (27:34)

Finally, we come to the law of the conclusion. Verse 34. *"These are the commandments which the LORD commanded Moses for the sons of Israel at Mount Sinai."* (27:34).

The LORD is finished with His commandments for the Nation of Israel. He started with the required offerings and ended with the required tithe. In between, He provided everything the people of the Nation of Israel needed to be His faithful servant. In so doing, the LORD provided all the laws that would still be in place for every Jews until the death, burial, and resurrection of the LORD and the Church's establishment. These laws will guide every bit of the rest of Jewish life as recorded in the Old Testament and the New Testament's Gospels.

Made in the USA
Columbia, SC
09 February 2024